Reading Grade 5

Table of Contents

How to Use This Book

1. This book can be used in a home or classroom setting. Read through each unit before working with the student(s). Familiarize yourself with the vocabulary and the skills that are introduced at the top of each unit activity page. Use this information as a guide to help instruct the student(s).

2. Choose a quiet place with little or no interruptions (including the telephone). Talk with the student(s) about the purpose of this book and how you will be working as a team to prepare for standardized tests.

3. As an option, copy the unit test and give it as a pretest to identify weak areas.

4. Upon the completion of each unit, you will find a unit test. Discuss the Helping Hand strategy for test taking featured on the test. Use the example on each test as a chance to show the student(s) how to work through a problem and completely fill in the answer circle. Encourage the student(s) to work independently when possible, but this is a learning time, and questions should be welcomed. A time limit is given for each test. Instruct the student(s) to use the time allowed efficiently, looking back over the answers if possible. Tell him to continue until he sees the stop sign.

5. Record the score on the record sheet on page 4. If a student has difficulty with any questions, use the cross-reference guide on the inside back cover to identify the skills that need to be reviewed.

Teach & Test

Introduction

Now this makes sense—teaching students the skills and strategies that are expected of them before they are tested!

Many students, parents, and teachers are concerned that standardized test scores do not adequately reflect a child's capabilities. This may be due to one or more of the factors italicized below. The purpose of this book is to reduce the negative impact of these, or similar factors, on a student's standardized test scores. The goal is to target those factors and alter their effects as described.

1. *The student has been taught the tested skills, but has forgotten them.* This book is divided into units that are organized similarly to fifth grade textbooks. Instructions for the skill itself are found at the top of each unit activity page, ensuring that the student has been exposed to each key component. The exercises include drill/practice and creative learning activities. Additional activity suggestions can be found in a star burst within the units. These activities require the student to apply the skills that they are practicing.

2. *The student has mastered the skills but has never seen them presented in a test-type format.* Ideally, the skills a student learns at school will be used as part of problem solving in the outside world. For this reason, the skills in this book, and in most classrooms, are not practiced in a test-type format. At the end of each unit in this book, the skills are specifically matched with test questions. In this way, the book serves as a type of "bridge" between the skills that the student(s) has mastered and the standardized test format.

3. *The student is inexperienced with the answer sheet format.* Depending on the standardized test that your school district uses, students are expected to use a fill-in-the-bubble name grid and score sheet. To familiarize students with this process, a name grid and score sheet are included for the review tests found at the midway point and again at the end of the book.

4. *The student may feel the anxiety of a new and unfamiliar situation.* While testing, students will notice changes in their daily routine: their classroom door will be closed with a "Testing" sign on it, they will be asked not to use the restroom, their desks may be separated, their teacher may read from a script and refuse to repeat herself, etc. To help relieve the stress caused by these changes, treat each unit test in this book as it would be treated at school by following the procedures listed below.

Stage a Test

You will find review tests midway through the book and again at the end of the book. When you reach these points, "stage a test" by creating a real test-taking environment. The procedures listed below coincide with many standardized test directions. The purpose is to alleviate stress, rather than contribute to it, so make this a serious, but calm event and the student(s) will benefit.

1. Prepare! Have the student(s) sharpen two pencils, lay out scratch paper, and use the restroom.

2. Choose a room with a door that can be closed. Ask a student to put a sign on the door that reads "Testing" and explain that no talking will be permitted after the sign is hung.

3. Direct the student(s) to turn to a specific page but not to begin until the instructions are completely given.

4. Read the instructions at the top of the page and work through the example together. Discuss the Helping Hand strategy that is featured at the top of the page. Have the student(s) neatly and completely fill in the bubble for the example. This is the child's last chance to ask for help!

5. Instruct the student(s) to continue working until the stop sign is reached. If a student needs help reading, you may read each question only once.

Helping Hand Test Strategies

The first page of each test features a specific test-taking strategy that will be helpful in working through most standardized tests. These strategies are introduced and spotlighted one at a time so that they will be learned and remembered internally. Each will serve as a valuable test-taking tool, so discuss them thoroughly.

The strategies include:

- Read all of the answer choices carefully before you choose your answer.
- If you cannot figure out an answer, skip the test item. Come back to it later.
- Reread the paragraphs if you cannot remember an answer.
- Read the directions carefully. Be sure you understand what you are supposed to do.
- Note the time allotment. Pace yourself.
- Take time to review your answers.
- If you are not sure which answer is correct, choose your best guess.
- If you become nervous, take deep breaths to relax.

Constructed-Response Questions

You will find the final question(s) of the tests are written in a different format called constructed response. This means that students are not provided with answer choices, but are instead asked to construct their own answers. The objective of such an "open-ended" type of question is to provide students with a chance to creatively develop reasonable answers. It also provides an insight to a student's reasoning and thinking skills. As this format is becoming more accepted and encouraged by standardized test developers, students will be "ahead of the game" by practicing such responses now.

Evaluating the Tests

Two types of questions are included in each test. The unit tests and the midway review test each consist of 20 multiple-choice questions, and the final review test consists of 30 multiple-choice questions. All tests include a constructed-response question which requires the student(s) to construct and sometimes support an answer. Use the following procedures to evaluate a student's performance on each test.

1. Use the answer key found on pages 125–128 to correct the tests. Be sure the student(s) neatly and completely filled in the answer circles.

2. Record the scores on the record sheet found on page 4. If the student(s) incorrectly answered any questions, use the cross-reference guide found on the inside back cover to help identify the skills the student(s) needs to review. Each test question references the corresponding activity page.

3. Scoring the constructed-response questions is somewhat subjective. Discuss these questions with the student(s). Sometimes it is easier for the student(s) to explain the answer verbally. Help the student to record his or her thoughts as a written answer. If the student(s) has difficulty formulating a response, refer back to the activity pages using the cross-reference guide. Also review the star burst activity found in the unit which also requires the student(s) to formulate an answer.

4. Discuss the test with the student(s). What strategies were used to answer the questions? Were some questions more difficult than others? Was there enough time? What strategies did the student(s) use while taking the test?

Record Sheet

Record a student's score for each test by drawing a star or placing a sticker below each item number that was correct. Leave the incorrect boxes empty as this will allow you to visually see any weak spots. Review and practice those missed skills, then retest only the necessary items.

Unit 1

1	2	3	4	5	6	7	8	9	10	11	12	13	14	15	16	17	18	19	20

Unit 2

1	2	3	4	5	6	7	8	9	10	11	12	13	14	15	16	17	18	19	20

Unit 3

1	2	3	4	5	6	7	8	9	10	11	12	13	14	15	16	17	18	19	20

Unit 4

1	2	3	4	5	6	7	8	9	10	11	12	13	14	15	16	17	18	19	20

Midway Review Test

1	2	3	4	5	6	7	8	9	10	11	12	13	14	15	16	17	18	19	20

Unit 5

1	2	3	4	5	6	7	8	9	10	11	12	13	14	15	16	17	18	19	20

Unit 6

1	2	3	4	5	6	7	8	9	10	11	12	13	14	15	16	17	18	19	20

Unit 7

1	2	3	4	5	6	7	8	9	10	11	12	13	14	15	16	17	18	19	20

Unit 8

1	2	3	4	5	6	7	8	9	10	11	12	13	14	15	16	17	18	19	20

Final Review Test

1	2	3	4	5	6	7	8	9	10	11	12	13	14	15	16	17	18	19	20

21	22	23	24	25	26	27	28	29	30

Name

Synonyms and antonyms

A **synonym** is a word that has the same or nearly the same meaning as another word. A word that may be used in place of another word and not change the meaning of a sentence is a synonym. Example: Our <u>guest</u> arrived with two suitcases and a large package. Our <u>visitor</u> arrived with two suitcases and a large package.

An **antonym** is a word that has the opposite meaning of another word. What one word means, the other means the reverse. Example: Mother <u>bought</u> an antique quilt at the flea market. Mother <u>sold</u> an antique quilt at the flea market.

Read the pairs of sentences and decide if the underlined words in each of the sentences are synonyms or antonyms. Circle your answers.

1. When the ship was in port, the deckhands <u>unloaded</u> the freight.

   Deckhands <u>loaded</u> the cargo before the passengers boarded the ship.

   synonyms   antonyms

2. Natalie was <u>satisfied</u> with the way the bakery decorated the cake.

   The baker was <u>displeased</u> with the decorated cake.

   synonyms   antonyms

3. Work was being done constantly on the old house to <u>maintain</u> its value.

   There was an order to <u>preserve</u> the old courthouse when all the other old buildings around it were demolished.

   synonyms   antonyms

4. Everyone <u>present</u> at the city council meeting voiced opinions about the new highway going through town.

   Bert was <u>absent</u> the day the class went to the wildlife refuge.

   synonyms   antonyms

5. The man <u>staggered</u> when he got out of the car after the accident.

   Martha <u>tottered</u> down the steps after riding the roller coaster.

   synonyms   antonyms

Synonyms and antonyms   Unit 1

Using the Word Banks below, choose synonyms for the Across clues and antonyms for the Down clues to complete the puzzle on page 7.

Across

1. entertain
4. arrived
6. discontinue
7. urge
8. extra
9. obtain
12. vase
13. hug
14. path
15. disbelief
16. brim
19. poke
21. cure
23. permit
25. appearance
26. flow
27. lengthy
29. each
30. powerful

Down

1. detest
2. above
3. entrance
4. gloom
5. wild
6. unite
10. maintain
11. remote
12. lovely
13. kind
15. fact
17. like
18. odd
19. fancy
20. whisper
22. arm
24. refreshed
25. busy
28. give

Synonyms

drive	pry	edge	earn	every
trail	allow	urn	stop	spare
long	strong	doubt	came	image
amuse	caress	heal	gush	

Antonyms

cruel	under	ugly	even	cheer
meek	exit	idle	separate	yell
adore	get	near	weary	leg
detest	plain	dream	alter	

Choose a paragraph from your favorite book. Rewrite the paragraph using synonyms for 10 of the words.

Name

Synonyms and antonyms

7

Homophones

Homophones are words that are pronounced the same, but are spelled differently and have different meanings.

Example: There is a <u>frieze</u> that goes across the front of city hall.
Water will <u>freeze</u> when the air temperature goes below 32 degrees.
The game warden at the wildlife refuge <u>frees</u> injured animals when they are well enough to live in the wild on their own.

Circle the homophone that completes each sentence.

1. The Native Americans taught the Pilgrims how to plant _____. (maze, maize)

2. The _____ of your company is requested at Sampson's party. (presence, presents)

3. The nurse had trouble finding my _____ when he drew my blood. (vein, vane)

4. We took a _____ ship through the Panama Canal. (crews, cruise)

5. Eric won a gold _____ in ice-skating for the third year in a row. (medal, metal, meddle)

6. The old _____ tree was struck by lightning. (beach, beech)

7. That post is _____ , so all furniture must be placed around it. (stationery, stationary)

8. A traditional _____ was held for the bishop when he passed away. (right, rite, write)

9. When we make bread, we let it rise and then we _____ it. (need, knead)

10. They cleared the grocery_____ in order to make room for the canned soup display. (isle, I'll, aisle)

11. I had never seen anyone play the _____ until I went to the concert. (lyre, liar)

12. Father received a letter that used _____ wax to secure the envelope closed. (ceiling, sealing)

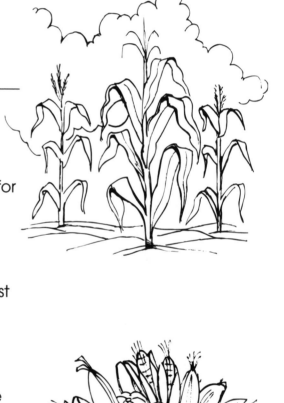

8

Name

Analogies

An **analogy** is a comparison or relationship between two or more things that may otherwise not be alike. To complete an analogy, you must first determine what the relationship is, and then determine what would complete it to keep the relationship the same. The relationships in the examples below are synonyms, antonyms, and homophones to demonstrate analogies.

Examples: Alone is to solo   Rear is to front   Week is to weak
 as one is to sole.   as back is to stomach.   as hour is to our.

Following are analogies using synonyms, antonyms, or homophones as the relationships. Circle the word that would best complete each analogy.

1. Mourn is to _____ as knight is to night.

   day   dark   morn   armor

2. _____ is to sculpture as picture is to painting.

   statue   pottery   clay   art

3. One is to several as _____ is to many.

   some   single   few   numerous

4. _____ is to answer as question is to response.

   comeback   reply   ask   what

5. Armor is to _____ as shield is to barrier.

   safe   shelter   protection   hide

6. _____ is to suppress as release is to restrain.

   free   hold   open   sleep

7. Pedal is to _____ as tense is to tents.

   medal   pump   cease   peddle

8. Clean is to immaculate as dirty is to _____.

   soiled   dark   pure   black

9. Explicit is to general as _____ is to widespread.

   here   place   common   exact

10. Strewn is to scattered as _____ is to fused.

    disband   nearly   fuss   combined

Write analogies using antonyms, synonyms, and homophones as the relationship.

Name

Analogies

Analogies may be written this way: Blue is to green as sky is to grass.
They may also be written this way: blue : green : : sky : grass.

Write the word that completes each analogy.

1. shower : _____ : : stove : kitchen

   bedroom   family room   office   bathroom

2. Mexico : _____ : : the United States : Canada

   North America   New England   California   the United States

3. _____ : bed : : cloth : table

   spread   place mat   pillow   towel

4. second : minute : : minute : _____

   day   month   week   hour

5. mouse : cheese : : _____ : acorn

   opossum   blue jay   rabbit   squirrel

6. sleep : _____ : : awake : day

   eat   nap   month   night

7. circle : wheel : : hexagon : _____

   triangle   stop sign   pentagon   rectangle

8. adornment : ornament : : embellishment : _____

   pictures   decoration   hangings   design

9. swimming : water polo : :
   _____ : ice hockey

   ice   skates   skating   winter

10. _____ : shoe : : shampoo : hair

    soap   polish   cleanser   lotion

11. teacher : student : : _____ : child

    adult   parent   grandparent   nurse

Analogies

Complete the analogies with words
from the Word Bank.

cow	neck
goat	sole
stalk	up
vine	year
hungry	four
lemon	aunt
fish	pool
transparent	haul
anatomy	court
mason	pride
write	place

1. rind : _____ : : skin : apple

2. day : week : : month : _____

3. _____ : niece : : uncle : nephew

4. pig : pork : : _____ : milk

5. push : shove : : pull : _____

6. read : _____ : : book : paper

7. palm : hand : : _____ : foot

8. _____ : down : : ascend : descend

9. collar : _____ : : cuff : wrist

10. when : time :: where : _____

11. celery : _____ : : lettuce : leaf

12. worm : _____ : : cheese : mouse

13. two : _____ : : four : eight

14. flower : pot : : _____ : trellis

15. clear : muddy : : _____ : cloudy

16. _____ : thirsty : : food : beverage

17. water : _____ : : ice : rink

18. carpenter : wood : : _____ : stone

19. golf : course : : tennis : _____

20. painting : art : : skeleton : _____

21. bear : cub : : _____ : : kid

22. _____ : lions : : gaggle : geese

Context clues

You may not recognize a word in a sentence or know its meaning, but there are different ways to figure it out. One is by its part of speech. Another is to use the other words in the sentence as clues to the word's meaning.

Example: The dreadful odor <u>permeated</u> the park and seemed to come from the direction of the garbage dump. (Permeated is a verb. Now use other words in the sentence to help determine its meaning.)

Use context clues to help you determine where the words from the Word Bank fit into the story.

Elephant Parts

An elephant's trunk is its nose and hands. It can find _____, pick up food, and put food in the elephant's mouth. The _____ is also a straw. It sucks up _____ to drink or to spray over itself as a _____. An elephant's eyes are very small, but its sense of smell is good.

An elephant's _____ are long incisor teeth growing from its _____ jaw. They are used to attack _____, knock down small trees, and dig and _____ into the ground. An elephant has four _____, one on each side of the upper and lower jaw. Because the elephant's food is _____ to chew, these molars _____ out, but they are _____ by others growing behind them. This happens five times during an elephant's _____. When the last molars are worn out, the elephant can no _____ feed itself, and it will die. An elephant _____ lives around 65 years.

enemies	upper	shower	molars	tusks
bore	usually	longer	food	water
trunk	difficult	replaced	life	wear

12

Name _____

Context clues   Unit 1

Context clues, along with your own ideas, will help you make a good guess at a word's meaning.

Read the passage. Then write each underlined word from the passage next to its definition below.

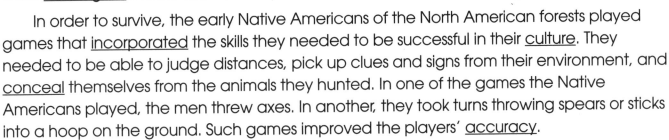

Early Native Americans in North America

The rocky land of the northern forests in North America was never good for farming. Without fish and game, the early <u>natives</u> would have starved. Their lives were <u>contingent</u> on the animals they hunted.

In order to survive, the early Native Americans of the North American forests played games that <u>incorporated</u> the skills they needed to be successful in their <u>culture</u>. They needed to be able to judge distances, pick up clues and signs from their environment, and <u>conceal</u> themselves from the animals they hunted. In one of the games the Native Americans played, the men threw axes. In another, they took turns throwing spears or sticks into a hoop on the ground. Such games improved the players' <u>accuracy</u>.

Moose and caribou were very important to the tribes. Moose usually lived and traveled by themselves. Caribou migrated in herds covering a large territory each season. The Native Americans <u>stalked</u> the moose from one <u>range</u> to another, but when hunting caribou they would wait for them at a place along the caribou's trails.

<u>Weirs</u>, nets, traps, hooks, and spears were used to catch fish. Whitefish and jackfish were caught in lakes, and Arctic grayling and trout were caught in rivers. The Native Americans fished from the shore or in canoes in summer and through holes cut in the ice in winter.

After the ice melted, the traps were set. Sometimes the Native Americans would discover a bear still hibernating in its den. Such a kill would feed the camp for a few days. Sometimes when meat was scarce, the Native Americans would eat rabbit, mink, or wolverine. When hunting became poor, they lived on dried meat and fish, and on pemmican, a mixture of dried berries, dried meat, and animal fat.

1. open area upon which animals roam   2. combined into one body

_____   _____

3. original inhabitants _____   4. dependent upon _____

5. to pursue prey _____   6. quality of being exact _____

7. to hide _____   8. enclosures set in a waterway for
                                                catching fish _____
9. one's social group _____

Name

Read or listen to the directions. Fill in the circle beside the best answer.

 Example:

Choose the homophone of the underlined word.

You can tell autumn is in the air because of the <u>chilly</u> morning.

(A) cold   (B) chili

(C) windy   (D) clear

Answer: B because they sound alike but have different meanings.

Now try these. You have 20 minutes. Continue until you see STOP .

Choose the homophone of the underlined words in sentences 1 and 2.

1. The city charged a <u>fare</u> to cross the bridge.

money	tariff	fair	tear
(A)	(B)	(C)	(D)

2. From the beautiful golf <u>links</u> we could see the ocean.

lines	lynx	link	chain
(A)	(B)	(C)	(D)

---

3. Select the sentence in which <u>peddle</u> would make sense.

(A) Tom is going to _____ magazines to make extra money.

(B) Larry had to _____ his bike quickly.

(C) The flower's_____ was a bright yellow color.

(D) Christine played in the _____ after the rainstorm.

GO ON ⟩

Unit 1 Test

Choose the synonym for the underlined words in sentences 4–8.

4. I was in a <u>melancholy</u> mood because I was not selected to be the class president.

ordinary
(A)

magnificent
(B)

satisfied
(C)

sorrowful
(D)

5. The cast was <u>ready</u> for the curtain to rise.

anxious
(A)

waiting
(B)

excited
(C)

prepared
(D)

6. The mouse <u>nibbled</u> at the cheese in the trap but did not get caught.

looked
(A)

gnawed
(B)

enjoyed
(C)

sniffed
(D)

7. Winning the primary was a huge <u>victory</u> for the candidate's party.

pleasure
(A)

event
(B)

success
(C)

happening
(D)

8. The director of the company was a <u>capable</u> businessman.

educated
(A)

retired
(B)

financial
(C)

competent
(D)

Choose the antonym for the underlined words in sentences 9–12.

9. <u>Numerous</u> people have signed the petition requesting a traffic light.

Several
(A)

Many
(B)

Few
(C)

Various
(D)

GO ON

10. Harry was so <u>proud</u> of his accomplishments he nearly burst his buttons.

loud
(A)

modest
(B)

pleased
(C)

indifferent
(D)

11. The <u>strong</u> man ran 10 miles with a hundred-pound pack on his back.

feeble
(A)

healthy
(B)

heavy
(C)

muscular
(D)

12. The city council <u>assembled</u> at the government center at 1:00 P.M.

dispersed
(A)

met
(B)

gathered
(C)

rescheduled
(D)

Complete the analogies in 13–16.

13. switch : light : : _____ : water

sink
(A)

bulb
(B)

hose
(C)

faucet
(D)

14. veterinarian : dog : : _____ : person

doctor
(A)

athlete
(B)

honorable
(C)

educator
(D)

15. Keyboard is to type as steering wheel is to _____ .

car
(A)

fuel
(B)

drive
(C)

ride
(D)

16. Vanish is to disappear as _____ is to abandon.

detect
(A)

desert
(B)

incorporate
(C)

release
(D)

GO ON ⟶

Unit 1 Test

Select the definition for the underlined words in sentences 17–20.

17. Venturesome travelers began to explore the Pacific coastline of North America four centuries ago.

Efficient
(A)

Sailing
(B)

Hesitant
(C)

Adventurous
(D)

18. The first European explorers that reached the extreme northwestern area of the North American continent saw high, steep cliffs rising above the ocean.

immediate
(A)

current
(B)

outermost
(C)

nearly
(D)

19. Upon landing on the western coast of the continent, they found prosperous Native American cultures living in fishing villages.

poor
(A)

thriving
(B)

existing
(C)

fishing
(D)

20. The Native Americans lived in wood homes called long houses. They had impressive totem poles that stood tall looking out over the ocean. The totem poles had hand-carved animals and gods of the ocean on them.

wooden
(A)

majestic
(B)

carved
(C)

tall
(D)

The land today does not look like it did years ago. Giant trees have been cut down and the extensive grasslands have become farmland for grazing cattle and raising crops. Some animals and plants have become endangered, but other species are still common.

Write the meaning of the underlined word. Then use the underlined word in a sentence.

_____

_____

_____

_____

STOP

Name

Multiple meanings

Unit 2

Some words have more than one meaning. The context of the sentence will help you determine the correct meaning of the word. Example: The cowboy wore spurs and chaps when he went on a roundup. Possible definitions: 1. leather leggings connected by a belt worn over regular pants 2. men (The sentence gives you clues to determine that the first definition is being used.)

Circle the definition of the underlined word in each sentence.

1. The featherbed was warm but very <u>light</u> to carry.

   set fire to   lamp   not heavy

2. Father took Jenny's picture riding <u>bareback</u> on her new pony.

   on a horse without a saddle   nothing covering the back   went back

3. Jerry ordered <u>lean</u> meat from the butcher.

   rest against   containing little fat   little nourishment

4. A woodwind player keeps extra <u>reeds</u> handy in case the one she is using splits.

   tall grasses   arrows   thin pieces of cane or metal attached to an air opening

5. The new <u>bureau</u> was put in Tim's room on the second floor.

   a department of government   a chest of drawers   an administrative unit

6. The teacher asked Susan to <u>divide</u> one-hundred five by fifteen.

   separate into equal parts   opposite of multiply   distribute parts

7. The voice teacher had her student sing the <u>scale</u> as a warm-up exercise.

   a machine to measure weight   a graduated series   climb

8. David did the <u>right</u> thing when he turned in the wallet he found.

   proper   opposite of left   show ownership

9. Chris always <u>trails</u> behind looking for wildlife when we go hiking.

   paths   pursues   lags

Write sentences showing the meanings of **swallow**. Then make a list of 10 other words with multiple meanings.

10. The boys were <u>loafers</u> who put off raking leaves and doing other chores to go fishing and sit around at the lake.

    shoes   lazy people   loaves of bread

Multiple meanings

Circle the correct definition for each underlined word. Then write a sentence using another meaning for the underlined word.

1. Mother attended a <u>function</u> at our neighbor's house where she met a candidate for mayor.

    a social gathering   a purpose for which something may be used

    _____

2. The mysterious woman walking in the mist drew her <u>hood</u> to hide her face.

    a part of an automobile   a protective covering

    _____

3. Taxes were an <u>issue</u> in the political campaign.

    a publication   the substance or main point of a policy

    _____

4. We found pieces of <u>petrified</u> wood on our trip in Arizona.

    turned to stone, fossilized   terrified

    _____

5. Two children on the seesaw were able to <u>balance</u> evenly by one sitting closer to the center of it.

    amount in bank account   equalized weight

    _____

6. George's friends could not help but <u>dwell</u> on his condition when they heard about the accident that rushed him to the hospital.

    continually think of   reside in

    _____

7. The newspaper was able to get a <u>scoop</u> on the hit-and-run accident.

    ice cream portion   news item

    _____

Multiple meanings: homographs   Unit 2

You have learned about homophones like to, too, and two. They are words that are pronounced alike, but are spelled differently and have different meanings.

Homographs are words that are spelled alike but have different pronunciations and meanings. They also are different parts of speech. Notice the differences in pronunciation, meanings, and parts of speech of "permit" in the example below.

Example: He has a <u>permit</u> that lets him through the gate.
          Do not <u>permit</u> him to come through the gate.

Use a homograph to complete each sentence pair. Then find the homographs in the word find. The words can be found horizontally, vertically, and diagonally.

1. Fred was going to _____ the play he wrote.

   My mother says that the Green Grocer sells the best _____ in town.

2. The _____ blew so hard that the windows in our house rattled.

   _____ up the string on the yo-yo before you begin to play with it.

3. The temperature of the pool's water was _____ .

   The union and company officers had to get someone in to _____ their labor negotiations.

4. Rachel and I went to shop for our father's _____ by ourselves.

   My mother is going to _____ our state governor at next week's Community Lecture Series.

5. The secretary kept a _____ of everything that was discussed at the meeting.

   We had our dad _____ the baseball game on television because we were going out to dinner.

6. I was chosen to _____ the symphony orchestra.

   The boy's _____ during the meeting was not appropriate.

E	E	M	C	N	T	C
P	R	O	D	U	C	E
M	R	D	R	E	A	S
R	S	E	I	O	R	D
E	T	R	S	C	C	A
C	P	A	O	E	O	T
O	D	T	R	C	N	E
R	S	E	L	E	D	T
D	T	N	B	S	U	U
R	E	F	D	E	C	D
P	R	O	E	S	T	T
P	R	P	W	I	N	D

Name _____

Prefixes

A **prefix** is a group of letters at the beginning of a base word that changes the word's meaning. Example: im + probable = improbable

Read the prefixes and their meanings below. Use them to complete the activities below.

mid - middle	im - not	tele - operate at a distance
post - after	micro - very small	super - above, outside
sub - below	uni - one, single	de - do the opposite of

Underline the base words in the words below. Then write the meanings of the words with their prefixes. Example: We eat lunch at mid<u>day</u>.   middle of the day

1. midstream _____

2. decode _____

3. postgraduate _____

4. improper _____

5. telephone _____

6. unicolor _____

7. microscope _____

8. subzero _____

9. supernatural _____

Write the words below on the blanks to complete the sentences.

microearthquakes	subcategory	midterm	telescope
superhuman	immobilize	decipher	postmodern

10. There was a man at the circus that performed _____ feats.

11. One can see the stars at night much better through a _____.

12. There are many _____ every day all over the world.

13. The enemy tried to _____ our messages during the war.

14. There was a show of _____ art at the museum.

15. All courts are a _____ of the justice department.

16. The doctor put a splint on my finger to _____ it.

17. My brother studied hard for his _____ exam in chemistry.

Suffixes
Unit 2

A **suffix** is a group of letters added to the end of a base word that changes its meaning.

Example: danger + ous = dangerous

Read the suffixes and their meanings below. Use them to complete the activities below.

ly – manner, relating

ance – condition or state of being

al – related to, time

ship – quality of or having the office of

ous – have qualities of

ish – likeness

ist – one who does or is, skilled at

ant, ent – one who performs

Underline the base words in the words below. Then write the meanings of the words with their suffixes.

1. contestant _____

2. fiendish _____

3. leadership _____

4. courageous _____

5. sweetly _____

6. attendance _____

7. frontal _____

8. lobbyist _____

Write the words from the Word Bank on the blanks to complete the paragraph.

timely	reddish	abruptly	mechanical	carefully
specialist	happily	resident	generous	patiently

The _____ of the _____ apartment building was

a _____ in his field at the hospital. On the way to work, his car stopped

_____ because of _____ problems. He

_____ waited for a tow truck. The serviceman _____

loaded the car onto his truck. The specialist _____ found another ride

to work from a _____ friend. The specialist's car was fixed in a

_____ manner.

Name

Similes and metaphors   Unit 2

Similes and **metaphors** are comparisons. Similes use like, as, or than to compare two things. Metaphors are implied comparisons. Both compare two unlike things.
Example of a simile: The runner <u>ran like a deer</u> the last 50 feet of the race.
Example of a metaphor: His hair <u>was an uncombed stringy mop</u>.

Write if the comparison is a **simile** or **metaphor**.

1. Meg babbled on and on like a brook about her baby brother. _____

2. The boys' eyes were as big as saucers when the magician pulled a mouse out of Larry's shirt. _____

3. Some news travels like the wind. _____

4. This piece of candy is hard as a rock. _____

5. The bald-headed moon lit up the night. _____

6. The dark clouds were dragons spitting fire. _____

7. Joe is a dirty rat to squeal about the surprise. _____

8. The fog is as thick as pea soup. _____

9. The soldier stood straight as an arrow. _____

10. The puppy ran around like a tornado. _____

11. After the fireworks, the sky was a red ceiling. _____

12. After the blizzard, the highway was smooth as glass. _____

13. The package was as light as a feather. _____

14. The flower bed is a rainbow on the ground. _____

15. The lawyer was a tiger concerning his client's innocence. _____

16. The soprano in the opera sings like a canary. _____

17. Michael is greased lightning on the ice. _____

Name _____

Idioms   Unit 2

An **idiom** is a figure of speech. It is often a phrase. It says one thing and means another.
Example: There was a long silence before Sam <u>broke the ice</u> by telling a funny story.
(Did Sam really break the ice? What did he do?)

Write the letter of the definition below that best describes the meaning of each underlined idiom.

a. a different subject

b. out of place

c. had the same problem

d. lost the opportunity

e. was undecided

f. talk a lot

g. did it right

h. cause trouble

i. try it out

_____ 1. The doctor was a <u>fish out of water</u> when he was at a meeting for hospital accountants.

_____ 2. The cousins at the family reunion stayed up late to <u>shoot the breeze</u>.

_____ 3. The factory worker did not want to <u>make waves</u> for fear he might lose his job.

_____ 4. The school's finance committee was discussing what playground equipment it would buy when Mrs. Jones raised a question about buying books for the library. The chairman of the committee said, "<u>That's a horse of another color</u>."

_____ 5. You should <u>test the waters</u> before making such a major decision.

_____ 6. The food committee <u>hit the nail on the head</u> when it planned the menu for the school picnic.

_____ 7. Everyone on the highway was <u>in the same boat</u> when the truck carrying eggs overturned during rush hour.

_____ 8. My father was angry at himself because he <u>missed the boat</u> when he did not buy property on the lake at half of the current cost.

_____ 9. Uncle Henry <u>ran hot and cold</u> about the candidates running for office.

Name

Personification

Personification is when an inanimate thing—like a plant, animal, or object—appears to have human qualities. It might have human characteristics or act or talk like a person.

Example: The daisies' faces smiled when they received a drink of water. (The daisies have the human qualities of having faces and smiling.)

Underline what is being personified in the sentences. Then write the word or words that identify the personification.

Example: The <u>trees</u> moaned as if they ached from the wind bending their branches.

moaned as if they ached

1. The first-place trophy proudly stood on the shelf in Charlie's room.

_____

2. Since we could not go out to play, we watched from our window as the heavens spit popsicles. _____

3. Autumn leaves seemed to sing as they danced across the lawn.

_____

4. Horns honked angrily as drivers became more impatient.

_____

5. The sun played hide-and-seek with me as it popped in and out of the clouds.

_____

6. The clouds marched across the sky ahead of the storm.

_____

7. The house eagerly waited for the new owners to arrive.

_____

Name

Read or listen to the directions. Fill in the circle beside the best answer.

 Example:

Identify the definition for the underlined word.

The boy had a tight <u>grip</u> on the rope.

(A) control   (B) feeling

(C) grasp   (D) knot

Answer: C because grip means to grasp.

Now try these. You have 20 minutes.

Continue until you see .

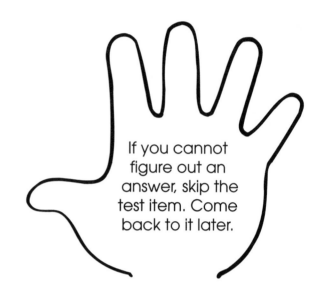

If you cannot figure out an answer, skip the test item. Come back to it later.

Choose the correct meanings for the underlined words in sentences 1–4.

1. The doctor gave me drops to clear up the infection in my <u>pupil</u>.

diagnosis	student	prescription	part of the eye
(A)	(B)	(C)	(D)

2. The champion wrestler won his 25th <u>match</u> in two years.

contest	equal	rival	fire stick
(A)	(B)	(C)	(D)

3. The scratch was so <u>minute</u> that one had to use a microscope to see it.

very small	magnification	unit of time	sizable
(A)	(B)	(C)	(D)

GO ON

Unit 2 Test

4. All the members of the Senate were <u>present</u> when the gavel sounded through Congress.

a gift	to introduce	in attendance	absent
Ⓐ	Ⓑ	Ⓒ	Ⓓ

Choose the correct meanings for the underlined prefixes and suffixes in 5–8.

5. <u>im</u>balance   <u>im</u>movable

more	after	not	never
Ⓐ	Ⓑ	Ⓒ	Ⓓ

6. <u>re</u>play   <u>re</u>store

do again	after	not	never
Ⓐ	Ⓑ	Ⓒ	Ⓓ

7. glori<u>ous</u>   victori<u>ous</u>

to make	one who performs	the study of	having qualities of
Ⓐ	Ⓑ	Ⓒ	Ⓓ

8. tour<u>ist</u>   biolog<u>ist</u>

relating to	likeness	one who does	a condition
Ⓐ	Ⓑ	Ⓒ	Ⓓ

Choose the answer that best describes the underlined similes, metaphors, or idioms in sentences 9–12.

9. The stalks of corn were <u>a sea of green</u> swaying in the breeze.

Ⓐ a moving, green field   Ⓑ getting watered

Ⓒ ready for picking   Ⓓ wind was blowing

GO ON ▷

10. Mother <u>flew off the handle</u> when Whiskers ate the family's dinner.

    (A) got very angry   (B) saw a hungry cat

    (C) used a frying pan   (D) threw Whiskers in the air

11. Sarah was <u>sharp as a tack</u> on the computer.

    (A) pointed   (B) very knowledgeable

    (C) fast   (D) piercing sound

12. Haddie had a <u>mountain of money</u> in her piggy bank.

    (A) a large hill   (B) dimes and quarters

    (C) a sizable amount   (D) a few coins

Identify the following underlined phrases as similes, metaphors, idioms, or personification in sentences 13–16.

13. The puppy was a <u>rubber ball bouncing down the street</u> on his leash.

    simile   metaphor   idiom   personification

    (A)   (B)   (C)   (D)

14. The children <u>tickled the slide</u> as they went down it.

    simile   metaphor   idiom   personification

    (A)   (B)   (C)   (D)

15. Ellen was <u>as quiet as a mouse</u> when she got up early to study for her test.

    simile   metaphor   idiom   personification

    (A)   (B)   (C)   (D)

16. The letter <u>danced down the alley</u> in the wind.

    simile   metaphor   idiom   personification

    (A)   (B)   (C)   (D)

GO ON

Choose the word that completes both sentences in 17–20.

17. Sarah is _____ the number of problems she still needs to complete.

The coach is _____ on Tyrone to score the winning goal.

cheering	finishing	counting	listing
Ⓐ	Ⓑ	Ⓒ	Ⓓ

18. There was a _____ in the attic with a lot of grandmother's old clothes.

The doctor studied the X-ray of his _____ .

chest	bureau	upper body	container
Ⓐ	Ⓑ	Ⓒ	Ⓓ

19. I used the clay to _____ an animal sculpture.

The _____ in the air makes me sneeze.

create	odor	mold	replicate
Ⓐ	Ⓑ	Ⓒ	Ⓓ

20. Tad wrote an article for the next _____ of our school newsletter.

Our class studied the political _____ involving the new tax law.

copy	party	article	issue
Ⓐ	Ⓑ	Ⓒ	Ⓓ

Write two sentences using different meanings for **charge** in each.

_____

_____

_____

_____

Main idea

The **main idea** identifies the main point (or points) in a story. The main idea in a paragraph is often stated in the first or second sentence and may be summed up in the final sentence. A title also tells what a story or passage is mostly about.

Circle the the main idea of each paragraph.

1. The ancient Egyptians used a reed, called papyrus, to make paper. They cut the stem into thin slices. They laid some pieces lengthwise and placed others across them. Next, they moistened the layers with water, put a heavy weight on the layers to press them together, and then dried them. When the layers were dry, they stuck together in a sheet. The Egyptians rubbed the dried sheet until it was smooth and ready to write on. Sometimes sheets were joined together to make long scrolls.

    how papyrus was made   how paper was made

    definition of papyrus   about ancient Egypt

2. In ancient times only a few people knew how to write. Most people who needed something written down had to ask a scribe to write for them. A scribe was someone who could write.

    ancient times   writing in ancient Egypt

    scribes   illiterate people in ancient times

3. Pyramids are large structures with square bases and four triangular sides that come to a point at the top. They were built by the ancient Egyptians as tombs in which the bodies of their kings and queens were placed. Before the bodies were placed in the tombs, they were mummified. Then they were placed in the tombs along with personal and household items. The Egyptians hoped to hide and preserve the bodies and to protect their souls so they could live forever. The remains of several pyramids can still be found in Egypt, but the tombs are empty. Grave robbers looted the graves.

    burying the dead in ancient Egypt   how pyramids were built

    use of pyramids in ancient Egypt   remains of the pyramids

Main idea   Unit 3

Read the passage and then follow the directions at the bottom of the page.

The Rosetta Stone

The Rosetta Stone was found among the ruins in Egypt a little more than 200 years ago. It unlocked the mystery that had been puzzling historians since the time of the Greeks and Romans: what did the symbols that covered the temples and tombs of ancient Egypt mean? The Rosetta Stone had been carved and set up for people to read around 196 B.C. It was named after the place it was found, called Rosetta.

Now that it has been translated, we know it tells about young King Ptolemy V of Egypt. He had been king for nine years and had passed laws giving more money to the priests. In return, the priests had decided to build statues of him in all the temples and to worship the statues three times a day.

There are three different kinds of writing on the stone. The writing on the top part of the stone is lines of small pictures, called hieroglyphics. Hieroglyphics were often carved on walls or on slabs of stone. The Egyptian priests were the ones who used hieroglyphics. The second script on the stone is now known as demotic script. Demotic means "popular." It was used by the Greeks in their everyday writing, like in letters. The third section at the bottom of the stone is written in Greek. By 196 B.C., a Greek family called the Ptolemies had been ruling Egypt for over a 100 years. Because of this, the Greek alphabet and language were being used in Egypt, along with Egyptian writing.

1. Write the main idea of the first paragraph. _____

   _____

2. Write the main idea of the second paragraph. _____

   _____

3. Write the main idea of the third paragraph. _____

   _____

4. Write the main idea of the passage. _____

   _____

Name

Main idea   Unit 3

All the ideas in a paragraph are clues to help you understand the main idea.

Read the groups of words. Decide how they would be related if they were found in a paragraph. Then write a paragraph using the words. Be sure to include a sentence telling the main idea. Underline this sentence.

1.   five candles   chocolate cake   Peter's day   lots of presents

_____

_____

_____

_____

_____

2.   amusement park   roller coaster   cotton candy   bumper cars

_____

_____

_____

_____

_____

3.   science fair   blue ribbon   judges   project

_____

_____

_____

_____

_____

_____

Main idea

Unit 3

The title of a paragraph tells what the paragraph is mostly about. This is your first clue about the main idea. The main idea is also usually stated in the first or second sentence. The other sentences of the paragraph support the main idea by telling who, what, when, where, why, and how. A summarizing sentence is usually at the end of the paragraph.

Read the paragraph and then follow the directions.

_____

When the United States Constitution was written in 1787, it established a government in which power was split between three branches: legislative, executive, and judicial. This kept any one branch from having more power than another. The legislative branch consists of the Congress—the House of Representatives and the Senate. Members of this branch are elected by their individual states. Congress makes the laws of the nation. The executive branch is headed by the president and is responsible for enforcing the laws of the nation. The Supreme Court is in charge of the federal court system. It also acts as a referee and makes sure that all laws and actions of the government follow the principles set forth in the Constitution. Although changes have been made to the Constitution over the past 200-plus years, the three branches of government remain as originally written.

1. Write a title above the paragraph.

2. Underline the sentence that expresses the main idea.

3. Circle a supporting sentence. Does it tell who, what, where, when, why, or how about the main idea?

_____

4. Write the summarizing sentence. _____

_____

_____

_____

Main idea

Unit 3

The **main idea** in a passage may be stated in the title, the first paragraph, or even in the first several paragraphs. The remaining paragraphs in the passage provide support for the main idea. The supporting paragraphs may explain who, what, where, when, why, and how about the main idea. There usually is a summarizing sentence at the end of the last paragraph or a summarizing paragraph at the end of the passage.

Read the passage and then follow the directions on page 35.

The Judiciary System

Laws are rules that we live by every day. If we did not have laws, we could do whatever we wanted without regard for the rights of others. Imagine if cars paid no attention to stop lights, if pedestrians crossed roads wherever and whenever they wanted, or if speed limits did not exist. Traffic laws maintain safety and also protect the rights of others.

Laws are enforced by the police and courts. Police officers see that the laws are obeyed, and courts enforce the laws. Judges in the courts see that laws are carried out fairly and "according to the law" (written rules and regular ways of punishing people who disobey the rules).

Courts in the United States have three responsibilities. First, they interpret the laws and see that they are followed by everyone. Second, the courts determine punishment for those who are found guilty of breaking the laws. Finally, they must protect the rights of every individual.

Laws can be changed to meet the needs of our nation. Although our laws have changed over the years, the principles that govern the judicial system have not. They ensure that everyone in the nation is protected equally under the laws and has a right to a fair trial with a fitting punishment for a crime. But most importantly, these principles guarantee every American the right to practice the many freedoms specified in the Constitution.

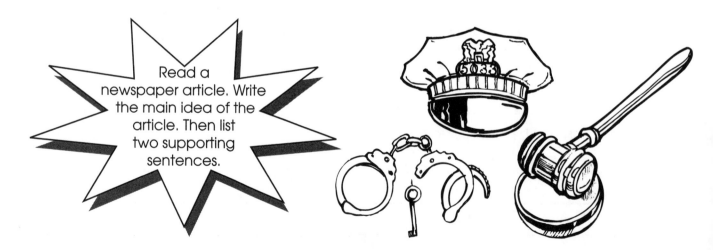

Read a newspaper article. Write the main idea of the article. Then list two supporting sentences.

Main idea   Unit 3

1. What is the main idea? _____

   _____

2. Circle the supporting idea in the first paragraph.

   Laws are rules.   Pedestrians travel on foot.   Traffic laws maintain safety.

3. Circle the supporting idea in the second paragraph.

   Judges see that laws are carried out.   People disobey rules.

   Laws need to be obeyed.

4. Circle the supporting idea in the third paragraph.

   The U.S. has a court system.   The courts must protect individual rights.

   Punishments may differ.

5. Circle the summation in the last paragraph.

   Though laws change, principles that govern the judiciary system do not.

   Laws change according to the needs of the nation.

   Everyone in the nation has equal rights.

6. Why do we have laws?

   for the judicial system   for punishment   to protect the rights of everyone

7. Who enforces the laws? _____

8. What are the courts' responsibilities? _____

   _____

   _____

   _____

9. Why must our laws sometimes change? _____

   _____

   _____

Main idea   Unit 3

Below are groups of three sentences in a mixed-up order. One is the main idea. One is a sentence to support the main idea, and one suggests the idea expressed by the other two sentences. Write **1** on the line following the main idea. Write **2** on the line following the supporting sentence. Write **3** on the line following the summarizing sentence.

Taking Care of the Environment

1. It is often used to describe where people or animals live. _____

   The word environment means the surroundings in which a living thing exists. _____

   The environment is made up of the soil, rock, water, vegetation, and air that surrounds us. _____

2. Therefore, people should not only learn to protect where they live, but they should become informed about other environments. _____

   Varied world environments, such as wetlands, tropical rain forests, and grasslands, need protection. _____

   If any part of the earth is harmed, all living things are affected. _____

3. Grasslands cover much of North America's midsection. _____

   If farmers grow too much food or keep too many cattle, the ground may become overworked and then require many years to recover. _____

   These lands are used mostly for grazing animals and growing crops. _____

4. People sometimes want to drain these areas so they can be developed. _____

   But the wetlands of the world should be protected because they contain rare animals and plants. _____

   Some environments, such as swamps and marshes, are wet. _____

5. They control where small areas of land may be cleared for growing food, and where nothing is planted so the land may rest. _____

   Large areas of forest land in tropical rain forests are being cut to make room for roads, towns, factories, and ranches . _____

   Some people realize how important the rain forests are and want to save them. _____

Name

Main idea

The main idea is supported by the sentences in a passage.

Read the supporting sentences below and then circle the main idea they support.

EXAMPLE:

A. As summer draws to an end, days get shorter.

B. Each morning the sun rises later. Each evening the sun sets a little earlier.

The sun provides light.   The temperature is cooler.   (Summer's nearly over.)

Fall Festivals

1. A. Farming was not always as efficient as it is today.

   B. Sometimes disease or bad weather ruined the crops before they were ready to harvest. Therefore, when there was a good harvest long ago, people had reason to celebrate.

   People would be hungry if there was a poor crop.
   Today, farmers use fertilizer to help grow better crops.
   Long ago, festivals were held when there was a good harvest.

2. A. They gave thanks because they had had a good harvest.

   B. The crops they gathered are now part of our Thanksgiving feast.
   Traditional Thanksgiving foods include turkey, cranberry sauce, and pumpkin pie.

   The Native Americans helped the settlers plant seeds.
   The first European settlers in America had a fall festival they named Thanksgiving.
   Turkey is served on Thanksgiving, along with the harvested crops.

3. A. Although farming has changed, the harvest is still celebrated.

   B. Different communities and countries celebrate in different ways. Some religious groups offer fruits and vegetables to the needy.

   Food is now grown in greenhouses year-round.
   Nearly all farmers today harvest their crops with machines.
   There is usually a celebration of some sort after a harvest.

Name

Unit 3 Test

Main Idea

Read or listen to the directions. Fill in the circle beside the best answer.

☐ Example:

Read the groups of words. Think about how they are related and what the main idea would be if they were put into a story or passage. Choose the main idea.

white tracks   wet whiskers   purr   spilled milk

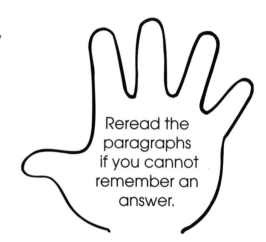

Reread the paragraphs if you cannot remember an answer.

(A) The cat has white whiskers.

(B) The cat is sleeping.

(C) The cat spilled the milk.

(D) The cat likes milk.

Answer: C

Now try these. You have 25 minutes. Continue until you see .

Decide how each group of words in 1–4 is related and choose the main idea of each.

1. dark clouds   trees bending   sirens sounding   go to safe place

   (A) Sirens warned of an impending storm.

   (B) We went to the basement.

   (C) The wind was blowing.

   (D) The clouds were scary.

2. check out books   date due   a quiet place   reading list

   (A) We went to market.

   (B) No one talks at the library.

   (C) We returned overdue books.

   (D) We got books on the list at the library.

GO ON

3. science lab   chemistry   terrible smell   opened windows

    (A) Our chemistry experiment caused a horrible smell.

    (B) The chemistry lab was a mess.

    (C) The teacher was angry.

    (D) Chemistry is fun.

4. hammer and nails   dad's workshop   small pieces of wood   gift for mom

    (A) Dad has a lot of tools.

    (B) Dad's workshop is neat.

    (C) Dad helped me make a gift for Mom.

    (D) I sawed wood into small pieces.

Choose the main idea for paragraphs 5–7.

5.   Mother gave Anne, Cathy, and Fran each a dollar. The girls went running off to the park. Each girl bought 10 red tickets for the rides, games, and food.

    (A) There was a carnival at the park.

    (B) The girls did not know what to do.

    (C) The girls won prizes.

    (D) The tickets were red.

6.   The waves lapped against the beach. Doug was walking barefoot in and out of the waves with his dog, Rex.

    (A) The waves made a lapping sound.

    (B) Doug and Rex went swimming.

    (C) Doug and Rex were at the beach.

    (D) Doug lost his shoes at the beach.

7.   Leslie wished upon a star last night, but she would not tell anyone what her wish was. When her mother came home from the hospital with a baby girl, Leslie got her wish.

(A) Wishes always come true.

(B) Leslie got her wish.

(C) It is better not to keep a secret.

(D) Leslie wanted a brother.

Select a title for paragraphs 8–10.

8.   Some waste must be sorted before it can be recycled. Glass bottles must be thrown into bins for glass. Plastic bottles should go in another bin, and aluminum cans and newspapers go in yet other bins. Trucks then come and carry away the different types of waste to places that process and make them reusable.

(A) All Waste Can Be Recycled   (B) All Bottles Go in the Same Bin

(C) The Recycling Process   (D) The Recycling Bins Are Pollution

9.   Mother could not find the socks that I had just given her for her birthday. When she opened the box and saw what was in it, she had put the socks on the table and thrown the box away. When she started to clean up, the socks were not there. She looked on the floor, inside the box in the trash can, and on the chair where she had been sitting. When she went into the kitchen, there was our puppy with something in his mouth.

(A) Opening Birthday Presents   (B) The Sock Mystery

(C) Mother Liked Her Presents   (D) The Puppy Looked Guilty

10.   All of a sudden I sat straight up in my bed. Sirens were breaking the night's silence as they sped past our house. I ran to the window and counted three ambulances, four police cars, and three fire engines racing toward the factory. I looked at the clock. It was two o'clock in the morning. Could anyone be there at that hour?

(A) Emergency Vehicles   (B) Two O'Clock in the Morning

(C) A Bedtime Story   (D) An Emergency at Night

GO ON

The sentences in 11–14 are in mixed-up order. Choose the sentences which state the main ideas.

11. (A) There were to be 13 alternating red and white stripes in a horizontal direction.

(B) The stars were to be white on a blue field.

(C) The Act fixed the number of stars to reflect the number of states in the Union.

(D) The Third Flag Act, passed in 1818, set the number of stripes and stars on the U.S. flag.

12. (A) Earth is the largest of the inner planets.

(B) All have rocky bodies.

(C) The four planets nearest the sun–Mercury, Venus, Earth, and Mars–are called the inner planets.

(D) They are closer together than the outer planets: Jupiter, Saturn, Uranus, Neptune, and Pluto.

13. (A) Tennis is played on a flat, rectangular area called a court.

(B) White lines on the court define its boundaries.

(C) Players on either side of the net hit the ball back and forth with a racket.

(D) A net, which stretches across the middle of the court, divides it in half.

14. (A) Natural camouflage may occur when an animal or plant makes itself difficult to see by changing its color.

(B) The chameleon is a good example of an animal changing its color.

(C) Some animals or plants have a design or patterning so they will blend in with their environment.

(D) Camouflage is a disguise.

GO ON

Choose the main ideas for passages 15 and 16.

15.　　After preparing for a three-day hike in the mountains, Rick and Bob took off. They drove to where the trail began, signed in, and put the date and time they expected to return. Then they put their huge packs with food supplies and camping gear on their backs and set out on their adventure.

On the last day Rick tripped and rolled about 50 feet down the mountain. Bob put down his pack and went to Rick. Rick was in pain and said he was afraid to move. Bob did not want to leave Rick, so he took off his pack, covered him, and made him as comfortable as possible.

When the boys did not return when they said they would, a search party set out looking for them. It was not too long before they spotted Bob's pack on the trail and saw the boys down below. The search party immobilized Rick's leg and carried him on a stretcher to a spot where a helicopter picked the boys up and took them the rest of the way home.

(A) Rick hurts his leg.

(B) The boys ride in a helicopter.

(C) The boys go on a three-day hike.

(D) The boys finish the hike with a happy ending.

16.　　New Year's Day is one of the world's oldest holidays, but it is not always celebrated like we do in the United States. It may be observed with different customs and at different times, but it always "sweeps out" the old and welcomes a new beginning.

Chinese New Year is around mid-January or February and lasts 15 days. It is that country's most celebrated holiday. In Israel Rosh Hashanah is celebrated in September or October. On the eve of Rosh Hashanah, families sit down together for a special meal that includes sweet foods in hopes of making the new year sweet and filled with happiness. Ethiopians celebrate the new year at the end of their rainy season in September. On New Year's Day they wash away the old year by bathing in the nearest body of water.

(A) The history of New Year's Day is interesting.

(B) New Year's Day is the world's oldest holiday.

(C) New Year's Day means the end of the rainy season.

(D) There are many New Year's customs around the world.

Read the passage to answer questions 17–20.

One important responsibility of the American cowboy was to drive herds of cattle north to the railroad stations in Kansas. The cowboys often followed the Chisholm Trail, which opened in 1867. Often two to three thousand cattle were herded at a time. Once they reached the railroad stations, the cattle were transported to the East.

The Chisholm Trail was named after Jesse Chisholm. In 1866, he drove his wagon north through Oklahoma to a trading post near Wichita, Kansas. The wheels of his wagon cut deep ruts into the land and marked a route that was followed by the cowboys for 20 years.

The trail drive became a major event in a cowboy's life. Usually the drive lasted about two to three months. The cowboys were hired by a trail boss. The trail boss also hired a wrangler, who looked after the horses, and a cook.

17. Choose the sentence that tells the main idea.

(A) Cowboys followed the Chisholm Trail.

(B) One important job of a cowboy was to herd cattle on long trail drives.

(C) The trail drive lasted two to three months.

(D) The trail boss hired cowboys, a wrangler, and a cook.

18. Which sentence would not belong in the second paragraph?

(A) Jesse Chisholm, who was part-Cherokee, was a trader.

(B) His wagon was loaded with buffalo hides.

(C) Every day a cowboy faced the danger of a broken bone.

(D) Chisholm drove through the Indian Territory.

19. Choose the best title for the passage.

(A) The Trail Drive

(B) Jesse Chisholm

(C) The Chisholm Trail

(D) Cowboys on the Ranch

GO ON

20. Which sentence could be added as a summarizing sentence for the passage?

(A) Cowboys needed to learn to rope and brand cattle.

(B) Trail drives are an important part of American folklore.

(C) A hat, chaps, lariat, and horse were all important equipment for a cowboy.

(D) Cowpokes and cowpunchers are other names for cowboys.

Write a sentence telling the main idea for the following supporting sentences. Then write another sentence adding another supporting idea.

The first trick Alexa taught her dog, Toby, was to sit. Toby then learned to roll over. Before long he could even jump through a hoop.

_____

_____

_____

_____

STOP

Finding the facts

Finding the **facts** of a passage means that given specific questions, you can respond with precise answers.

Read the passage and then find the facts to answer the questions.

Early Pioneer Travel in America

The pioneers followed several different routes on their way west. One route went through the Cumberland Gap, a natural pass in the Appalachian Mountains that ended near where Kentucky, Tennessee, and Virginia met. In 1775, several woodsmen led by Daniel Boone cut the Wilderness Road. Pioneers from New England traveled across New York on the Mohawk Trail.

The first groups of settlers crossed the Appalachian Mountains in the late 1700s and early 1800s and followed these early trails. Usually pioneer families joined several others who wanted to move west. Some traveled on foot carrying only a rifle, an ax, and a few supplies, but most went by wagon. Either way they did not take many belongings, especially anything that could be made along the way. They hunted and fished, and also used dried staples they carried with them.

The pioneers were able to only travel short distances every day. Most trips took several weeks.

1. Who followed the Mohawk Trail?_____

2. Where did the trail that went through the Cumberland Gap end? _____

_____

3. How did the pioneers get food? _____

_____

4. Who was responsible for the Wilderness Road? _____

5. When did the first groups of settlers head west?_____

6. Which trail crossed New York? _____

7. How did the pioneers travel? _____

8. How long did most trips take? _____

45

Name

Read the passage and then circle the facts that complete the sentences on page 47.

The Supreme Court

Originally the number of justices who sat on the Supreme Court varied from six to ten. But from 1869 to this day the Court has had nine justices: one chief justice and eight associate justices.

The Court may consider 5,000 cases, but usually only several hundred cases come before it. The cases are either of national importance or they challenge a law based on constitutional grounds.

Every case that comes before the Court is given the name of the parties involved. If Mr. Jones is suing the U.S. government, the case is called *Jones v. the U.S. Government*. When the justices decide a case, it becomes a precedent, which means that the decision becomes the basis of future rulings.

All Supreme Court justices are appointed by the president and approved by the Senate. Supreme Court justices may hold their seats until they die. If a justice acts improperly or shows corruptness, the justice may be impeached and removed from the Court.

The Court's most important duty is to maintain the laws as laid out in the Constitution. The authors of the Constitution could not have known what life would be like in the twenty-first century. Therefore, it is up to the Court to make adjustments as they relate to every individual's constitutional rights. The justices interpret the Constitution in light of today's times.

Finding the facts

1. Justices may be _____ from the Court if they act improperly.

   accused and barred   blamed and banned

   fired   impeached and removed

2. Currently there are _____ justices on the Court.

   more   one chief justice and eight associate

   fewer   one chief justice and nine associate

3. The Court hears _____ cases in a year.

   five thousand   one hundred

   several hundred   about one hundred

4. The Court must make _____ to the U.S. Constitution so it relates to current practices.

   adjustments   variations   reversals   distinctions

5. The cases that come before the Court are either _____ or they challenge laws based on constitutional grounds.

   constitutional law   of national importance   not important   state laws

6. The Court's most important function is to _____ as defined in the U.S. Constitution.

   keep law and order   appoint federal court judges

   maintain the laws   update the laws

7. Every case that comes before the Court is given the name of the _____.

   U.S. government   person suing   deciding justice   parties involved

8. The Supreme Court justices are named by the president and _____ by the Senate.

   appointed   announced   approved   applauded

9. Originally there were _____ justices on the Court.

   six to ten   seven to nine   ten   nine

10. A case decided by the Court becomes the _____ of future rulings.

    law   basis   impression   point

Name

Finding facts using a chart

Unit 4

Often facts about a certain subject are listed in a chart. This makes it easier to compare the facts. Be sure to read all the information carefully.

Twenty-nine percent of Earth is land. The land is divided into seven continents. Use this chart to record information about the continents on page 49.

	Area (in sq. mi.)	Highest Mountain (in feet)	Lowest Point (ft. below sea level)	Longest River (in miles)
Africa	11,7000,000	Kilimanjaro (19,340)	Lake Assal (512)	Nile (4,145)
Antarctica	5,400,000	Vinson Massif (16,864)	not known	no rivers
Asia	17,200,000	Everest (29,028)	Dead Sea (1,312)	Yangtze (3,915)
Australia	3,071,000	Kosciusko (7,310)	Lake Eyre (52)	Murray-Darling (2,310)
Europe	3,800,000	Elbrus (18,510)	Caspian Sea (92)	Volga (2,194)
North America	9,400,000	McKinley (20,320)	Death Valley (282)	Missouri (2,540)
South America	6,900,000	Aconcagua (22,834)	Valdes Peninsula (131)	Amazon (4,000)

Name

Finding facts using a chart

1. List the continents according to size from largest to smallest.

   a. _____

   b. _____

   c. _____

   d. _____

   e. _____

   f. _____

   g. _____

2. Which continent has the highest mountain and the lowest point? _____

3. What are the two longest rivers? _____ and _____

4. Which continents are about the same size?

   _____ and _____

5. Which continent has the shortest mountain and the highest lowest point? _____

6. List the mountains that are greater than 20,000 feet high.

   _____

   _____

   _____

7. List the rivers from shortest to longest.

   a. _____

   b. _____

   c. _____

   d. _____

   e. _____

   f. _____

Write two questions using the chart.

Name

Reading for details

An author includes many details to help you better understand a story. **Details** provide you with a clearer picture of all the story elements, such as characters, setting, and plot.

Read the summary of <u>Shiloh</u> by Phyllis Reynolds Naylor (Bantam Doubleday Dell Publishing Group, Inc., 1991). Use details from the summary to complete the puzzle. The bold spaces will tell you what award this book received.

Shiloh

In <u>Shiloh</u>, an award-winning book, 11-year-old Marty Preston tells about what happens when a dog follows him home. Marty lives with his parents and two sisters, Becky and Dara Lynn, in the hills above Friendly. Friendly is a small town in West Virginia near Sisterville. On a Sunday afternoon, after a big dinner of rabbit and sweet potatoes, Marty goes for a walk along the river. During his walk, Marty spies a short-haired dog. The dog, a beagle with black and brown spots, does not make a sound as he watches and follows Marty. From the dog's behavior, Marty suspects that the dog has been mistreated. Since he found the dog near the old Shiloh schoolhouse, Marty calls the dog Shiloh. Marty soon discovers that Shiloh belongs to mean Judd Travers. After returning Shiloh to Judd, Marty contemplates how he can earn enough money to buy the dog. Before Marty can solve this problem, he is faced with a difficult decision.

1. In what town does Marty live? ☐☐☐☐☐☐☐☐

2. How old is Marty? ☐☐☐☐☐☐

3. What kind of potatoes did the family eat on Sunday? ☐☐☐☐☐

4. What kind of meat did they eat? ☐☐☐☐☐☐

5. What kind of dog is Shiloh? ☐☐☐☐☐☐

6. Write the last name of Shiloh's owner. ☐☐☐☐☐☐☐

7. Name one of Marty's sisters. ☐☐☐☐☐☐

8. What adjective was used to describe Judd Travers? ☐☐☐☐

9. What is Marty's last name? ☐☐☐☐☐☐☐

10. What day does Marty find Shiloh? ☐☐☐☐☐☐

11. Who is telling the story? ☐☐☐☐☐

12. Marty finds the dog by what schoolhouse? ☐☐☐☐☐☐

Name

Understanding characters

The most important characters in a story are called main characters. They seem to be brought to life by their actions. Details from the story help you to better understand the personalities of the characters.

Read the story and then follow the directions.

Frosty

Emily saw a gray, longhaired cat on her way to the park. She stopped to pet it and see if it had a collar with an identification tag. It did not. Emily walked on to meet her friends, and the cat followed her. Emily and her friends played on the swings and other playground equipment. The cat followed the girls from one place to another and watched them play. When it was time to go home, Emily waved good-bye to her friends and walked home. She noticed the cat did not stay at the park but rather followed her.

When Emily got to her house, she went in the kitchen door. The cat sat outside the closed screen door watching Emily eat her lunch. Emily knew it was not a good idea to feed a stray pet, but the poor cat had not had any food in at least several hours. So Emily gave it a saucer of milk.

After lunch Emily decided to clean up the cat. When she began to brush it, its fur got lighter as the dirt came out along with some of its hair. It seemed the gray cat was really a white cat!

When she finished brushing the cat, Emily made some sketches of it. With a poster pen she wrote its description, where it was found, and a phone number where the owner could find the cat. That afternoon Emily put her notices up in the neighborhood. She also called the animal shelter to report the found cat.

There were no responses after a few days, and the cat had become her friend. Emily asked her parents if she could keep the cat, and they agreed it was a nice pet. Emily decided to call it Frosty because it was now as white as snow.

1. Who was the main character in this story? _____

2. Circle the words that describe this character.

   frustrated   careless   caring   tough   resourceful

3. List three ways she demonstrates the above character traits.

   _____

   _____

   _____

51

Name

Read the story and then follow the directions.

Becoming Good Neighbors

Billy and Roger were next-door neighbors and were in the same class at Central School. Billy was probably the brightest student in the class. Roger was definitely the strongest and the best athlete in the school. The boys often got a ride to school in the morning from one of their parents, but in the afternoon they came home separately. Roger usually stayed and played either touch football or basketball with some of the older boys. Sometimes Billy watched, but usually he came home and did his homework and read a book.

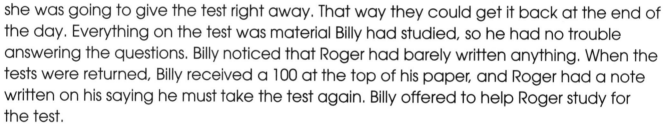

One day, Billy asked if he could join in Roger's after-school games. Roger answered, "No, you are too small and not strong enough." The other boys laughed as they all headed out to the field. Billy was crushed. He went home and studied for the next day's science test.

When Billy and Roger got to the classroom the next day, their teacher said she was going to give the test right away. That way they could get it back at the end of the day. Everything on the test was material Billy had studied, so he had no trouble answering the questions. Billy noticed that Roger had barely written anything. When the tests were returned, Billy received a 100 at the top of his paper, and Roger had a note written on his saying he must take the test again. Billy offered to help Roger study for the test.

The next morning on their way to school, Roger invited Billy to play with him and his friends after school. He encouraged Billy by telling him he would teach him how to play the games.

1. Who were the main characters in the story? _____

2. Circle two of Billy's characteristics.

       helpful   athletic   selfish   studious   average student

3. Circle two of Roger's characteristics.

       unfriendly   unkind   athletic   a bully   studious

4. Circle two of Roger's characteristics after the science test.

       frustrated   hard worker   considerate   appreciative   threatening

Name

Read or listen to the directions. Fill in the circle beside the best answer.

☐ Example:

Ming began jumping up and down and shouting with glee when her team won.

Choose the word that best describes Ming.

(A) timid   (B) sad

(C) elated   (D) frustrated

Answer: C

Now try these. You have 25 minutes.

Continue until you see ⬡STOP.

Read the directions carefully. Be sure you understand what you are supposed to do.

Select a word or phrase that best describes the characters in 1–4.

On Forrest's way to the party, he tripped over Mr. Preston's hose stretched across the sidewalk. He fell on top of the present he was carrying and also scraped his elbow. Mr. Preston heard Forrest crying and came to see what happened. Mr. Preston cleaned up Forrest, rewrapped the gift, and drove him to the party.

1. Mr. Preston was _____.

(A) considerate   (B) annoyed

(C) thoughtless   (D) comical

Andrew would not clean up his room, so his father would not let him go to the ball game. Andrew stayed in his room while the rest of the family went.

2. Andrew was _____.

respectful   stubborn   happy   indifferent
(A)   (B)   (C)   (D)

GO ON ⇒

Maggie said the referee made a bad call, the team did not use all their time-outs, and the other team was not fair.

3. Maggie was _____.

discouraged Ⓐ   rude Ⓑ   a bad sport Ⓒ   a good athlete Ⓓ

The fifth-grade teacher let her students have an extra recess because they had worked so hard in the morning practicing for the upcoming play.

4. The teacher _____.

Ⓐ knew the class liked to run   Ⓑ appreciated their hard work

Ⓒ was in charge   Ⓓ was helpful

Use the chart to answer questions 5–8.

Northwest States

	Date State Entered Union	Area in Square Miles	Population in 1995	% Population Change from 1980–1995
Alaska	Jan. 3, 1959	570,374	604,000	50.2
Idaho	July 3, 1890	82,751	1,163,000	23.2
Oregon	Feb. 14, 1859	96,003	3,141,000	19.3
Washington	Nov. 11, 1889	66,582	5,431,000	31.4

5. Which state is the largest in size with the smallest population?

Alaska Ⓐ   Idaho Ⓑ   Oregon Ⓒ   Washington Ⓓ

GO ON

Name

6. Which two states entered the union approximately 100 years apart?

(A) Idaho and Washington   (B) Oregon and Washington

(C) Alaska and Oregon   (D) Idaho and Alaska

7. Which state's population changed the least from 1980 to 1995?

Alaska	Idaho	Oregon	Washington
(A)	(B)	(C)	(D)

8. Which state is the smallest in size but has the greatest population?

Alaska	Idaho	Oregon	Washington
(A)	(B)	(C)	(D)

Choose the correct answers for questions 9–14.

The U.S. president and vice president are elected every fourth year on the first Tuesday after the first Monday in November.

9. How often is the presidential election held?

(A) every other November   (B) the first Tuesday after the first Monday

(C) every four years   (D) when called for by Congress

The number of elected officials to Congress from any state is determined by its number of senators plus its number of representatives. Every state has two senators. A senator's term is six years. The number of representatives from each state varies according to the state's population. Every state has at least one representative. The most populous state has fifty-two representatives. A representative's term is only two

10. What is the smallest representation any state has in Congress?

one	two	six	three
(A)	(B)	(C)	(D)

GO ON

11. How often are senators elected to office?

(A) every four years   (B) every two years

(C) every six years   (D) varies according to the state's population

The Electoral College actually determines the outcome of a presidential election. It consists of electors from each state. The number of electors from each state is determined by the number of senators and representatives it has in Congress. The electors meet the first Monday after the second Wednesday in December to officially elect the two highest officers in the nation. Although registered voters throughout the U.S. vote for president and vice president, their votes may not count when their state electors meet in their state capitals. This happened in the year 2000. Al Gore won the popular vote because more people in the country voted for him. However, George Bush received more votes in the states that had larger numbers of Electoral College members.

12. Who has the final say about the winner in a presidential election?

(A) the president and vice president   (B) registered voters

(C) the Electoral College   (D) senators and representatives

13. When does the Electoral College meet?

(A) the first Monday in December

(B) the second Monday after the first Wednesday in December

(C) the first Wednesday after the second Monday in December

(D) the first Monday after the second Wednesday in December

14. What is the representation of electors from each state on the Electoral College?

(A) number of voters from the winning party

(B) number of senators plus representatives from each state

(C) number of representatives in each state capital

(D) same number of electors from each state

GO ON

Unit 4 Test

Read the following paragraph and answer questions 15 and 16.

There were Seven Wonders of the Ancient World, but the only one that remains is in Egypt. The three Great Pyramids built of stone were erected approximately 4,600 years ago at Giza on the west bank of the Nile River, north of Cairo. They were built as royal tombs. The largest of the three, called Khufu, is built of solid limestone blocks and covers about 13 acres. It is estimated this pyramid contains 2,300,000 stone blocks and that each one averages two and one-half tons. One hundred thousand laborers are said to have worked to build this pyramid.

15. What is the name of the largest pyramid?

      Cheops   Khafra   Chephren   Khufu
        (A)   (B)   (C)   (D)

16. Where are the three Great Pyramids located?

(A) at Cairo on the west bank of the Nile River above Giza

(B) at Giza on the west bank of the Nile River above Cairo

(C) at Giza on the east bank of the Nile River above Cairo

(D) at Cairo on the west bank of the Nile River above Giza

Read the following story and answer questions 17–20.

There was going to be a test on Friday covering the meteorology unit. Ethan was determined to get at least 95 percent on the test. He had several days to study. On Monday, he made study cards with all the definitions of the vocabulary words he needed to know. That evening he took the cards with him and reviewed them as his mom drove him to soccer practice. He made an outline of the unit on Tuesday afternoon. Ethan's dad then quizzed him from the outline. His friend Zach came home with him after school on Wednesday. They each made 25 game cards with questions from their science books. The boys kept track of the number of questions they each answered correctly. Ethan won; his hard work was paying off! Ethan went to his room on Thursday evening and studied quietly for an hour. The next day he confidently answered every question on the test.

GO ON

17. Which is not a way Ethan prepared for the test?

(A) He made a game with his friend Zach.

(B) His mom quizzed him from the study guide.

(C) He made an outline of the unit.

(D) He made vocabulary study cards.

18. How many days did Ethan study?

two	three	four	five
(A)	(B)	(C)	(D)

19. Where did Ethan review the vocabulary words?

in the car	at home	at school	at soccer practice
(A)	(B)	(C)	(D)

20. Select the word that best describes Ethan.

idle	studious	dignified	isolated
(A)	(B)	(C)	(D)

Write a short paragraph that shows that a character, Jerome, is frightened. Then write a question using details from the paragraph.

_____

_____

_____

_____

_____

_____

_____

(STOP)

Midway Review Test Name Grid

Write your name in pencil in the boxes along the top. Begin with your last name. Fill in as many letters as will fit. Then follow the columns straight down and bubble in the letters that correspond with the letters in your name. Complete the rest of the information the same way. You may use a piece of scrap paper to help you keep your place.

STUDENT'S NAME		SCHOOL

LAST · **FIRST** · **MI**

The name grid consists of lettered bubble columns (A–Z) with blank boxes at top for writing letters.

SCHOOL

TEACHER

FEMALE ○   MALE ○

DATE OF BIRTH

MONTH	DAY	YEAR
JAN ○	⓪ ⓪	⓪ ⓪
FEB ○	① ①	① ①
MAR ○	② ②	② ②
APR ○	③ ③	③ ③
MAY ○	④	④ ④
JUN ○	⑤	⑤ ⑤
JUL ○	⑥	⑥ ⑥
AUG ○	⑦	⑦ ⑦
SEP ○	⑧	⑧ ⑧
OCT ○	⑨	⑨ ⑨
NOV ○		
DEC ○		

GRADE ③ ④ ⑤

Midway Review Test Answer Sheet

Pay close attention when transferring your answers. Fill in the bubbles neatly and completely. You may use a piece of scrap paper to help you keep your place.

SAMPLES
A Ⓐ Ⓑ ● Ⓓ
B Ⓕ ● Ⓗ Ⓙ

1 Ⓐ Ⓑ Ⓒ Ⓓ   7 Ⓐ Ⓑ Ⓒ Ⓓ   13 Ⓐ Ⓑ Ⓒ Ⓓ   19 Ⓐ Ⓑ Ⓒ Ⓓ
2 Ⓕ Ⓖ Ⓗ Ⓙ   8 Ⓕ Ⓖ Ⓗ Ⓙ   14 Ⓕ Ⓖ Ⓗ Ⓙ   20 Ⓕ Ⓖ Ⓗ Ⓙ
3 Ⓐ Ⓑ Ⓒ Ⓓ   9 Ⓐ Ⓑ Ⓒ Ⓓ   15 Ⓐ Ⓑ Ⓒ Ⓓ
4 Ⓕ Ⓖ Ⓗ Ⓙ   10 Ⓕ Ⓖ Ⓗ Ⓙ   16 Ⓕ Ⓖ Ⓗ Ⓙ
5 Ⓐ Ⓑ Ⓒ Ⓓ   11 Ⓐ Ⓑ Ⓒ Ⓓ   17 Ⓐ Ⓑ Ⓒ Ⓓ
6 Ⓕ Ⓖ Ⓗ Ⓙ   12 Ⓕ Ⓖ Ⓗ Ⓙ   18 Ⓕ Ⓖ Ⓗ Ⓙ

Name _____

Read or listen to the directions.
Fill in the circle beside the best answer.

☐ Example:

Choose the homophone that completes the sentence.

What _____ can you play on the guitar?

(A) cords

(B) notes

(C) chords

(D) songs

Answer: C

Now try these. You have 25 minutes.

Continue until you see ⬡STOP .

1. Read all of the answer choices carefully before you choose your answer.

2. If you cannot figure out an answer, skip the test item. Come back to it later.

3. Reread the paragraphs if you cannot remember an answer.

4. Read the directions carefully. Be sure you understand what you are supposed to do.

5. Fill in the answer sheet carefully. Be sure the problem number from the test matches the problem number on the answer sheet.

Choose the relationship of the underlined words in 1–3.

1. The prominent landmark on the highway warned us that we were nearing the rest area.

   The path in the forest became obscure because of the overgrowth on the forest's floor.

   synonyms   antonyms   homophones   homographs
   (A)   (B)   (C)   (D)

2. Because of all the rain, there was an exceptional display of spring flowers.

   There was a phenomenal antique car show at the arena.

   synonyms   antonyms   homophones   homographs
   (F)   (G)   (H)   (J)

GO ON

Midway Review Test

3. Sometimes <u>sealing</u> wax may be used to close an envelope.
   The <u>ceiling</u> in my bedroom needs to be painted.

synonyms	antonyms	homophones	homographs
Ⓐ	Ⓑ	Ⓒ	Ⓓ

Select the word to complete each analogy in 4–6.

4. Bell : telephone : : _____ : lightbulb

Morse	Edison	Marconi	Whitney
Ⓕ	Ⓖ	Ⓗ	Ⓙ

5. Spaniel : canine : : Siamese : _____

culture	Asian	feline	dog
Ⓐ	Ⓑ	Ⓒ	Ⓓ

6. Data is to research as _____ is to scientific study.

specimen	lab	notebook	conclusion
Ⓕ	Ⓖ	Ⓗ	Ⓙ

Choose the words that complete sentences 7 and 8.

7. The developer _____ the land into seven lots.

subdivided	envisioned	inflated	submerged
Ⓐ	Ⓑ	Ⓒ	Ⓓ

8. The naval officer's mission was very _____ and secretive.

outrageous	marvelous	humorous	dangerous
Ⓕ	Ⓖ	Ⓗ	Ⓙ

GO ON ▷

Midway Review Test

Identify the kinds of phrases the underlined words are in sentences 9–11.

9. The tree <u>was a ball of fire</u> with its autumn leaves.

      simile   metaphor   idiom   personification

       (A)   (B)   (C)   (D)

10. The winner of the race ran <u>like a gazelle</u>.

      simile   metaphor   idiom   personification

       (F)   (G)   (H)   (J)

11. The <u>leaves whispered</u> to the boy, "Hurry home before the storm."

      simile   metaphor   idiom   personification

       (A)   (B)   (C)   (D)

Select the main idea of paragraphs 12 and 13.

12.   Barry and his sister were taking lunch to their grandmother because she was not feeling well. When they got there, the door was open. They went into her bedroom, but she was not there. At first they were afraid something may have happened, but they noticed that her nightgown was on the bed, and there was a note next to it. It read, "Do not worry. I feel better, and I have gone to the market. Wait for me, and we can eat together. I will bring you a surprise dessert."

    (F) Grandmother was missing.

    (G) The children took lunch to their grandmother.

    (H) Grandmother goes to the market.

    (J) The children discover that their grandmother feels better.

GO ON ⟹

Midway Review Test

13. Everyone in the world lives by rules. If there were no rules, or laws, everyone would do what he or she pleased regardless of how it might affect another person. Imagine if you worked all day and wanted to get a good night's sleep, but your neighbor slept all day and wanted to play loud music all night. You would have a right to complain because most communities have a "disturbing the peace" law. Your neighbor could be prohibited from playing the music so loud, and you could get your sleep. That is an example of why there are laws and how they can work.

(A) Rules are for everyone.   (B) Think before you act.

(C) Play only soft music.   (D) Obey all the rules.

Read the paragraph to answer questions 14–16.

Thrushes are songbirds that have many similarities and differences. Their young have spotted breasts. They all eat worms, insects, and berries. There are several kinds of thrushes. The robin is probably the most common. Solitaires and bluebirds also belong to this group. The family name for this group of birds is *Turdidae.* All members of this family, except bluebirds, can be seen standing or running on the ground. As winter approaches, most thrushes migrate in flocks at night, but robins and bluebirds travel in the daytime. Most of these birds build nests in trees or shrubs, but the bluebird builds its nest in tree cavities or birdhouses.

14. Which statement is true about thrushes?

(F) Solitaires are the most common.   (G) Bluebirds run on the ground.

(H) Thrushes only live in North America.   (J) Most thrushes can be seen running on the ground.

15. Which sentence best tells the main idea of the article?

(A) Thrushes have many similarities and differences.

(B) Thrushes all eat worms, insects, and berries.

(C) The robin is probably the most common.

(D) Thrushes are songbirds.

16. Which fact is not included in the article?

(F) *Turdidae* is the family name for thrushes.

(G) The wood thrush has a spotted, white breast.

(H) Bluebirds build nests in birdhouses.

(J) Robins migrate during the daytime.

Read the story to answer questions 17–20.

Marta wanted to earn some extra money so she could buy a new CD. Finally, Marta's mother agreed to let her baby-sit her six-year-old younger brother, Trent. Marta promised to watch Trent carefully. After their mother had left, Marta and Trent played catch outside. Then they made a fort in the basement. Trent pretended he was king of the basement. Marta let Trent order her around. After Trent became bored being king, Marta read him six different books while they camped out in the fort. Then she fixed him a big bowl of chocolate ice cream. Finally, they watched Trent's favorite movie. When their mother returned, Marta was exhausted!

17. Why did Marta want to earn extra money?

(A) to buy a book

(B) to go to a movie

(C) to buy a new CD

(D) to help her mother

18. How did Marta feel after her mother returned?

(F) tired

(G) relieved

(H) prosperous

(J) energetic

19. Which activity did Marta and Trent not do?

(A) read books

(B) play catch

(C) watch a movie

(D) play hide-and-seek

20. Choose the best title for the story.

(F) A Big Bowl of Ice Cream   (G) The Basement Fort

(H) Marta's Day Baby-sitting   (J) The New CD

Write a paragraph about someone you admire. Use a simile in your paragraph. Underline the sentence that tells the main idea.

_____

_____

_____

_____

_____

_____

_____

Sequencing with a time line

Unit 5

A **time line** shows dates and events in the order they happened.

Study the time line and complete the activities on page 67.

Oct. 4, 1957 (The U.S.S.R. launched *Sputnik 1*, the first man-made satellite.)

Nov. 3, 1957 (The U.S.S.R. launched *Sputnik 2*, which carried the first space traveler, a dog.)

April 12, 1961 (The U.S.S.R. launched *Vostok 1*, the first manned flight, with Major Yuri Gagarin.)

Feb. 20, 1962 (John Glenn, aboard *Mercury 6*, was the first American to orbit Earth.)

Oct. 16–19, 1963 (The U.S.S.R.'s Valentina Tereshkova, who was aboard *Vostok 6*, was the first woman in space.)

Mar. 18, 1965 (The U.S.S.R. completed the first space walk from *Voskhod 2*.)

Dec. 21–27, 1968 (*Apollo 8* from the U.S. was the first manned flight to orbit the moon.)

July 16–24, 1969 (Neil Armstrong and Edwin Aldrin, aboard the U.S.'s *Apollo 11*, made the first moon landing.)

May 14, 1973 (The first U.S. space station was established.)

Dec. 4, 1978 (The *Pioneer Venus* from the U.S. entered the orbit of Venus.)

April 12–14, 1981 (The U.S. flew the space shuttle *Columbia*, a reusable spacecraft.)

Name

Sequencing with a time line

1. Number the space missions in the order they occurred.

_____ *Vostok 6*

_____ *Sputnik 2*

_____ space shuttle *Columbia*

_____ *Apollo 8*

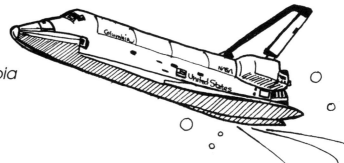

2. Write the letter of the space explorer in front of the date of the mission.

_____ July 16–24, 1969   A. Yuri Gagarin

_____ February 20, 1962   B. Neil Armstrong

_____ April 12, 1961   C. Valentina Tereshkova

_____ October 16–19, 1963   D. John Glenn

3. Number the events in the order they happened.

_____ the first U.S. space station

_____ the first man-made satellite

_____ the first woman in space

_____ the first manned flight to orbit the moon

_____ the first space walk

_____ the first moon walk

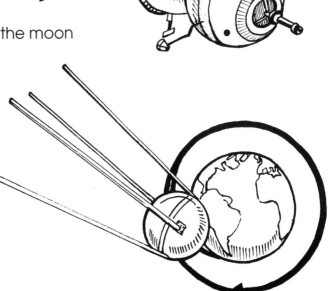

Make a time line of important events at your school or home.

Sequencing
Putting a series of events in order is called **sequencing**.

Read the passage and then number the events on page 69 in the order they occurred.

The Anasazi

One of the better-known prehistoric peoples of the southwestern United States are the Anasazi. We do not know what the Anasazi called themselves. It is the name given them by those who have studied prehistoric Native Americans of the Southwest. Anasazi is a Navajo word that means "ancient ones."

The Anasazi most likely came to the Southwest around 100 B.C. They built their simple homes of sticks and mud in shallow caves along canyon walls. They relied on food they grew such as corn and squash. They were expert basket weavers, and therefore this first phase is named the Early Basket Maker Period. They existed until around 400 A.D.

The next Anasazi phase is named the Modified Basket Maker Period. These Anasazi wanted to be closer to their crops, so they built their homes in open areas near the land they farmed. Their homes were called pit houses because they were built partially underground. During this period, the Anasazi still made baskets, but they also began making clay pots. Beans become a more important crop because they could now be cooked over a fire in a clay pot. During this time, they began using a bow and arrow for hunting and wearing turquoise jewelry.

The Anasazi's third phase began around 700 A.D. It is named the Developmental Pueblo Period. Their homes were now aboveground, but they built kivas, partly underground rooms for ceremonies. They made pottery for two purposes: cooking and beauty.

The Great Pueblo Period began around 1100 A.D. During this period, the Anasazi built cliff dwellings that look like today's apartment buildings. They used ladders to get into the upper stories. They could pull these ladders inside to keep enemies from entering. Sometimes several of these cliff dwellings were built near one another to form communities. These communities sometimes became the center for an entire region. Trade with other nearby tribes began during this period.

What became of the Anasazi remains somewhat a mystery. Was it a drought, warring nomadic tribes, the lack of good topsoil, or a combination? It is believed that perhaps they drifted into the areas now occupied by other pueblo dwellers of New Mexico and the Hopi and Zuni.

Name

Number the events from **1** to **10** to show the correct sequence.

_____ a. The third phase began around 700 A.D., and it is named the Developmental Pueblo Period.

_____ b. This first phase is named the Early Basket Maker Period.

_____ c. What actually happened to the Anasazi remains a mystery.

_____ d. The Anasazi probably came to the Southwest around 100 B.C.

_____ e. The Great Pueblo Period began around 1100 A.D.

_____ f. The second phase began after 400 A.D., and it is named the Modified Basket Maker Period.

_____ g. When several of the "apartment buildings" were built near one another, they formed a larger community.

_____ h. They grew corn and squash and were excellent basket makers.

_____ i. The homes of the last phase are similar to today's apartment buildings.

_____ j. During the Developmental Pueblo Period, the Anasazi's homes were aboveground and ceremonial rooms, called kivas, were partly underground.

Name

The following groups of sentences are out of order. Number them to show the correct order.

1. _____ He did not know anyone in the neighborhood.

   _____ Freddie did not live too far from the park. He thought if he walked there, perhaps he might meet some new friends.

   _____ Freddie had just moved into his new home on Elm Street.

2. _____ When he got to the park, Freddie saw some boys playing kickball.

   _____ The boys reluctantly agreed to let him play.

   _____ He introduced himself and asked if he could play with them.

3. _____ His team ended up winning.

   _____ And when his team was up, Freddie was responsible for four runs.

   _____ When Freddie's team was in the field, he made a couple of spectacular outs.

   _____ After that the boys were ringing his doorbell and asking him to come to the park and play kickball.

4. _____ They found out they shared some of these interests.

   _____ For the rest of the summer, Freddie enjoyed playing with the boys.

   _____ At the end of the summer, all the boys were good friends— on and off the kickball field.

   _____ Freddie also had the boys over to his house, so they could learn more about his other interests.

Following directions
Unit 5

Often directions are sequenced steps which help you do something or get somewhere.
Directions should be read one at a time and followed exactly.

There are several appliances in your house you use frequently, but probably rarely consider what you do to make them work. Imagine that you have rented your house to someone, and you need to leave instructions about how the appliances work.

Number the instructions in a logical order.

1. How to Use the Washing Machine

_____ Next, determine the size of your wash and set the knob to small, medium, or large.

_____ Gently lay the dirty laundry around the center agitator.

_____ Depending on the size of your wash load, pour between a quarter to half a cup of liquid detergent onto the wash.

_____ Set the type of wash (regular, permanent press, delicate) for the machine, close the lid, and pull out the knob to start the machine.

2. How to Use the VCR

_____ Press PLAY.

_____ To get the cassette out, press EJECT.

_____ To rewind the film after it is over, press REWIND.

_____ Insert the cassette, and the VCR power will come on automatically.

_____ When you are finished watching, press STOP.

3. How to Set Up and Use the Telephone/Answering Machine

_____ Next, hold down the day-and-time button to set the day and stop on the day.

_____ Once the time and day are set, record your greeting by pressing down the announce button and speaking after the tone.

_____ After listening to a message, press the erase button.

_____ To listen to messages, press the review button.

_____ First, set the time by pressing the hour button and stopping at the correct hour, and then pressing the minute button and stopping at the correct minute.

Name

Following directions
Remember to always read all the directions and follow them in the order listed.

Unit 5

Complete the steps in the spaces below for each set of directions.

A. 1. Draw two vertical parallel lines.

2. Draw two parallel lines that intersect the vertical lines.

3. Draw a circle that intersects every line.

4. Make an X in the center box.

B. 1. Write the name of a building that rhymes with **mouse**.

2. Change the middle letter to N.

3. Switch the order of the last two letters.

4. Add the twentieth letter of the alphabet to the end of the word.

5. What is the word?

C. 1. Draw a hexagon.

2. Inside of the hexagon, write the number of sides it has.

3. Draw three different-sized triangles below it.

4. Shade in the middle triangle.

D. 1. Write the word that means "words with the same or nearly the same meaning."

2. Beginning with the S, cross out every other letter.

3. Add the second letter remaining between the last two letters.

4. What is the word?

5. Add a hyphen between the second and third letters.

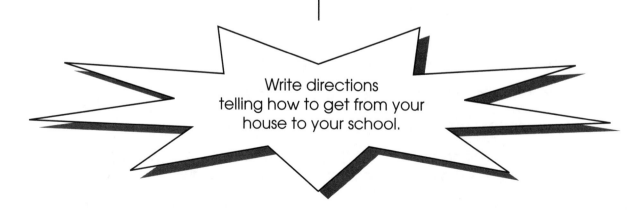

Write directions telling how to get from your house to your school.

Name

Read or listen to the directions. Fill in the circle beside the best answer.

 Example:

Select the picture that followed the directions correctly.

Draw a square. Divide the square in half with a vertical line. Write 6 in the right half. Write 7 in the left half.

(A)

(B)

(C)

(D)

Note the time allotment. Pace yourself.

Answer: A

Now try these. You have 20 minutes. Continue until you see .

Choose the correct sequences for the numbered sentences in 1–4.

1.
  1. They also experiment to find the answers.
  2. People who study Earth, how it was formed and how it changes, are called geologists.
  3. They learn about Earth by making observations and by asking questions.

3, 1, 2	2, 1, 3	2, 3, 1	1, 3, 2
(A)	(B)	(C)	(D)

2.
  1. Earth is constantly changing.
  2. However, water erodes riverbanks and shorelines, and wind and rain wear away the mountains to change their shapes.
  3. Your eye cannot see it happen because changes take hundreds of thousands of years to occur.

1, 3, 2	2, 3, 1	3, 2, 1	1, 2, 3
(A)	(B)	(C)	(D)

GO ON

3. 1. Igneous rocks form when hot, liquid rock, called molten rock, hardens and then cools. Sedimentary rock forms when sand or silt is pressed together. Metamorphic rock forms when igneous and sedimentary rocks are heated and compacted together.
   2. These types of rock are named based on the way the rock is formed.
   3. Lava is an example of igneous rock, sandstone is an example of sedimentary rock, and marble is an example of metamorphic rock.
   4. Geologists classify rocks into three types: igneous, sedimentary, and metamorphic.

2, 4, 1, 3	4, 3, 2, 1	3, 1, 4, 2	1, 2, 4, 3
Ⓐ	Ⓑ	Ⓒ	Ⓓ

4. 1. The more they learn about them from the past and from current observations, the more they can tell about future ones.
   2. They measure how strong an earthquake is on a machine called a seismograph.
   3. Geologists study earthquakes.
   4. The seismograph tells the force of an earthquake, with a number from 1 to 10, on what is called the Richter Scale.

2, 3, 4, 1	1, 4, 3, 2	3, 2, 4, 1	4, 2, 1, 3
Ⓐ	Ⓑ	Ⓒ	Ⓓ

Select the correct order of the directions in 5 and 6.

Brushing Your Teeth

5. 1. Rinse out your mouth.
   2. Remove the cap from the toothpaste and squeeze some paste on the brush.
   3. Then wet it under running water.
   4. Put the cap back on the tube and rinse off the brush before putting both away.
   5. Brush your upper teeth from the gum down and your lower teeth from the gum up.

4, 2, 3, 5, 1	2, 4, 1, 3, 5	3, 2, 1, 5, 4	2, 3, 5, 1, 4
Ⓐ	Ⓑ	Ⓒ	Ⓓ

GO ON

Unit 5 Test

Making a Milk Shake

6.
1. Add one cup of milk.
2. Pour into a glass and enjoy.
3. Get all of the supplies: blender, ice cream, ice cream scoop, milk, chocolate sauce, and a glass.
4. Blend until completely mixed.
5. Squirt the desired amount of chocolate sauce into the ice cream and milk.
6. Put five scoops of ice cream in the blender.

(A) 2, 5, 4, 3, 1, 6

(B) 3, 6, 1, 5, 4, 2

(C) 6, 5, 1, 3, 4, 2

(D) 5, 3, 6, 1, 2, 4

Use the week's class schedule to answer questions 7–10.

Time	Monday	Tuesday	Wednesday	Thursday	Friday
8:30	attendance, plans for the day, any necessary business, etc.				
8:45	Social Studies report due	Social Studies discussion		Discuss trip to Museum	Social Studies review
9:45	Math long division	Math drill	Field Trip to History Museum	Math remainders	Math test
10:45	recess, restrooms, etc.			recess, restrooms, etc.	
11:15	Spelling new words	Write spelling sentences		Spelling workbook	Spelling test
12:00	lunch, recess, patrol duty, etc.				
12:45	Creative Writing lesson	Group reading Willow book	Group reading about H. Keller	English use of adverbs	Creative Writing
2:00	Music	Poetry	Art	Music	Study Period
2:30	Science seed types	Study Period	Science plant seeds	Science records	"Show & Tell"
3:15	dismissal				

7. How many times a week does the class have science?

five	four	three	two
(A)	(B)	(C)	(D)

8. At what time of day does the class have math?

8:45	9:45	10:45	11:15
(A)	(B)	(C)	(D)

GO ON

Unit 5 Test

9. What does not occur before lunch?

    (A) social studies   (B) spelling

    (C) attendance   (D) poetry

10. Which two subjects are both studied for an hour?

    (A) social studies and math   (B) math and spelling

    (C) music and science   (D) English and reading

11. Which directions were followed correctly?

1. Draw a circle and color it gray.
2. Add a smaller white circle in front of the gray circle.
3. Draw a vertical line through the center of both circles.
4. Draw a perpendicular line that intersects the vertical line above the circles.

Choose the sentence which would be first in each paragraph in 12–14.

12.   (A) The Hall family moved from the city to a home out in the country.

    (B) Jackson's parents recognized his loneliness.

    (C) Eight-year-old Jackson missed his old neighborhood where he could walk outside and find a playmate.

    (D) But his parents loved the quiet surroundings where all they could hear were the songs of birds and rustling leaves in the gentle breeze.

13.   (A) First, his mom fished with him in the creek that ran through their property.

    (B) But Jackson still missed his old playmates.

    (C) They tried many things to make him happy.

    (D) Next, his father put up a basketball net and shot baskets with him.

GO ON

14.
(A) Jackson did like the dog.

(B) Finally, his parents got Jackson a dog.

(C) They became best friends, and Jackson did not miss the old neighborhood anymore.

(D) They went everywhere together and played together.

Use the time lines of these baseball legends to answer questions 15–19.

Babe Ruth

Born February 6 in Baltimore, Maryland.	Began baseball career with the Boston Red Sox.	Red Sox won World Series.	Was sold to the New York Yankees.	Hit 60 home runs in one season.	Hit home run 714 and retired from baseball.
1895	1914	1915	1920	1927	1935

Jackie Robinson

Born January 31 in Cairo, Georgia.	Tried out for the Chicago White Sox.	Discharged from U.S. Army.	Signed contract with Brooklyn Dodgers organization.	Named Most Valuable Player of the National League.	Announced retirement from baseball.
1919	1942	1944	1945	1949	1957

Stan Musial

Born November 21 in Donora, Pennsylvania.	Joined the St. Louis Cardinals at Sportsman's Park.	Cardinals won the World Series.	Began military service with the U.S. Navy.	Named Player of the Decade by the Sporting News.	Announced retirement from baseball.
1920	1941	1942	1945	1956	1963

Joe DiMaggio

Born November 25 in Martinez, California.	Played first season with New York Yankees.	Voted Most Valuable Player of American League.	Began military service with the U.S. Army.	Won third MVP honor and the World Series.	Announced retirement from baseball.
1914	1936	1939	1943	1947	1951

15. Put these events in order.

1. Jackie Robinson tried out for the Chicago White Sox.
2. Joe DiMaggio played his first season with the Yankees.
3. Babe Ruth hit home run #714.
4. Stan Musial joined the St. Louis Cardinals at Sportsman's Park.

(A) 4, 1, 3, 2

(B) 3, 4, 1, 2

(C) 2, 3, 4, 1

(D) 3, 2, 4, 1

Name

16. Which event happened first?

(A) Jackie Robinson was born.

(B) Joe DiMaggio began his military service

(C) Stan Musial and the Cardinals won the World Series.

(D) Babe Ruth hit 60 home runs in one season.

17. Whose birthday is celebrated last during the year?

Babe Ruth (A)   Jackie Robinson (B)   Stan Musial (C)   Joe DiMaggio (D)

18. Who began his military service last?

Babe Ruth (A)   Jackie Robinson (B)   Stan Musial (C)   Joe DiMaggio (D)

19. Who was the first to be born?

Babe Ruth (A)   Jackie Robinson (B)   Stan Musial (C)   Joe DiMaggio (D)

20. Which directions were not followed correctly?

1. Draw a square.
2. Draw a horizontal line through the square.
3. Shade the upper part of the square gray.
4. Draw a circle to the left of the square.

(A) (B) (C) (D)

List the steps you would take to prepare a sack lunch for a field trip.

_____

_____

_____

_____

STOP

Name

Compare and contrast

To **compare** means to note the similarities and differences of the subjects in a passage.
To **contrast** means to show the differences of the subjects. By comparing and contrasting,
you will better understand the material you are reading.

Ships of the Desert

Camels were once wild animals in
Arabia and Asia, but long ago they were
domesticated. There are two kinds of camels:
the one-humped Arabian camel and the two-
humped Bactrian camel. Both can carry heavy
loads, but the Bactrian camel is sturdier, can
carry heavier loads, and can withstand cooler
climates. Arabian camels, which can be trained
for racing, have shorter hair than the Bactrian
camels. Camels are called "ships of the desert"
because of their swaying motion when they
walk and carry their loads.

A camel's hump is actually fat that the camel's body uses for food when plant food
is not available on long desert walks. Water is not stored in a camel's hump. Water is
stored in body tissues and in pouches inside its stomach.

Nomadic people in North Africa and Asia still use camels. They carry loads where
there are no roads. Camels are more than beasts of burden. Their hair, hides, bones,
meat, and milk are used for clothing and food.

List the similarities and differences of the camels using the following facts.

*water stored in body tissue   *one hump   *shorter hair
 and pouches   *trained for racing   *swaying motion
*also used for food and clothing   *sturdier   *hump stores food
*can withstand cooler climates   *two humps

Arabian Camel	Both	Bactrian Camel
_____	_____	_____
_____	_____	_____
_____	_____	_____
_____	_____	_____
_____	_____	_____
_____	_____	_____

Compare and contrast   Unit 6

Completing a chart showing similarities and differences of subjects helps to organize the information and make it easier to compare and contrast.

Racket Sports

Tennis is played on a flat, rectangular area called a court. The court is outside most of the time, but in cold or inclement weather, indoor courts may be available. A tennis court's size is the same for singles and doubles. The court's boundaries are marked with white lines on its floor. A net, which stretches across the middle of the court, divides it in half. There is a forecourt and a backcourt on each side of the net. Players on either side of the net hit the ball back and forth. Tennis is played with a strung racket and hollow rubber ball covered with a fuzzy cloth. Only four points are needed to win a game. Tennis is played with either two players (singles) or four players (doubles).

Squash is played indoors on a four-walled court. Red lines are painted on the floor and walls of the court to show the boundaries. A different-sized court and a different ball are used for singles and doubles. The singles' ball is soft and hollow. The doubles' ball is hard and hollow. Players use strung rackets to hit the ball against the four walls. In order to win, one side must win 15 points.

Write the phrases below on the chart on page 81 to explain how the games are similar and different. (Some phrases will be used twice.)

usually outdoors	four walls
red boundary lines on court and walls	two or four players
hit ball back and forth across net	four
soft and hollow (singles)	strung
hit ball against walls	flat, rectangular
hollow rubber ball covered with fuzzy cloth	always indoors
hard and hollow (doubles)	net stretched across
	fifteen

Name

	Tennis	Squash
Court		
Racket		
Ball		
Points to win		
How game played		

Make a chart showing the similarities and differences of two characters in a book.

Name

Cause and effect   Unit 6

There are times when one event causes another event to happen. Recognizing the **cause** (the reason) and **effect** (the result) of a story event helps you to better understand a story.

Example: Margaret fell from her tree house and broke her arm.
"Fell from the tree house" is the cause. "Broke her arm" is the effect.

Finish the sentences by choosing the causes or effects from the Word Bank. Then circle the causes and underline the effects in the sentences.

1. The overhead light of the car was left on overnight and when Father

   tried to start the car in the morning, the _____.

2. Mother put _____ in the dishwasher, and when

   she came to unload it there was foam all over the kitchen floor.

3. The employees of the electric company _____ restoring

   electricity to the city because of the high winds yesterday.

4. The house on the hill _____ and needed a lot of

   restoring before it could open as a restaurant.

5. Main Street had a lot of potholes because of all the _____

   during the winter.

6. When Mother opened the vacuum cleaner to see why it _____

   _____, she found a sock blocking the air passage.

snow and ice

too much
detergent

was not picking
up the dirt

battery was dead

was very old

worked all night

Name

Finish the chart by writing the matching causes and effects.

The regular path was blocked by a fallen tree.

It made fishing in the stream difficult.

It made it easy for the blue team to score.

A batter hit a home run into the stands.

The water was running so fast.

The red team's goalie was out of position.

The pitcher threw a high ball.

It made John's horse buck and throw him from the saddle.

The hikers took a longer route.

There was a sharp sound like a gun being fired.

I hit golf balls at the practice range.

I had my best golf score.

Cause

A stray dog kept trying to eat our food.

Effect

We moved our picnic spot from under the tree.

1.	
2.	
3.	
4.	
5.	
6.	

Name

Fact or opinion   Unit 6

A **fact** is real. It will always be proven true.
Example: President John Kennedy was killed by an assassin's bullet.

An **opinion** is what a person thinks. Someone else may think differently. It will not always be the same.
Example: If President Kennedy had lived, he would have been the greatest president the United States ever had.

Write an **F** before the sentences that state a fact and an **O** before the sentences that state an opinion.

_____ 1. Utah, Arizona, New Mexico, and Colorado form the Four Corners of the United States.

_____ 2. It has the most beautiful scenery in America.

_____ 3. The Colorado River carved the Grand Canyon in Arizona.

_____ 4. Denver is the state capital of Colorado.

_____ 5. It seems most people who live in Colorado ski all the time.

_____ 6. Geronimo is the most famous Native American from Arizona.

_____ 7. The first atomic bomb was exploded in New Mexico in 1945.

_____ 8. Lots of people thought the atom bomb was horrendous.

_____ 9. Santa Fe, New Mexico, is the oldest capital in the United States.

_____ 10. Some people think Georgia O'Keeffe's paintings of New Mexico are beautiful.

_____ 11. People who go rafting think riding the Rio Grande River through New Mexico is the most exciting ride.

_____ 12. Others disagree. They think the ride on the Colorado is the most exciting and the most spectacular.

_____ 13. Four major U.S. rivers, the Platte, Rio Grande, Arkansas, and Colorado, begin in Colorado.

_____ 14. Arizona was the last of the 48 contiguous states to become a state.

_____ 15. The states that make up the southwestern United States have more history and interesting sights than all of the other states combined.

Fact or opinion

Read the passages and then write **F** before the statements that are facts and
O before the statements that are opinions.

The Great Barrier Reef is considered by many people to be the eighth natural
wonder of the world. It is the largest coral structure in the world and the
largest structure ever constructed by living organisms.

The Great Barrier Reef consists mostly of coral, a
rocklike substance made by tiny animals. These tiny
animals, called polyps, are too numerous to count. New
polyps are constantly being born through a continuous
cycle of reproducing, eating, and dying. New coral is
added to the reef through this process.

The reef is constantly changing its shape and color. This
is caused by the polyps' constant activities, and by people
who visit the reef whose activities cannot help but destroy it.

_____ 1. The tiny animals that make the Great Barrier Reef are called polyps.

_____ 2. People should not be allowed to visit the reef.

_____ 3. It is a good thing that there are so many polyps.

_____ 4. It is the largest coral structure in the world.

Tropical rain forests lie near the equator. Rain falls almost every day, and there is
little variation in temperature. Tropical rain forests are packed with all kinds of dense
vegetation, including trees, vines, shrubs, and brightly colored flowers. About half the
world's species of plants and animals live in tropical rain forests.

The world's tropical rain forests are in great danger. They are being cut down to
provide timber and firewood and to make room for homes, roads, farms, and factories.
Some areas are being cleared for the mining of oil and valuable minerals. The habitats
of thousands of species of animals and plants have already vanished. The way of life for
many rain forest people is also threatened by these changes.

_____ 5. There is too much vegetation in the rain forests.

_____ 6. Tropical rain forests are wet.

_____ 7. All development should stop in the tropical rain forests.

_____ 8. A tropical rain forest is a densely packed area
of trees and plants.

Name

Fiction, nonfiction, and biography   Unit 6

Fiction is a story invented by someone's imagination that may be based on some real experiences but nothing actually documented. **Nonfiction** includes all writings that are not fiction. Stories about factual, documented events are nonfiction. A **biography**, which is a written account of another person's life, is a type of nonfiction.

Decide in what kind of stories the events below would be found. Write **F** for fiction, **NF** for nonfiction, and **B** for biography.

_____ 1. Most early Americans wanted their own government and fought for their freedom.

_____ 2. Samuel Clemens grew up along the Mississippi River in Hannibal, Missouri.

_____ 3. The world's first atomic bomb was built at a top secret test site in Los Alamos, New Mexico.

_____ 4. When Bobby was watching a television show, the electricity went out just as it got to the scary part.

_____ 5. The ball rolled up to the boys and said, "If you want to play, I know some good games."

_____ 6. George Washington Carver, who made more than 300 products from peanuts, went to Simpson College in Indianola, Iowa.

_____ 7. The earthquake that disrupted the World Series in San Francisco occurred in 1989.

_____ 8. Marnie took pictures of the unmanned spacecraft launch when she was in Florida.

_____ 9. The giraffe ducked its head way down to get into Theo's house.

_____ 10. In 1932, Amelia Earhart became the first woman to fly nonstop across the Atlantic.

_____ 11. When he was just a baby, Richard moved west with his family by wagon train.

_____ 12. In 1969, Apollo 11 astronauts Neil Armstrong and "Buzz" Aldrin became the first men to walk on the moon.

_____ 13. The Hershey Plant, the world's largest chocolate factory, is located in Hershey, Pennsylvania.

_____ 14. Arnie knew how to put a tourniquet on Ed to stop the bleeding.

_____ 15. Leonardo da Vinci was a painter, sculptor, architect, and engineer.

Name

Unit 6 Test

Page 1

Relationships in Reading

Read or listen to the directions. Fill in the circle beside the best answer.

📩 Example:

Which sentence states an opinion?

(A) The flag had 13 stars.

(B) They make the best pizza.

(C) The girls took violin lessons every Thursday.

(D) Mr. Grayson owns the building.

Answer: B

Take time to review your answers.

Now try these. You have 25 minutes. Continue until you see .

Choose what is different about the subjects in paragraphs 1–4.

1.   Soccer and field hockey are played outdoors on a field. The field is divided by a center line. There is a goal cage at either end. Two teams play against each other, and 11 players are on each team. The object of the game is for a team to score a goal against its opponent. In soccer, a goal is scored by kicking the ball into the opponent's goal. In field hockey, a goal is scored by hitting the ball with a stick into the opponent's goal.

(A) number of players

(B) object of the game

(C) method of scoring

(D) type of field

2.   Pat and Cathy live on the same street and go to the same school. They are the smartest students at their grade levels.

(A) street name

(B) school

(C) achievement level

(D) grade level

GO ON ⟩

© Carson-Dellosa CD-4319

87

Teach & Test Reading: Grade 5

3. Robert E. Lee and Ulysses S. Grant graduated from West Point and served in the U.S. Army before the Civil War. Both were generals in the Civil War. General Lee led the Confederate Army (the South), and General Grant led the Union Army (the North).

(A) rank in Civil War   (B) army experience before Civil War

(C) sides during Civil War   (D) military education

4. The Browns and the Friedmans adopted their kittens at the same animal shelter. Although they came from the same litter and were the same size, the Brown's kitten was orange with white stripes, and the Friedmans' kitten was white with orange spots.

(A) appearance   (B) size

(C) age   (D) where they came from

Choose what is similar about the subjects in paragraphs 5–8.

5. Tales of American folk heroes Paul Bunyan and Pecos Bill have been passed down from generation to generation. It is said Paul Bunyan grew so big that prints of his feet made the Great Lakes. It is also said he was able to level an acre of trees when he was learning to crawl. Tales of Pecos Bill included that he could fight off three bears at one time by slinging mud in their eyes.

(A) tales generations old   (B) their size

(C) their feats   (D) how they changed America

6. Alaska is the newest member of the Union. It is not contiguous to the first 48 states, but it ranks number one in the territory that it covers. Hawaii is the second newest state. It ranks 47th in the territory that it covers. It is not attached to the United States as it is an island state.

(A) island states   (B) rank in size

(C) not contiguous to the first 48 states   (D) newest members of the Union

Unit 6 Test

7. Tornadoes are violent storms that often occur in the lower Mississippi Valley, but any state could experience them. Their average path of destruction is rarely wider than a quarter of a mile. Their speeds can reach 150 to 200 miles an hour, though the average speed is 20 to 40 miles per hour. Hurricanes are violent storms that usually begin over water and move inland. They can be as wide as 400 miles. They move slowly, but their winds may reach 150 miles an hour.

speed	violent storms	origin	width
(A)	(B)	(C)	(D)

8. Of the several kinds of transportation, going by car is my favorite. I can see a lot of the land up close. I can see the landscape up close on a train, too, but a train will not stop whenever I want to. Most of my friends like to fly because a plane is fast. A boat can be fun, but a boat cannot go inland.

(A) good for sightseeing   (B) making friends

(C) speed   (D) modes of travel

Select the causes for the numbered and underlined effects in the paragraph.

The calendar has not always been what it is now. It evolved through several forms. In ancient times, the people observed the sunrise and sunset. This daily event gave them (9) a basic unit of time—a day, or 24 hours. Then they noticed the moon went through shape changes on a regular cycle. The time from one full moon to the next became (10) a month. They also noticed seasonal changes had a regular pattern and therefore planted and harvested their crops accordingly. The pattern of the seasons became (11) a solar year—the time it takes Earth to go around the sun.

9. (A) sunrise and sunset   (B) moon changed shapes on regular cycle
(C) calendar changes   (D) regular pattern of seasons

10. (A) sunrise and sunset   (B) moon changed shapes on regular cycle
(C) calendar changes   (D) regular pattern of seasons

11. (A) sunrise and sunset   (B) moon changed shapes on regular cycle
(C) calendar changes   (D) regular pattern of seasons

GO ON

Select the effects for the numbered and underlined causes in the paragraph.

The first reliable calendar may have been invented by the Sumerians. It was (12) <u>shorter than a solar year,</u> so they added a month. The Egyptians' calendar was nearly the same as a solar year. It had 12 months of 30 days plus five days. The early Roman calendar (13) <u>had only 10 months,</u> which made it very inaccurate. When Julius Caesar became emperor, he designed the Julian calendar. It had 365 days, plus an extra day every four years. It was wrong too, but not by much—11 minutes. But the 11 minutes over centuries caused the calendar to be inaccurate. Pope Gregory XIII changed the calendar in 1582 to be the calendar we use today—the Gregorian calendar.

12. (A) 365 days   (B) 12 months of 30 days
     (C) made it very inaccurate   (D) added a month

13. (A) 365 days   (B) 12 months of 30 days
     (C) made it very inaccurate   (D) added a month

Identify the statement that is an opinion in 14 and 15.

14. (A) Our local newspaper is called the <u>Bee and Herald</u>.

     (B) The <u>Bee and Herald</u> has been published for over 50 years.

     (C) The paper is published twice a week.

     (D) It seems to always take a middle-of-the-road stance about important issues to the community.

15. (A) The equator is an imaginary, horizontal line that circles the middle of Earth.

     (B) Because of the hot climate along the equator, it is difficult to live there.

     (C) It divides the Northern Hemisphere from the Southern Hemisphere.

     (D) The equator crosses both South America and Africa.

GO ON

16. Choose the title of a fiction story.

(A) A Special Invitation   (B) Types of Electric Motors

(C) Planting a Garden   (D) The Life of Henry Ford

17. Which sentence would most likely be from a book of fiction?

(A) Almost 90 percent of Maine is covered by forests.

(B) Jim Thorpe won the pentathlon and decathlon in the 1912 Olympics.

(C) Seth climbed the tree to rescue the kitten.

(D) One way to display shells is to mount them on cardboard.

Select the statement that is a fact in 18 and 19.

18.   (A) The movie will be showing at the theater for three weeks.

(B) The ending of the movie is the best part.

(C) It will probably win several awards.

(D) It cost too much to produce the movie.

19.   (A) The city council met to discuss the budget.

(B) The city should spend money fixing its streets instead of planting flowers.

(C) The meeting lasted too long.

(D) The council should meet every week.

GO ON

20. Choose the subject of a biography.

    (A) my neighbor's bird   (B) Walt Disney

    (C) the Roman Empire   (D) the Missouri River

Write a fact and an opinion about the state where you live.

_____

_____

_____

_____

_____

Name

Drawing conclusions

To **draw conclusions** means to consider the information you have, and from the information, come up with answers which have not been directly stated.

Example: We saw one of the zookeepers training an animal that swims and lives on the rocks in one of the zoo's ponds. This animal was learning to balance a ball on its nose. Was it a tiger, monkey, giraffe, or seal?

Conclusion: It would not be a tiger, monkey, or giraffe because they do not swim or live in a zoo pond. So the answer would be seal.

Circle the clothing accessory described in the paragraphs.
Then write the clue(s) that helped you decide.

1.   Sharon was looking for something to carry on her business trip. She wanted it large enough to hold her money, glasses, address book, and a small cosmetic bag. She preferred that it had a shoulder strap and would go with all the clothes she was taking.

   wallet   purse   suitcase   backpack

   What clue(s) made you select this accessory? _____

   _____

2.   Sharon went to buy something she could wear after work. She knew how hot Florida could get in the summer, and she wanted to be able to cool off and relax at the beach after work. She found the perfect thing—light blue with little yellow fish swimming around each leg opening.

   beach towel   tennis shorts   bathing suit   golf shirt

   What clue(s) made you select this article? _____

   _____

3.   Sharon stopped at a store. She told the salesman where she was going, what clothes she was taking, and how she would be on her feet a lot. She explained how she would like for everything to match, but the most important thing was for her to be comfortable when standing all day and demonstrating her product. Sharon sat down to try on some of the things the salesman brought her.

   hat   shoes   luggage   belt

   What clue(s) made you select this accessory? _____

   _____

   _____

Name

Drawing conclusions

Read the descriptions of the characters. Circle their occupations. Then tell why you made your selections.

1.   Veronica usually sits at a desk in the front of the office answering phones, making appointments for clients, and greeting them when they enter the law office. Her appearance is important to her job because Veronica is the first person people see when they come into the office.

   administrative assistant   lawyer   receptionist   telephone operator

   Why did you select the profession you did?_____

   _____

2.   Nathan never knows what to expect when he goes to work. Some days he just patrols his route. Other days the dispatcher radios him to go to a specific address because of some trouble.

   chauffeur   police officer   firefighter   dog catcher

   Why did you select the profession you did?_____

   _____

3.   Grant does not have an office, but he goes to work every day. He works in a tall building where he always has something to do for the good of the building. He might fix an out-of-order elevator or replace a pipe.

   maintenance man   janitor   plumber   electrician

   Why did you select the profession you did?_____

   _____

4.   Tobie loves her work. On days that she does not have surgery, Tobie might see as many as 40 patients. Many of them come for yearly checkups and shots. But sometimes they are sick. Tobie cannot always tell what is wrong from a temperature reading or from listening to a patient's chest. Tobie sometimes has to get more information about the patient's current symptoms from the person to whom the patient belongs.

   dentist   surgeon   veterinarian   medical doctor

   Why did you select the profession you did?_____

   _____

Making inferences   Unit 7

To make an **inference** means to make judgments about a story based on the given information.

Read the story and then circle the words or phrases that complete the sentences.

When Jenny came home from school, there was an unopened envelope addressed to her on the front hall table. She tore it open and read it.

Dear Jenny,

I can't wait to meet you. Your grandparents have known me since the day I was born. I am four years old now and was raised in their neighbor's barn. I'm sure you and I are going to have many good times together. I can't wait to go on a walk with you and see your neighborhood. I'm getting a ride from your grandparents, and I'll be at your house a week from today. Maybe I can even give you a ride.

Signed, a new "Pal"

1. When Jenny saw the letter addressed to her, she was _____.

    thrilled   relieved   not interested

2. The letter was actually written by _____.

    her parents   her grandparents   a new playmate

3. "Pal" is a _____.

    sheep   horse   dog

4. "Pal" will arrive _____.

    next month   in three days   in a week

Pal arrived as promised. Jenny learned how to care for Pal, and Pal gave her hundreds of rides for many years. They won a lot of awards together. When Pal got too old to ride, Jenny kept him in the pasture and let him live an easy life, grazing and sleeping. But every morning and night, Jenny would sit on the pasture fence and pat Pal. He would then nuzzle her.

5. Jenny and Pal _____.

    were in a lot of horse shows   grew old together

6. You could tell Jenny loved Pal because _____.

    they were in a lot of shows   she did not ride Pal when he got too old

Making inferences   Unit 7

Circle the situation that led to the ending described in the sentences.

1. Finally, a taxi pulled over to the curb, and the traveler climbed in with his drenched suitcase.

   The traveler had just arrived.   The traveler called for a taxi.

   The traveler had been standing in the rain trying to hail a taxi.

2. Mickey left the doctor's office with her arm in a sling.

   Mickey had gone to the doctor to get some new medicine.

   Mickey had tripped and fallen on her shoulder.

   Mickey went to see the doctor because the sling was uncomfortable.

3. The cafeteria's line was at a standstill.

   There were too many people in line.   The food was very good.

   The server had gone to refill the chicken tray.

4. The students slept on the bus all the way back to school.

   The class had been camping for three days.   The bus was late getting them.

   The class had gone to the high school band concert for two hours

5. When we opened the door, we heard the "culprit" who had made the mess in the house.

   The wind blew through an open window.   There had been an earthquake.

   A bird had flown inside through the open window and had become frightened.

6. The meat was not on the counter where Mother had left it.

   The family had finished dinner.   Mother had put it in the refrigerator.

   The dog had been left alone in the kitchen.

7. Chris heard the doors lock when he stepped outside with a stack of books.

   Chris was the last to finish the test.   Chris had been at the library.

   Chris shopped until the store closed.

Predicting outcomes

Unit 7

Using the information in a story, you can often **predict** what will happen.

Read the following situations and explain why you think the characters made their choices.

1.   Sally Ann was over 80 years old. She lived in a small house with a very small fenced-in yard. She had just lost her 16-year-old dog and decided to get another dog right away. Sally Ann went to the animal shelter, and after looking at all the dogs, she narrowed her choice down to two. The first was a large, black, one-year-old retriever. He had a lot of energy and was used to running on acres of land. The second dog was a small, three-year-old mix. The people who had owned him said he stayed home alone all day and knew how to use a doggy door to go out to the yard.

Which dog do you think Sally Ann chose? _____

Why do you think she did that? _____

_____

2.   Harry's weekend was very busy. Friday evening he had spent the night at Justin's house. They had stayed up late watching movies and playing cards. Harry left early the next morning for baseball practice. He was exhausted when he finally returned home, but he helped his mom get ready for the neighborhood party they were hosting that evening. When all the preparations were finished, Harry decided to take a short nap.

What will probably happen? _____

_____

_____

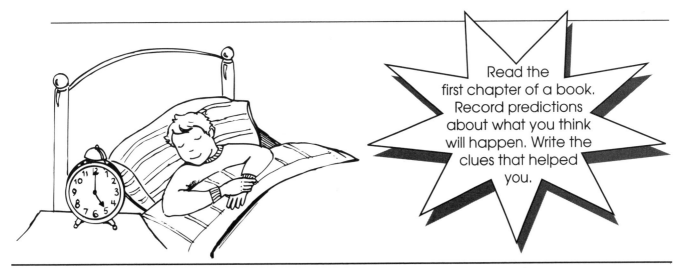

Read the first chapter of a book. Record predictions about what you think will happen. Write the clues that helped you.

Name

Predicting outcomes

Circle what you consider to be the best outcomes under the circumstances.

1. Fifteen students were on the school bus when it had a flat tire. The driver put on the emergency flashing lights and _____.

    waited for a tow truck   stopped to let the students off

    kept going slowly   pulled off to the side of the road

2. Not until Marnie sat down to do her math homework did she realize she had left it in her desk at school. Marnie _____.

    called a friend to get the assignment   told her younger brother

    made up the answers   did not do it

3. The girls skated leisurely around the ice rink until Billy, a bully from school, pushed them into the fence that went around the rink. The girls _____.

    skated with Billy   chased Billy and pushed him into the fence

    went to get the rink manager   screamed and yelled at Billy

4. There was a water shortage in the southwestern states because there had been very little precipitation the past two years. So the people of the area _____.

    did not brush their teeth   did all they could to conserve water

    dug for well water   hoped it would rain soon

5. The traffic light at the top of the ramp off the busy highway was not working. A police officer _____.

    closed the street   put up a detour sign

    gave a ticket to any car that honked   was there to direct traffic

6. Reggie hit a baseball into the street. He ran to get it and _____.

    stopped at the curb to look both ways   saw a dog running away with it

    saw it hit a car and break its window   played with another ball

Name

Unit 7 Test

Analytical Thinking in Reading

Read or listen to the directions. Fill in the circle beside the best answer.

☐ Example:

When we were finally allowed outside, tree branches were strewn all over lawns and streets.

What had been the problem?

(A) trees were trimmed

(B) dead trees

(C) a windstorm

(D) a beaver

Answer: C

If you are unsure which answer is correct, choose your best guess.

Now try these. You have 25 minutes. Continue until you see .

Choose why the actions are taking place in 1–4.

1. Muriel was saying her multiplication tables over and over to herself.

  (A) studying for a test   (B) counting money

  (C) jumping rope   (D) amusing herself

2. The football player was jumping up and down, screaming, and waving his arms at the referee.

  (A) needed exercise   (B) wanted a time-out

  (C) angry at the referee's call   (D) won the coin toss

3. The audience stood and applauded while the cast took a curtain call.

  (A) glad play ended   (B) liked the play

  (C) kept time to music   (D) needed to stretch

---

4. Before placing his order, Kent reached in his back pocket.

   (A) just washed his pants   (B) was tired of standing in line

   (C) wanted to take out his wallet   (D) forgot what he was going to order

Choose what you think happened in 5–8.

5. Yesterday Meg and Laurie were best friends, but today they are not talking.

   (A) Meg did not like what Laurie was wearing today.

   (B) Laurie could not think of anything to say.

   (C) Laurie was not at school today.

   (D) They had a fight, and neither one would apologize.

6. Last night our family spent a couple of hours in the basement.

   (A) The all clear sounded.

   (B) It was raining very hard.

   (C) The warning siren on our street went off.

   (D) Our electricity went out, and we had candles in the basement.

7. Mother fixed a plain baked potato and hot tea for Faye's dinner.

   (A) Faye told her mother she did not like what they were having for dinner.

   (B) Faye had an upset stomach earlier in the day.

   (C) The doctor put Faye on a special diet to gain weight.

   (D) Mother had not gone to the grocery store, and there was nothing else to eat.

GO ON

8. It was 6:00 P.M. Mother told everyone to come sit down.

(A) Dinner was ready.

(B) Mother wanted to have a family meeting.

(C) Mother needed help preparing dinner.

(D) The family was going out to eat.

Choose what you consider to be the best outcomes under the circumstances in 9–12.

The van was packed full, and some things were attached to the luggage rack on top. My mom and dad, two sisters, and I left early Saturday morning for a one-week vacation. We were going about halfway, 400 miles, the first day. My dad had made a reservation at a motel just off the highway. We were moving along on schedule, when all of a sudden there was a bang, and the car lurched. My father grasped the steering wheel tightly to keep the car under control, and then drove it onto the shoulder of the road out of the way of traffic.

9. (A) We were out of gas. (B) The things on top of the car had fallen off.

(C) The car hit a rock. (D) We had a blowout.

10. Why do you think that?

(A) There was a thud. (B) There was a bang and a pull.

(C) The car stopped. (D) We were hungry and were going on a picnic.

GO ON

Dad said that we had to unload the back of the van to get the spare tire. We all helped unload the van, and my dad replaced the tire. After he replaced the tire, we put everything back and tied the damaged tire, which would need to be fixed, on top of the things on the luggage rack. We noticed a billboard sign that said there was a gas station at the next highway exit. I said it was too bad we had not had our blowout a few minutes later, and we could have gone to the gas station.

11. (A) They threw the tire away.   (B) They had another blowout.

(C) Dad got off at the next exit.   (D) They stopped for dinner.

12. Why do you think that?

(A) Dad wanted to fix the damaged tire.

(B) Dad wanted gas.

(C) Dad wanted to rearrange the luggage.

(D) We all wanted a cold drink.

What are the subjects of the book titles in 13–16?

13. A Day Deep in the Ocean

(A) living on a submarine   (B) deep-sea fishing

(C) animal life on a coral reef   (D) shark attacks

14. Fun and Games

(A) jokes and riddles   (B) game suggestions

(C) funny movies   (D) mysteries

15. A Journey to the Peak

(A) bike riding   (B) mountain climbing

(C) fishing and camping   (D) river rafting

GO ON

Unit 7 Test

16. Growing up with Friends in Higgenstown

(A) early story of Higgenstown

(B) life as a four-year-old in Higgenstown

(C) family's story in Higgenstown

(D) a young person's life in Higgenstown

Identify what the characters are in 17–20.

Shameka practices every night after school. She always begins by warming up her fingers with special exercises. Her mother enjoys listening to her practice.

17.   (A) a softball player   (B) a gymnast

(C) a dancer   (D) a pianist

Tony stays after school on Thursdays to help his teacher. This responsibility earns him service hours for his club.

18.   (A) a volunteer   (B) a teacher

(C) an employee   (D) the club's president

The streets just outside of town were littered with trash. Bucky decided he was going to clean them up himself. One Saturday morning he rode his bike to the edge of town and took along several empty trash bags. As he began to pick up the litter, he found some interesting things. Anything that he thought he would like to keep he put in a separate trash bag. It took Bucky longer to pick up the trash because he examined every piece. Bucky is a _____.

19.   collector   good friend   slow worker   bike racer

(A)   (B)   (C)   (D)

GO ON ⟩

20.   Sam was very excited for the last football game of the season that was to be played Saturday afternoon. His team had a chance to win the city championship. On Monday the coach had announced that every player was required to be at practice on Wednesday evening. Wednesday morning Sam's mom informed him that neither she nor his dad would be able to take him to practice because they both had a meeting. Sam will _____.

    (A) miss practice

    (B) ask a friend for a ride

    (C) tell his mom to miss her meeting

    (D) go to the meeting with his dad

One morning six little chipmunks were singing inside their home in the tree trunk as they ground berries and nuts to make bread. A very clever, hungry fox heard them and wondered how he might get a piece of bread. He thought that if he took them some berries to use in their bread, they would let him in.

The fox sprinted off to pick some berries. He put them in a basket made of leaves and ran to the chipmunks' door and knocked. The fox could smell the bread baking.

Sometimes the chipmunks were very foolish. Without thinking, they responded to the knock and said, "Come in." When they saw the fox, they scampered up the hollow trunk and out an opening onto a tree branch.

What do you think the fox did next? Use information from the story to support your answer.

_____

_____

_____

_____

_____

Name _____

Alphabetizing

Most reference work requires the skill of **alphabetizing**. Dictionaries, encyclopedias, and other reference materials are organized alphabetically.

Sometimes it is only necessary to look at the first letter when alphabetizing a list.
Example: banana   grapefruit   lime   peach

Other times you have to look at the second letter when the first letter is the same.
Example: shift   sign   slant   spot

When the first two letters are the same, you have to look at the third letter.
Example: coat   color   company   corn

And when the first three letters are the same, you have to look at the fourth letter.
Example: process   program   promise   proud

Number the lists below alphabetically.

1.		2.		3.		4.	
___	antilog	___	most	___	anchor	___	contest
___	antigen	___	mosaic	___	annex	___	contact
___	antic	___	mosquito	___	analyze	___	contrary
___	antique	___	mosey	___	anytime	___	confusion
___	antidote	___	moss	___	angel	___	continue

Dictionary skills

Guide words are the two words found at the top of each dictionary page. Use guide words to help you locate a word in a dictionary. Any entry word listed on that page will fall alphabetically between the guide words.

Examples: engage — equal   happen — hassle
                    entrance   hardware

Printed below are sets of guide words. Circle the entry words that would be found on those pages.

5. report—resolve	6. honor—howl	7. pucker—put	8. dice—digit
require	horn	push	decide
restrain	hover	pulley	diesel
resist	hoist	public	differ
reply	honey	pudding	digital
reserve	hound	purple	digest
represent	hoop	putt	dictate

Key words   Unit 8

When looking up information in reference materials such as an encyclopedia or almanac, decide what question you are trying to answer. Write down the question and notice the **key words**. Looking up information about the key words will help you answer your question.

Examples: Under what circumstances did <u>Harry Truman</u> become president?
(Usually when looking up a person, use the last name.)

Who was <u>Galileo</u>? (Some people are best known by their first names.)

Why did <u>Alexander Hamilton</u> and <u>Aaron Burr</u> duel?
(Sometimes more than one reference or key word is given.)

Underline the key words in each question.

1. What war did the United States enter after an attack on Pearl Harbor?

2. In what state is Mount Rushmore located?

3. Who invented the radio and the phonograph?

4. What is ozone, and of what importance is it to the environment?

5. What kind of clothing did people wear in the late 1700s?

6. In what movie did Mickey Mouse first appear?

7. How was Harriet Tubman affiliated with the Underground Railroad?

8. In what country did croquet originate?

9. In what kind of a climate does the cactus grow best?

10. What function does the liver have in your body?

11. Which animals are endangered and what is being done to save them?

12. What is the immigration policy of the United States?

13. What changes did the Industrial Revolution bring to America?

14. What is the history of political parties in the United States?

Name _____

Encyclopedias

An **encyclopedia** is a book or set of books containing information on various subjects. The subjects are organized alphabetically. On the outside of each book is a letter or letters showing alphabetically what subjects will be found inside the book. Encyclopedias also have guide words at the top of each page to help you locate the subjects inside.

Write the number(s) of the volume(s) you would look in to find the answers to the questions.

1. _____ What kind of vegetation grows in the Arctic?

2. _____ From what country do pandas come, and what do they like to eat?

3. _____ On what continent is Luxembourg located?

4. _____ Make a time line showing the history of transportation.

5. _____ What part did the Alamo play in Texas's history?

6. _____ Make a list of reptiles in the U.S. and the characteristics they share.

7. _____ What is the difference between a tornado and a hurricane?

8. _____ What did Louis Pasteur invent?

9. _____ Who was president when the U.S. negotiated the Louisiana Purchase?

10. _____ What discoveries did Magellan make?

11. _____ List England's monarchs from William the Conqueror to the present.

12. _____ Who were the allies in World War II?

13. _____ What is the life cycle of salmon?

14. _____ Who were the Etruscans, and what were their accomplishments?

15. _____ When did printing begin, and how did it change the culture?

Name

Atlas   Unit 8

An **atlas** is a specialized reference book which includes a collection of maps. The maps may be of states, countries, or the world. Sometimes an atlas includes informative tables or other factual matter. Some atlases are specialized. They might include maps of the night sky, rivers, or populations.

Use the map of Missouri to answer the questions.

1. What is the state's capital? _____

2. How many states border Missouri? _____

3. Which states border Missouri on the west? _____

   _____

4. Which cities have three major highways going through them?_____

   _____

MISSOURI

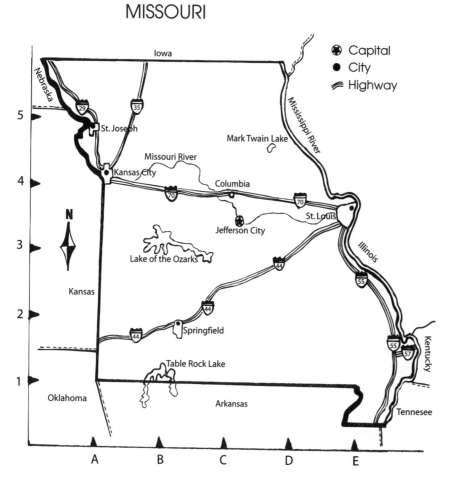

5. What river borders Missouri on the east?

   _____

6. Springfield is what direction from the capital?_____

7. What city is just east of the capital? _____

   _____

Use the number and letter pairs to identify the cities by going across from the numbers and up from the letters.

8. 2, B _____

9. 5, A _____

10. 4, C _____

Glossary

A **glossary** is a specialized dictionary. It is usually at the back of a specialized reference book and has words pertaining only to the subjects covered in the book. The words are arranged alphabetically as in a dictionary.

Several words are listed together as they would be in a glossary. Decide what the subject of the book is and then underline the title of the book.

Example: Glossary: Akita   golden retriever   poodle   rottweiler
          Book's title: <u>Dogs as Pets</u>   Hunting Dogs   Miniature Dogs

1. hickory   maple   oak   sycamore
   Wild Flowers   Trees in Your Backyard   Forest Lands

2. Lincoln Memorial   The Pentagon   U.S. Capitol   White House
   Washington, D.C.   Springfield, Illinois   Seattle, Washington

3. Argentina   Brazil   Chile   Venezuela
   North American Countries   European Countries   South American Countries

4. Arctic Circle   equator   Greenwich meridian   international date line
   Longitude and Latitude   Traditional Landmarks   Places on a Street Map

5. baseball   basketball   football   hockey
   Ball Games   Competitive Team Sports   Winter Games

6. Columbus, OH   Jefferson City, MO   Lincoln, NE   Madison, WI
   United States Cities   Cities Named for Presidents   U.S. Capital Cities

7. heart   kidneys   liver   lungs
   The Respiratory System   Organs of the Body   The Nervous System

8. Mid-Atlantic   New England   Northwest   Rocky Mountain States
   Western Universities   Regions of the United States   Midwestern Culture

9. Newton, Sir Isaac   Pasteur, Louis   Salk, Jonas   Van Allen, James
   Twentieth Century Inventions   American Biographies   Famous Scientists

10. Apache   Cherokee   Iroquois   Navajo
    America's Past   Native Americans   America's European Beginnings

11. Amazon   Congo   Mississippi   Nile
    Major World Rivers   Water Transportation   Rivers in America

12. Beethoven   Chopin   Mozart   Wagner
    Famous Painters   Famous Musicians   Famous Composers

Name

The **table of contents** and the **index** in a book are directories.

The table of contents is found in the front of a book. It lists each chapter by its title or subject.

If a book has an index, it is at the end of the book. The index lists specific names and subjects in alphabetical order and the page or pages on which information about them can be found.

Using the table of contents and index, write the page numbers you would look on to answer the questions. If there are no listings, leave the lines blank.

Table of Contents

Index

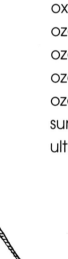

	Table of Contents	Index
1. What things destroy ozone in the atmosphere?	_____	_____
2. What are the layers of the atmosphere?	_____	_____
3. What is ozone?	_____	_____
4. Are there solutions to the ozone problem?	_____	_____
5. What is the connection between ozone and cancer cells?	_____	_____
6. Where are definitions of words relating to the ozone?	_____	_____

Name _____

Where to look

When you have to look something up, you should first know precisely what you want to know and then decide what sources would contain the information you need.

Circle the sources you would use to locate the following information.

1. life in Russia under Joseph Stalin

    atlas   encyclopedia   dictionary   glossary

2. words in a book associated with computer science: download, byte, RAM, Internet

    dictionary   encyclopedia   glossary   table of contents

3. locations of the oceans of the world

    atlas   dictionary   index   glossary

4. desert wildlife

    index   table of contents   glossary   encyclopedia

5. definitions of spelling words: breezy, eldest, grateful, merry, oriental, stackable

    glossary   index   dictionary   table of contents

6. the chapter pertaining to French artists

    encyclopedia   dictionary   index   table of contents

7. pages relating to the constellations

    index   encyclopedia   glossary   dictionary

8. distance from Indianapolis, IN, to San Diego, CA

    table of contents   index   atlas   glossary

9. definitions of words found in the second chapter of a science book

    encyclopedia   glossary   table of contents   index

10. military career of General George McClellan

    dictionary   glossary   atlas   encyclopedia

11. pages showing the rivers of Mexico

    glossary   index   atlas   dictionary

12. chapter discussing the digestive system

    table of contents   index

    encyclopedia   glossary

List three subjects you would find in an encyclopedia, atlas, and glossary.

Name

Read or listen to the directions. Fill in the circle beside the best answer.

☐ Example:

Read the sentence. Which word will go on the page with the guide words shown?

fleck—flicker

(A) flier

(B) flea

(C) fleece

(D) flimsy

If you become nervous, take deep breaths to relax.

Answer: C

Now try these. You have 20 minutes. Continue until you see ⬡STOP .

Choose the words that are first in alphabetical order in 1–3.

1. formidable   formerly   formula   formulate
       (A)   (B)   (C)   (D)

2. tough   toupee   touched   tourism
       (A)   (B)   (C)   (D)

3. grill   grit   grind   grime
       (A)   (B)   (C)   (D)

Select between which guide words you would find the words in 4–6.

4. Hanoi

   (A) haddock—hail   (B) hair—halibut

   (C) Halifax—harbor   (D) hardball—harem

GO ON ➡

Unit 8 Test

5. ocelot

- (A) ocean—octane
- (B) October—Odin
- (C) odyssey—office
- (D) offset—ogres

6. insect

- (A) Iceland—iguana
- (B) Iliad—immune
- (C) imprint—Indian
- (D) indigo—insecure

Select the key word(s) that you would use to look up the answers in questions 7–9.

7. Where does the Nile River start in Africa?

- (A) River, Africa
- (B) major rivers
- (C) Nile, Africa
- (D) Nile, start

8. In what city did the Continental Congress meet to declare the American colonies' independence from England?

- (A) American colonies, Continental Congress
- (B) England, Continental Congress
- (C) city, independence
- (D) declare, Continental Congress

9. Why is the state of Delaware's nickname "First State"?

- (A) First State
- (B) United States
- (C) nickname
- (D) Delaware

GO ON

Choose what you would use to look for the specific information in 10–13.

10. Our teacher assigned a different Spanish explorer to each one of us to research.

encyclopedia
(A)

table of contents
(B)

index
(C)

dictionary
(D)

11. I need the exact page where the book discussed adding fractions.

table of contents
(A)

index
(B)

glossary
(C)

guide words
(D)

12. We pointed out all the countries that surrounded the Mediterranean Sea.

dictionary
(A)

encyclopedia
(B)

atlas
(C)

index
(D)

13. The teacher told each one of us to look up our favorite short story in the book and to list three things we liked about it.

index
(A)

table of contents
(B)

glossary
(C)

encyclopedia
(D)

Use the city map to answer questions 14–17.

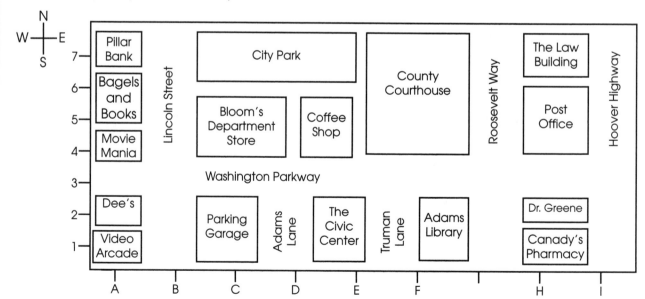

GO ON

14. What business is located at 5, C?

(A) Movie Mania   (B) Bloom's Department Store

(C) Coffee Shop   (D) Bagels and Books

15. What is the grid reading for the Civic Center?

2, E   4, D   6, F   2, F

(A)   (B)   (C)   (D)

16. The County Courthouse is what direction from the Parking Garage?

NW   SE   NE   SW

(A)   (B)   (C)   (D)

17. What direction is Pillar Bank from Canady's Pharmacy?

NW   SE   NE   SW

(A)   (B)   (C)   (D)

Choose the volume of the encyclopedia you would use to answer questions 18 and 19.

18. How many varieties of insects are in North America?

A– Ant Vol. 1   Hit– Jal Vol. 5   Mep– Nur Vol. 7   Tos– Wik Vol. 11

(A)   (B)   (C)   (D)

19. What is the climate of northern Denmark?

Ban– Cli Vol. 2   Clo– Dek Vol. 3   Del– Fah Vol. 4   Nir– Peb Vol. 8

(A)   (B)   (C)   (D)

GO ON

20. Which word would not be found in the glossary of a book about rocks and minerals?

stalagmite   crystal   meteorite   satellite

Ⓐ   Ⓑ   Ⓒ   Ⓓ

Circle the question you might ask a librarian if a teacher gave you the following assignment.

Find a book in the library about nutrition. Use the book to make your own personal spelling list of 10 words for next week.

What is nutrition?   Does the book have a glossary?

What food is good for you?

Explain your answer.

_____

_____

_____

_____

STOP

Final Review Test Name Grid

Write your name in pencil in the boxes along the top. Begin with your last name. Fill in as many letters as will fit. Then follow the columns straight down and bubble in the letters that correspond with the letters in your name. Complete the rest of the information the same way. You may use a piece of scrap paper to help you keep your place.

STUDENT'S NAME		SCHOOL
LAST / FIRST / MI		TEACHER

FEMALE ○   MALE ○

DATE OF BIRTH

MONTH	DAY	YEAR
JAN ○	⓪ ⓪	⓪ ⓪
FEB ○	① ①	① ①
MAR ○	② ②	② ②
APR ○	③ ③	③ ③
MAY ○	④	④ ④
JUN ○	⑤	⑤ ⑤
JUL ○	⑥	⑥ ⑥
AUG ○	⑦	⑦ ⑦
SEP ○	⑧	⑧ ⑧
OCT ○	⑨	⑨ ⑨
NOV ○		
DEC ○		

GRADE ③ ④ ⑤

Name grid with bubbles A–Z for each letter column of the student's name.

Final Review Test Answer Sheet

Pay close attention when transferring your answers. Fill in the bubbles neatly and completely. You may use a piece of scrap paper to help you keep your place.

SAMPLES
A Ⓐ Ⓑ ● Ⓓ
B Ⓕ ● Ⓗ Ⓙ

1 Ⓐ Ⓑ Ⓒ Ⓓ	7 Ⓐ Ⓑ Ⓒ Ⓓ	13 Ⓐ Ⓑ Ⓒ Ⓓ	19 Ⓐ Ⓑ Ⓒ Ⓓ	25 Ⓐ Ⓑ Ⓒ Ⓓ
2 Ⓕ Ⓖ Ⓗ Ⓙ	8 Ⓕ Ⓖ Ⓗ Ⓙ	14 Ⓕ Ⓖ Ⓗ Ⓙ	20 Ⓕ Ⓖ Ⓗ Ⓙ	26 Ⓕ Ⓖ Ⓗ Ⓙ
3 Ⓐ Ⓑ Ⓒ Ⓓ	9 Ⓐ Ⓑ Ⓒ Ⓓ	15 Ⓐ Ⓑ Ⓒ Ⓓ	21 Ⓐ Ⓑ Ⓒ Ⓓ	27 Ⓐ Ⓑ Ⓒ Ⓓ
4 Ⓕ Ⓖ Ⓗ Ⓙ	10 Ⓕ Ⓖ Ⓗ Ⓙ	16 Ⓕ Ⓖ Ⓗ Ⓙ	22 Ⓕ Ⓖ Ⓗ Ⓙ	28 Ⓕ Ⓖ Ⓗ Ⓙ
5 Ⓐ Ⓑ Ⓒ Ⓓ	11 Ⓐ Ⓑ Ⓒ Ⓓ	17 Ⓐ Ⓑ Ⓒ Ⓓ	23 Ⓐ Ⓑ Ⓒ Ⓓ	29 Ⓐ Ⓑ Ⓒ Ⓓ
6 Ⓕ Ⓖ Ⓗ Ⓙ	12 Ⓕ Ⓖ Ⓗ Ⓙ	18 Ⓕ Ⓖ Ⓗ Ⓙ	24 Ⓕ Ⓖ Ⓗ Ⓙ	30 Ⓕ Ⓖ Ⓗ Ⓙ

Name

Final Review Test

Read or listen to the directions. Fill in the circle beside the best answer.

 Example:

Choose a synonym for **principle**.

(A) important

(B) dominant

(C) belief

(D) principal

Answer: C because belief has a similar meaning.

Now try these. You have 35 minutes.

Continue until you see .

Remember your Helping Hand Strategies:

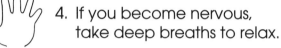

1. Note the time allotment. Pace yourself.

2. Take time to review your answers.

3. If you are not sure which answer is correct, choose your best guess.

4. If you become nervous, take deep breaths to relax.

5. Fill in the answer sheet carefully. Be sure the problem number from the test matches the problem number on the answer sheet.

Read the paragraph to answer questions 1 and 2.

The currency system in colonial times was not systematic. The early settlers from England exported crops to their native country, and instead of receiving English money, their pay was in goods. Most of the currency in the new country was actually foreign money injected into the economy through trade in the West Indies and from seaport purchases. In settlements away from the coast, crops, animal skins, and musket balls were the legal currency. Some states eventually printed their own paper money, but England banned this currency. This became one of the causes of the American Revolution.

1. Which title best describes the main idea?

(A) Early Currency in America

(B) British Control in Early America

(C) A Cause of the American Revolution

(D) Need for Currency System in Early America

Final Review Test

2. Which statement is not true about the currency system in colonial times?

(F) It lacked a system or method.

(G) Crops and animal skins were a type of currency.

(H) Foreign money was not used.

(J) Paper money was printed by some states.

Choose the meaning of the underlined words in sentences 3 and 4.

3. The recipe recommended a <u>moderate</u> oven setting.

(A) preside over a meeting   (B) temperate

(C) excessive   (D) extremely low

4. The time John spent studying for the test was <u>superfluous</u> because he already had an A as a final grade.

(F) more than enough   (G) unnecessary

(H) useful   (J) not fair

5. Select the statement that is not an opinion.

(A) Our family is going hiking and camping in the mountains next week.

(B) Hiking is the best form of exercise.

(C) Camping is the cheapest way to vacation.

(D) My dad fries the tastiest fish over a campfire.

6. Complete the analogy.

physiology : living organisms : : astronomy : _____

Jupiter   telescope   research   space

(F)   (G)   (H)   (J)

GO ON

Read the paragraph to answer questions 7–10.

John left his house early for the airport. He was flying to Phoenix to interview for a new job. He was very excited about this opportunity and the possible move to Phoenix where many of his friends lived. The highway leading to the airport was being widened. Traffic was moving extremely slowly because several lanes had been shut down for the new construction. Consequently, John arrived at the airport late and missed his flight.

7. What caused John to arrive late to the airport?

(A) He left early for the airport.   (B) The highway was being widened.

(C) Traffic was moving slowly.   (D) He was excited about his trip.

8. What do you think John will do next?

(F) He will go back home.   (G) He will go to work.

(H) He will catch another flight.   (J) He will move to Phoenix.

9. How do you think John felt when he arrived at the airport?

frustrated   embarrassed   enthusiastic   remarkable
(A)   (B)   (C)   (D)

10. Choose the sentence that supports the main idea.

(F) There was also road construction near the airport in Phoenix.

(G) The airport was 15 miles from John's house.

(H) Next, roads were to be widened near the stadium.

(J) John brought his golf clubs with him.

11. Postwar means _____.

(A) during the war   (B) before the war

(C) a single war   (D) after the war

12. Over 200 firefighters had been fighting the raging fire in the mountainous forest for two days. Just when they thought it was under control, the winds picked up.

What do you think happened next?

(F) The fire will stop.

(G) They will put out the fire again.

(H) The wind will cause the fire to spread.

(J) The firefighters will stop working.

13. There had always been a wait at the Corner Restaurant, but ever since it was reviewed in the paper it has been easy to get seated.

Why do you think the popularity of the restaurant changed?

(A) The review about the restaurant was not complimentary.

(B) People got tired of waiting to be seated.

(C) The service has gotten faster.

(D) The restaurant added more seating.

14. Where would you look to find out what countries are between the tropic of Cancer and the tropic of Capricorn?

encyclopedia (F)   atlas (G)   dictionary (H)   index (J)

15. Frank's birthday party was a lot of fun. We played games until everyone was there. Prizes were given out to the winners of every game. After everyone had arrived, Frank opened his presents. Before we went home, Frank's mother brought a cake with 11 lighted candles, and we then sang to Frank. Finally, we ate the cake with ice cream.

What was the second to last event that happened at the party?

cake brought in (A)   won prizes (B)   sang to Frank (C)   opened gifts (D)

GO ON

Name

Read the paragraph to answer 16–19.

Tomorrow was the day of the long race. Jackie had been preparing for the race for months. She was determined to finish in record time. The few items she needed for the race were carefully set beside her bed. Stamina would be the most important factor, and Jackie knew with a good night's sleep she would have the energy to compete with the best.

16. In what kind of race was Jackie going to compete?

bicycle (F)   automobile (G)   horse (H)   marathon (J)

17. Choose the word that best describes Jackie.

feeble (A)   committed (B)   cynical (C)   incapable (D)

18. What is a synonym for **stamina**?

endurance (F)   excitement (G)   excursion (H)   emotion (J)

19. Select the word that expresses the main idea.

victorious (A)   competition (B)   preparation (C)   restlessness (D)

20. Between which guide words would you find **forest**?

flour – fluoride (F)   flurry – focus (G)   fodder – food (H)   force – formal (J)

21. Choose the word with the same meaning as **abolish**.

eliminate (A)   comprise (B)   include (C)   abandon (D)

GO ON

Read the paragraph to answer 22 and 23.

The Constitution of the United States states what age an elected, national official must be to run for office and how long a term the official may serve. A person elected to the House of Representatives is elected every two years and must be 25 years old to hold office. Senators are elected every six years and must be 30 years old. The president and vice president's term is four years. In order to run for president, a candidate must be 35 years old.

22. Which elected official's term is the longest?

representative	vice president	senator	president
(F)	(G)	(H)	(J)

23. How old must someone be to be elected to the House of Representatives?

22	25	30	35
(A)	(B)	(C)	(D)

24. What is an antonym for **hopeless**?

optimistic	negative	desperate	stillness
(F)	(G)	(H)	(J)

25. Identify the statement that is not from a nonfiction book.

(A) Susan B. Anthony campaigned for women's rights.

(B) The snow leopard is an endangered animal.

(C) A padlock requires a key or a combination to be opened.

(D) The howling wind frightened the young girl.

26. Which picture follows the directions correctly?

1. Draw a rectangle.
2. Write an X inside the rectangle.
3. Draw two circles next to the rectangle.
4. Shade one-half of one circle.

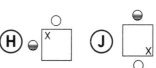

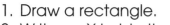

Final Review Test

27. Where would you look in an anatomy book to find the meaning of **histology**?

table of contents
(A)

dictionary
(B)

glossary
(C)

encyclopedia
(D)

28. Choose the correct order for the directions on how to wrap a present.

1. Secure the paper around the box with tape.
2. Put the present into a box.
3. Tape a card to the wrapped present.
4. Measure wrapping paper around the box and then cut the paper.
5. Tie some ribbon around the box.

(F) 2, 4, 1, 5, 3   (G) 4, 1, 2, 4, 5

(H) 3, 2, 1, 4, 5   (J) 1, 2, 4, 5, 3

29. Identify the word that would come last in alphabetical order.

marigold
(A)

marinade
(B)

marimba
(C)

maritime
(D)

30. Complete the analogy.

Biography is to nonfiction as _____ is to social studies.

encyclopedia
(F)

fiction
(G)

geography
(H)

meteorology
(J)

Choose two summer activities. List three ways they are similar and three ways they are different.

_____

_____

_____

_____

_____

STOP

Page 5

1. antonyms; 2. antonyms;
3. synonyms; 4. antonyms;
5. synonyms

Pages 6–7

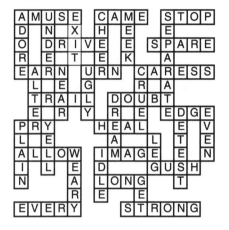

Page 8

1. maize; 2. presence; 3. vein;
4. cruise; 5. medal; 6. beech;
7. stationary; 8. rite; 9. knead;
10. aisle; 11. lyre; 12. sealing

Page 9

1. morn; 2. Statue; 3. single; 4. Ask;
5. protection; 6. Free; 7. peddle;
8. soiled; 9. exact; 10. combined

Page 10

1. bathroom; 2. the United States;
3. spread; 4. hour; 5. squirrel;
6. night; 7. stop sign; 8. decoration;
9. skating; 10. polish; 11. parent

Page 11

1. lemon; 2. year; 3. aunt; 4. cow;
5. haul; 6. write; 7. sole; 8. up;
9. neck; 10. place; 11. stalk; 12. fish;
13. four; 14. vine; 15. transparent;
16. hungry; 17. pool; 18. mason;
19. court; 20. anatomy; 21. goat;
22. pride

Page 12

food; trunk; water; shower; tusks;
upper; enemies; bore; molars;
difficult; wear; replaced; life; longer;
usually

Page 13

1. range; 2. incorporated; 3. natives;
4. contingent; 5. stalked;
6. accuracy; 7. conceal; 8. weirs;
9. culture

Unit 1 Test

1. C; 2. B; 3. A; 4. D; 5. D; 6. B; 7. C;
8. D; 9. C; 10. D; 11. A; 12. A; 13. D;
14. A; 15. C; 16. B; 17. D; 18. C;
19. B; 20. B; Constructed-response
answers will vary.

Page 18

1. not heavy; 2. on a horse without
a saddle; 3. containing little fat;
4. thin pieces of cane or metal
attached to an air opening; 5. a
chest of drawers; 6. opposite of
multiply; 7. a graduated series;
8. proper; 9. lags; 10. lazy people

Page 19

1. a social gathering; 2. a protective
covering; 3. the substance or main
point of a policy; 4. turned to stone,
fossilized; 5. equalized weight;
6. continually think of; 7. news item

Page 20

1. produce; 2. wind; 3. moderate;
4. present; 5. record; 6. conduct

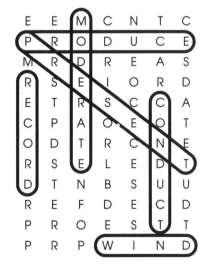

Page 21

1. stream, middle of the stream;
2. code, opposite of code;
3. graduate, after graduation;
4. proper, not proper; 5. phone,
carry sound over a distance;
6. color, one color; 7. scope, very
small scope; 8. zero, below zero;
9. natural, above natural;
10. superhuman; 11. telescope;
12. microearthquakes; 13. decipher;
14. postmodern; 15. subcategory;
16. immobilize; 17. midterm

Page 22

1. contest, one who performs in a
contest; 2. fiend, like a fiend;
3. leader, quality of being a leader;
4. courage, having qualities of
courage; 5. sweet, relating to sweet;
6. attend, condition of attending;
7. front, relating to the front;
8. lobby, one who lobbies; resident,
reddish, specialist, abruptly,
mechanical, patiently, carefully,
happily, generous, timely

Page 23

1. simile; 2. simile; 3. simile;
4. simile; 5. metaphor; 6. metaphor;
7. metaphor; 8. metaphor; 9. simile;
10. simile; 11. metaphor; 12. simile;
13. simile; 14. metaphor;
15. metaphor; 16. simile;
17. metaphor

Page 24

1. b; 2. f; 3. h; 4. a; 5. i; 6. g; 7. c;
8. d; 9. e

Page 25

1. first-place trophy, proudly stood
on the shelf in Charlie's room;
2. heavens, splitting popsicles;
3. Autumn leaves, sing as they
danced; 4. Horns, honked angrily;
5. sun, played hide-and-seek;
6. clouds, marched across the sky;
7. house, eagerly waited for the
new owners to arrive

Answer Key

Unit 2 Test

1. D; 2. A; 3. A; 4. C; 5. C; 6. A; 7. D; 8. C; 9. A; 10. A; 11. B; 12. C; 13. B; 14. C; 15. A; 16. D; 17. C; 18. A; 19. C; 20. D; Constructed-response answers will vary.

Page 30

1. how paper was made; 2. writing in ancient Egypt; 3. burying the dead in ancient Egypt

Page 31

Answers will vary. Possible answers include: 1. The Rosetta Stone was found in Egypt more than 200 years ago.; 2. The Rosetta Stone tells about King Ptolemy V.; 3. There are three different kinds of writing on the stone.; 4. The Rosetta Stone unlocked the mystery that had been puzzling historians since the time of the Greeks and Romans: what did the symbols say that covered the temples and tombs of Ancient Egypt.

Page 32

Answers will vary.

Page 33

1. Titles will vary.; 2. When the United States Constitution was written in 1787, it established a government in which power was split between three branches: legislative, executive, and judicial.; 3. Answers will vary.; 4. Although changes have been made to the Constitution over the past 200-plus years, the three branches of government remain as originally written.

Pages 34–35

Answers may vary. Possible answers include: 1. Laws are rules that we live by every day.; 2. Traffic laws maintain safety.; 3. Judges see that laws are carried out.; 4. The courts must protect individual rights.; 5. Though laws change, principles that govern the judiciary system do not.; 6. to protect the rights of everyone; 7. police and courts; 8. They interpret the laws and see that they are followed by everyone, they determine punishment for those who are guilty, and they protect the right of every individual.; 9. Laws can be changed to meet the needs of our nation.

Page 36

1. 2, 1, 3; 2. 3, 2, 1; 3. 1, 3, 2; 4. 2, 3, 1; 5. 3, 1, 2

Page 37

1. Long ago, festivals were held when there was a good harvest.; 2. The first European settlers in America had a fall festival they named Thanksgiving.; 3. There is usually a celebration of some sort after a harvest.

Unit 3 Test

1. A; 2. D; 3. A; 4. C; 5. A; 6. C; 7. B; 8. C; 9. B; 10. D; 11. D; 12. C; 13. A; 14. D; 15. C; 16. D; 17. B; 18. C; 19. A; 20. B; Constructed-response answers will vary.

Page 45

1. pioneers from New England; 2. where Kentucky, Tennessee, and Virginia met; 3. hunted, fished, and carried dried staples; 4. Daniel Boone; 5. late 1700s and early 1800s; 6. Mohawk Trail; 7. by foot or wagon; 8. several weeks

Pages 46–47

1. impeached and removed; 2. one chief justice and eight associates; 3. several hundred; 4. adjustments; 5. of national importance; 6. maintain the laws; 7. parties involved; 8. approved; 9. six to ten; 10. basis

Pages 48–49

1. a. Asia; b. Africa; c. North America; d. South America; e. Antarctica; f. Europe; g. Australia; 2. Asia; 3. Nile River and Amazon River; 4. Europe and Australia; 5. Australia; 6. Everest, McKinley, Aconcagua; 7. a. Volga; b. Murray-Darling; c. Missouri; d. Yangtze; e. Amazon; F. Nile

Page 50

1. Friendly; 2. eleven; 3. sweet; 4. rabbit; 5. beagle; 6. Travers; 7. Becky; 8. mean; 9. Preston; 10. Sunday; 11. Marty; 12. Shiloh; Newbery Medal

Page 51

1. Emily; 2. caring, resourceful; 3. Answers will vary.

Page 52

1. Billy and Roger; 2. helpful, studious; 3. unkind, athletic; 4. considerate, appreciative

Unit 4 Test

1. A; 2. B; 3. C; 4. B; 5. A; 6. C; 7. C; 8. D; 9. C; 10. D; 11. C; 12. C; 13. D; 14. B; 15. D; 16. B; 17. B; 18. C; 19. A; 20. B; Constructed-response answers will vary.

Midway Review Test

1. B; 2. F; 3. C; 4. G; 5. C; 6. F; 7. A; 8. J; 9. B; 10. F; 11. D; 12. J; 13. A; 14. J; 15. A; 16. G; 17. C; 18. F; 19. D; 20. H; Constructed-response answers will vary.

Answer Key

Pages 66–67

1. 2, 1, 4, 3; 2. B, D, A, C; 3. 6, 1, 2, 4, 3, 5

Pages 68–69

a. 5; b. 3; c. 10; d. 1; e. 7; f. 4; g. 9; h. 2; i. 8; j. 6

Page 70

1. 2, 3, 1; 2. 1, 3, 2; 3. 3, 2, 1, 4; 4. 3, 1, 4, 2

Page 71

Answers may vary. Check for logical sequences. 1. 2, 1, 3, 4; 2. 2, 5, 4, 1, 3; 3. 2, 3, 5, 4, 1

Page 72

1. 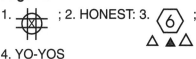 ; 2. HONEST: 3. ; 4. YO-YOS

Unit 5 Test

1. C; 2. A; 3. B; 4. C; 5. D; 6. B; 7. C; 8. B; 9. D; 10. A; 11. B; 12. A; 13. C; 14. B; 15. D; 16. A; 17. D; 18. C; 19. A; 20. D; Constructed-response answers will vary.

Page 79

Arabian Camel: one hump, trained for racing, shorter hair; Both: water stored in body tissue and pouches, also used for food and clothing, swaying motion, hump stores food; Bactrian Camel: can withstand cooler climates, sturdier, two humps

Pages 80–81

	Tennis	Squash
Court	• usually outdoors • flat, rectangular • net stretched across	• red boundary lines on court and walls • four walls • always indoors
Racket	• strung	• strung
Ball	• hollow rubber ball covered with fuzzy cloth	• soft and hollow (singles) • hard and hollow (doubles)
Points to win	• four	• fifteen
How game played	• hit ball back and forth across net • two to four players	• hit ball against walls • two to four players

Page 82

Words in bold should be circled.
1. battery was dead; **The overhead light of the car was left on overnight**; battery was dead; 2. too much detergent, **Mother put too much detergent in the dishwasher**; there was foam all over the kitchen floor; 3. worked all night; **high winds yesterday**; The electric company worked all night; 4. was very old; **The house on the hill was very old**; needed a lot of restoring; 5. snow and ice; **snow and ice during the winter**; Main Street had a lot of potholes; 6. was not picking up the dirt; **a sock blocking the air passage**; opened the vacuum cleaner to see why it was not picking up the dirt

Page 83

1. The regular path was blocked by a fallen tree. The hikers took a longer route.; 2. The water was running so fast. It made fishing in the stream difficult.; 3. The red team's goalie was out of position. It made it easy for the blue team to score.; 4. The pitcher threw a high ball. A batter hit a home run into the stands.; 5. There was a sharp sound like a gun being fired. It made John's horse buck and throw him from the saddle.; 6. I hit golf balls at the practice range. I had my best golf score.

Page 84

1. F; 2. O; 3. F; 4. F; 5. O; 6. O; 7. F; 8. O; 9. F; 10. O; 11. O; 12. O; 13. F; 14. F; 15. O

Page 85

1. F; 2. O; 3. O; 4. F; 5. O; 6. F; 7. O; 8. F

Page 86

1. NF; 2. B; 3. NF: 4. F; 5. F; 6. B; 7. NF: 8. F; 9. F; 10. B; 11. F; 12. NF: 13. NF; 14. F; 15. B

Unit 6 Test

1. C; 2. D; 3. C; 4. A; 5. A; 6. C; 7. B; 8. D; 9. A; 10. B; 11. D; 12. D; 13. C; 14. D; 15. B; 16. A; 17. C; 18. A; 19. A; 20. B; Constructed-response answers will vary.

Page 93

Clues will vary. 1. purse; 2. bathing suit; 3. shoes

Page 94

Clues will vary. 1. receptionist; 2. police officer; 3. maintenance man; 4. veterinarian

Page 95

1. thrilled; 2. her grandparents; 3. horse; 4. in a week; 5. were in a lot of horse shows; 6. she did not ride Pal when he got too old

Answer Key

Page 96

1. The traveler had been standing in the rain trying to hail a taxi.; 2. Mickey had tripped and fallen on her shoulder; 3. The server had gone to refill the chicken tray.; 4. The class had been camping for three days.; 5. A bird had flown inside through the open window and had become frightened.; 6. The dog had been left alone in the kitchen.; 7. Chris had been at the library.

Page 97

Answers will vary.

Page 98

1. pulled off to the side of the road; 2. called a friend to get the assignment; 3. went to get the rink manager; 4. did all they could to conserve water; 5. was there to direct traffic; 6. stopped at the curb to look both ways

Unit 7 Test

1. A; 2. C; 3. B; 4. C; 5. D; 6. C; 7. B; 8. A; 9. D; 10. B; 11. C; 12. A; 13. A; 14. B; 15. B; 16. D; 17. D; 18. A; 19. A; 20. B; Constructed-response answers will vary.

Page 105

1. 4, 3, 1, 5, 2; 2. 5, 1, 3, 2, 4; 3. 2, 4, 1, 5, 3; 4. 3, 2, 5, 1, 4; 5. require, resist, reserve, represent; 6. horn, hover, hound, hoop; 7. push, pulley, pudding, purple; 8. diesel, differ, digest, dictate

Page 106

1. United States, Pearl Harbor; 2. Mount Rushmore; 3. radio, phonograph; 4. ozone; 5. clothing; 6. Mickey Mouse; 7. Harriet Tubman, Underground Railroad; 8. croquet; 9. cactus; 10. liver; 11. endangered; 12. immigration policy; 13. Industrial Revolution; 14. political parties, United States

Page 107

1. 1; 2. 8; 3. 6; 4. 11; 5. 1, 11; 6. 9; 7. 5, 11; 8. 9; 9. 6; 10. 7; 11. 3; 12. 12; 13. 10; 14. 3; 15. 9

Page 108

1. Jefferson City; 2. 8; 3. Nebraska, Kansas, Oklahoma; 4. St. Louis, Kansas City; 5. Mississippi River; 6. SW; 7. St. Louis; 8. Springfield; 9. St. Joseph; 10. Columbia

Page 109

1. Trees in Your Backyard; 2. Washington, D.C.; 3. South American Countries; 4. Longitude and Latitude; 5. Competitive Team Sports; 6. U.S. Capital Cities; 7. Organs of the Body; 8. Regions of the United States; 9. Famous Scientists; 10. Native Americans; 11. Major World Rivers; 12. Famous Composers

Page 110

1. 12; 6, 12–18; 2. 4; 4–5; 3. 6; 24; 4. 20; 21–22; 5. 18; 19; 6. 24; NA

Page 111

1. encyclopedia; 2. glossary; 3. atlas; 4. encyclopedia; 5. dictionary; 6. table of contents; 7. index; 8. atlas; 9. glossary; 10. encyclopedia; 11. index; 12. table of contents

Unit 8 Test

1. B; 2. C; 3. A; 4. C; 5. A; 6. D; 7. C; 8. A; 9. D; 10. A; 11. B; 12. C; 13. B; 14. B; 15. A; 16. C; 17. A; 18. B; 19. C; 20. D; Constructed-response answers will vary.

Final Review Test

1. A; 2. H; 3. B; 4. G; 5. A; 6. J; 7. C; 8. H; 9. A; 10. G; 11. D; 12. H; 13. A; 14. G; 15. C; 16. J; 17. B; 18. F; 19. C; 20. J; 21. A; 22. H; 23. B; 24. F; 25. D; 26. F; 27. C; 28. F; 29. D; 30. H; Constructed-response answers will vary.

Editor
Eric Migliaccio

Managing Editor
Ina Massler Levin, M.A.

Illustrator
Alexandra Artigas

Cover Artist
Tony Carrillo

Art Manager
Kevin Barnes

Art Director
CJae Froshay

Imaging
Rosa C. See

Publisher
Mary D. Smith, M.S. Ed.

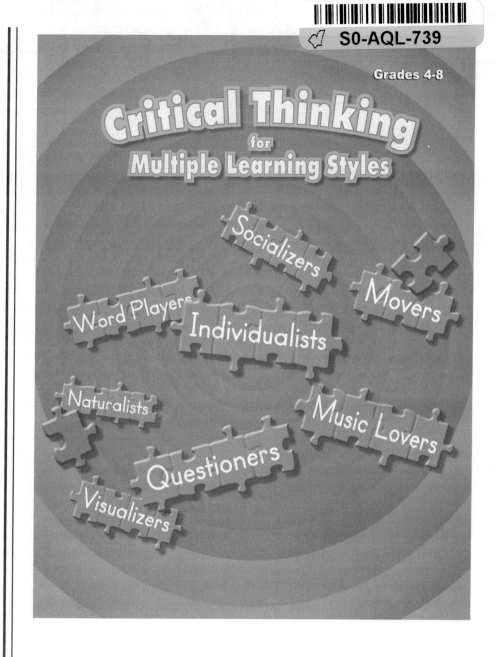

Grades 4-8

Critical Thinking
for
Multiple Learning Styles

Socializers

Movers

Word Players

Individualists

Naturalists

Music Lovers

Questioners

Visualizers

S0-AQL-739

Author

Karen M. Streeter

Teacher Created Resources

Teacher Created Resources, Inc.
6421 Industry Way
Westminster, CA 92683
www.teachercreated.com

ISBN-0-7439-3400-8

©2005 Teacher Created Resources, Inc.

Made in U.S.A.

Table of Contents

Table of Contents (cont.)

Introduction

Welcome to *Critical Thinking for Multiple Learning Styles*. The purpose of this book is to help make meaningful personal and professional connections for the teacher and student in a thinking classroom.

Brain research tell us that our brain is first a social brain—it grows and changes from interactions with the world within which it lives. Consequently, learning begins with how we feel about ourselves and the relationships we have with others: the care connection. In the thinking classroom, the over-arching emphasis on "care-fronting" students honors what makes them human and special. Genuine regard and dignity, plus activities and experiences that celebrate individuality within a safe-yet-challenging environment, help to create the personal care connection. It is not enough for the learner to feel good about one's self (self-esteem); the learner must also feel capable and contributing (self-efficacy). In the care-fronting, thinking classroom, each individual learner is valued as unique, one-of-a-kind, prized, and smart! Opportunities to create and to experience personal success help build the care connection. This book will share ideas that nurture learners as "human beings, not human doings" and help learners contribute to—not just cope with—the world they live in. In short, this book will encourage teachers to focus on the student as a unique child first, a capable learner second. Kids don't care how much you know until they know how much you care.

Learning is making connections between what we know and what we do not know. Learning is making connections between self and the world of others. Learning is making connections between the school world and the real world. In short, learning is making sense of the world in which we live. Brain research tells us that our brain innately does this; it is a natural pattern maker. So what does that mean to the educator? A goal of this book is to help the educator create options for a thinking classroom where the learner naturally makes his/her own connections to the world rather than be confined to regurgitation of trivia. It is important to remember that learning actually takes place in the brain, not the classroom. Learning is a child's response to education and/or experience. In addition, this book will address the fact that people are smart in different ways and use a variety of learning-thinking styles to make sense of the world. Howard Gardner's *Theory of Multiple Intelligences* is an effective way to explore these differences. Specific chapters of *Critical Thinking for Multiple Learning Styles* are prefaced with a child portrait and a designated "T" chart to exemplify each of the eight smarts or intelligences identified by Gardner. The "T" chart highlights an **SOS** (*Significantly Out-of-Sync*) child in a particular kind of intelligence and illustrates what you would see a SOS child doing and what you would hear a SOS child saying.

What do you hear this SOS child saying?	**What do you see this SOS child doing?**

Introduction *(cont.)*

Examples of real-life role models will be given. These chapters will then elaborate on warm-ups, teaching activities, and games that nurture a specific intelligence. The "M" chart will be a reflective tool at the end of the chapter to emphasize how the SOS learner feels as he or she makes meaningful connections in a thinking classroom geared to his or her special abilities.

What do you *see* this SOS child saying?   **What do you *hear* this SOS child saying?**   **How will this SOS child be *feeling*?**

Another goal of *Critical Thinking for Multiple Learning Styles* relates to differentiation, the key to effective education. Differentiation involves creating options for the learner by tailoring or personalizing the learning process so that it makes sense to him or her. Differentiation is dependent on a learner's learning-thinking style, readiness to learn, and interest. Focusing on a student's interest and passion will help make meaningful connections. An array of options must exist within a thinking classroom, especially for the SOS child (one who is Significantly-Out-of-Sync with his or her peers). The SOS child may: talk in paragraphs, use elaborate vocabulary, create unique designs and inventions, participate in a social circle well beyond his years, be "street smart," grasp unusual inferences, be intuitively sensitive, observe nuances, relish in self discovery, challenge truth, learn differently. *Critical Thinking for Multiple Learning Styles* provides options for differentiation in instruction and curriculum (content, process, and product), especially for the SOS child.

A professional connection is another purpose of this book: to "plug into" the roles and responsibilities of teachers. Teachers are building our future because they are teaching our future leaders, designers, engineers, artists, teachers, problem solvers. Teachers can make a difference in the lives of our children, and so they need to walk tall and be proud of their profession. Yet today teachers walk "short" because of the job demands and changes.

Today, teachers have a broader curriculum to teach (including technology, drugs and alcohol, human growth and development, character development, and personal safety), yet a stricter expectation for accountability of the basics. They also have a greater range of abilities in the classroom, yet a mandate toward conformity. In turn, the classroom has a richer diversity because of mobility, changing demographics of the population, and emphasis on the immersion philosophy, yet limited opportunities for staff development and professional growth. Today's teachers feel threatened and unsafe because of the waning respect for authority in our society. It is easy to see why teachers walk "short."

Critical Thinking for Multiple Learning Styles is "teacher-friendly" in implementing ideas that demonstrate best practices in education. It features ideas that highlight experiential "hands on" learning; higher-order-thinking (**HOT thinking**) strategies; cooperative, collaborative projects; plus real-life problem solving and decision making. In short, *Critical Thinking for Multiple Learning Styles* offers genuine options and choices for the thinking classroom. The ideas thrive within an "intelligence-friendly" classroom where the priority will be to ask "How are you smart?" rather than "How smart are you?"

Introduction *(cont.)*

"SOS" Kid

significantly-out-of-sync

HOT (Higher Order Thinking) Strategies

Analogy

Brainstorming
- Elaboration
- Flexibility
- Fluency
- Originality

Decision and Outcomes

Encapsulation

Metacognition
- Evaluation
- Prediction
- Reflection

Mind Mapping

Plus, Minus, Interesting

Point-of-View

Visualization

"T" Chart

What do you *see* the child doing?	What do you *hear* the child saying?

"M" Chart

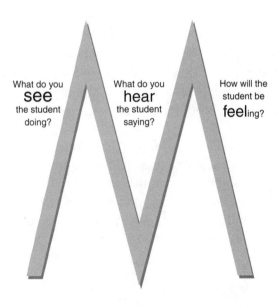

What do you **see** the student doing?

What do you **hear** the student saying?

How will the student be **feel**ing?

Warm-Ups

In a thinking classroom it is important to warm up the brain, to do some mental jogging to prime the neurons. Throughout the book, selective warm-ups will be shared that nurture multiple intelligences or different kinds of smart. Here is an example of a mental jogging warm-up.

Figure Drawing

- Draw a figure that represents you. Write down ideas for each part of the body.

- **Head:** List things you like to think about.

- **Heart:** List things you love.

- **Hands:** List things you like to do.

- **Feet:** List things you want to stomp out of this world.

- Share your drawing with others.

This activity is beneficial because it:

1. focuses on the learner as a "human being" not a "human doing"

2. applies brain research: there is a link between the cognitive and affective parts of our brain

3. addresses the *whole* child: head, heart, body, spirit

4. practices intrapersonal intelligence and self-reflection

5. allows for differentiation: plugs into student interest/passion

6. develops teamwork: "we stick together" bulletin board format

7. presents a timeless activity with little teacher preparation

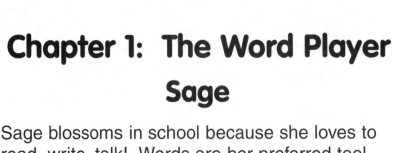

Chapter 1: The Word Player
Sage

Sage blossoms in school because she loves to read, write, talk! Words are her preferred tool. She easily talks in paragraphs and enjoys elaborating with new vocabulary or adding ideas to stimulating discussions. She prefers oral or written reports, rather than interpretive drawings or skits. Sage feels at home in the library; loves research; and finds the biographies of Maya Angelou, Shel Silverstein, Toni Morrison, and Louis Braille captivating. Sage's game shelf includes *Scrabble*®, *Balderdash*®, *Boggle*®, *Trivial Pursuit*®, and *Taboo*®. Competing in spelling bees and playing word games delights her. She was fascinated with school field trips to the local newspaper business and the community courtroom. She conscientiously uses a New-Word-A-Day calendar. A career in law or journalism intrigues Sage but an acting career also beckons.

How would you differentiate for Sage in the classroom?

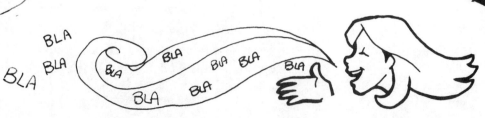

Verbal/Linguistic Connections

The Word Player

See	Hear
• carrying stacks of encyclopedias	• using large vocabulary
• sleeping with a thesaurus	• talking in paragraphs
• reading books	• telling stories
• enjoying New-Word-A-Day calendars	• using puns, idioms, humor
• playing word games	• asking "May we go to the library?"
• writing reports	• elaborate discussions
• researching unusual topics	• singing "Supercalifragilisticexpialidocious"
• creating word games	• saying "Let's play *Trivia Pursuit*"
• pursuing journalist, lawyer, author, poet, actress careers	• reciting poetry
	• recalling, memorizing facts
	• brainstorming ideas

SOS People: William Shakespeare, Maya Angelou, Shel Silverstein, Toni Morrison, Shirley Temple, Robert Frost

Warm-Ups: How many words can you make out of *encyclopedia*? List words that begin and end with the same letter.

Games: *Spill and Spell*®, *Taboo*®, *Scrabble*®, *Balderdash*®, *Boggle*®, *Hangman*®, *Scattergories*®, *Trivia Pursuit*®

Option #	Activity Name	Page #
1.	Word Volley	10
2.	Password	11
3.	Headline Contest	11
4.	Book Bites	12
5.	What You Don't Say!	13
6.	Silly Words & Daffy Definitions	14
7.	Puzzlers	14

In addition, see Chapter 9 for the following activities: "ABC Puzzlers" (pages 136 and 137), "Colorful Puzzlers" (pages 141–145), "Connections" (page 146), "Name That Country!" (page 166), and "Wordles" (pages 167).

Word Volley

Students, grouped in duos (pairs) or trios (threesomes), brainstorm words to create a word bank for a selected topic. The teacher gives a topic such as "name mammals." Students think of ideas that will fit the category. Verbal responses are bounced back and forth from one player to the next in a given amount of time. The teacher listens for appropriateness of response and for unusual verbal connections. The responses may be written down for further analysis and application.

Benefits of "Word Volley"

- Increases vocabulary
- Useful in any content area or grade level
- Allows students to do the talking
- Promotes interactive learning
- Provides a quick assessment
- Teaches the components of (HOT) creative thinking, fluency, flexibility, originality

Curriculum Examples

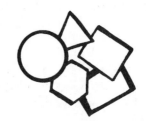

- ✧ *Math:* name geometric shapes
- ✧ *Social Studies:* name states and capitals
- ✧ *Science:* name herbivores
- ✧ *Chemistry:* name elements on the periodic table
- ✧ *Literature:* name authors
- ✧ *English:* name homonyms
- ✧ *PE:* name sports played with a ball
- ✧ *Art:* name colors
- ✧ *Health:* name fruits
- ✧ *Geography:* name islands

Johnson, Nancy (1990). *Questioning Makes the Difference.* Beavercreek, OH. Pieces of Learning.

Something to think about: Do you use *fat* questions *or skinny* questions? Fat questions are more open-ended—for example, "Name things that measure other things." (Answer would include *metronome, Richter scale, hand, acre-feet,* etc.) Skinny questions are more finite—for example, "Name math measurement tools." (Answer would include *ruler, compass, tape measure, meter stick,* etc.)

Password

The teacher selects relevant vocabulary terms from a topic of study. Each term is written on a large index card. The teacher displays a card over the head of one student so that he or she cannot see it. Other participants are asked to give one-word clues to make the student say the selected word (HOT: encapsulation). The contestant puts the various one-word clues together to guess the selected term (HOT: inductive thinking). The winning clue-giver becomes the next contestant for Password.

Benefits of "Password"

- Increases vocabulary understanding

- Inspires healthy competition among students

- Encourages HOT (encapsulation and inductive thinking)

- Provides a quick learning assessment

- Useful in any content area and various grade levels

- Little teacher preparation needed

Headline Contest

The teacher selects a photograph or a picture from a magazine or a newspaper and posts the selection on a bulletin board. During the week students generate ideas for the headline, write them on paper, and put them in a ballot box. At the end of the week, the ballot box and picture are given to another classroom for evaluation. Criteria are determined for evaluation such as relevance, conciseness, creativity, and intrigue. Students vote on the winning selection for the headline. The picture with the winning headline is posted in the classroom headline gallery. The winner gets to select the picture for the next week.

Another format may be to display book jackets or to play current songs. Students must generate new Headline titles for these products.

Benefits of "Headline Contest"

- Exposure to a variety of media

- Reinforces HOT (encapsulation and evaluation)

- Promotes independent and group processing

- Provides a learning center differentiation activity

- Adaptable to different grade levels

Book Bites

Students read a self-selected library book and write clues about the book. Four to five clues are written about each book. The clues are put into an envelope and then given to a classmate to solve. Or, the clues can be given to a group of students, each student getting one clue. The group must work together to solve the puzzle: the name of the book.

Students may also write clues about plays, movies, television shows, heroes, countries, careers, inventions, or sports.

Examples of a Book Bite

1. Story takes place in a house in the woods.

2. The house is vandalized.

3. A main character is a taste-tester and does research on chairs and beds.

4. Family vows to lock their door next time.

Answer: "Goldilocks and the Three Bears"

Example of a Hero Bite

1. He grew up in Texas.

2. He overcame cancer.

3. He wrote the book titled *It's Not About the Bike*.

4. He has won the Tour de France several times.

Answer: Lance Armstrong

Example of a Country Bite

1. Country is in the Southern Hemisphere.

2. Country is composed of two islands.

3. It has fiords, geysers, and sand beaches.

4. Maori are the indigenous people.

5. It is the jumping-off place to the South Pole.

Answer: New Zealand

Benefits of "Book Bites"

• Offers choice and variety of student products

• Reinforces HOT: encapsulation, deductive-inductive thinking, problem solving

• Promotes individual or group process

• Extends knowledge of literature

What You Don't Say!

In every curriculum study there are famous people connected with the content. This option helps students become more familiar with these selected individuals. The teacher writes the name of a famous person where only one team member can see it. That student must then give clues about the name of the person to help his or her teammate solve the identity. (Clues should only be about the person's name, not his or her accomplishments.) Classmates may work in teams to guess the identity of the VIP person.

For instance, if the category is "Presidents," the name might be Franklin Pierce. Clues could include:

1. Cupid's arrow may stab, cut, or _____ the heart. (*pierce*)

2. If you use language that is very direct and honest, you are being very _____ . (*frank*)

3. The opposite of out is _____ . (*in*)

Frank + in + Pierce = **Franklin Pierce**

If the category is "Scientists," the clues for Galileo might be:

1. A casual term for a man and woman may be a guy and a _____ . (*gal*)

2. A floral necklace worn in Hawaii is called a _____ . (*lei*)

3. The zodiac sign for an early August birthday is _____ . (*Leo*)

Gal + lei + leo = **Galileo**

Various categories of famous people may be studied or reviewed, such as athletes, Olympians, authors, artists, mathematicians, musicians, or inventors. At the beginning of the year this activity may even be used to acquaint students with the names of their classmates or their teachers.

Benefits of "What You Don't Say!"

- Fun, challenging activity

- Unique introduction to VIPs in any content area

- Accents HOT: elaboration, originality

- Provides healthy competition and teamwork

Silly Words & Daffy Definitions

Students may exercise their creative-thinking skills by using silly words in a vocabulary study. The teacher may put a made-up silly word on the board and ask students to define, elaborate on, or illustrate the word. Or students may invent their own daffy definitions. For instance, as a warm-up, the teacher writes this teaser on the board:

> Please illustrate a GEGENFLETZ and tell what it does.

Students visualize, draw, design their own interpretation of a GEGENFLETZ and then explain what a GEGENFLETZ does. Ideas are shared in class.

Benefits of "Silly Words & Daffy Definitions"

- Stimulates creativity (originality, elaboration, flexibility)

- Provides humor and enjoyment in the classroom

- Highlights visual-spatial and verbal skills

- Applies to any content area; silly words may be used in writing math word problems or creating new Olympic events

Puzzlers

Many word puzzles can be intriguing options for word smart learners. Crossword puzzles, word searches, and Jumbles (scramble word puzzles) are favorite choices.

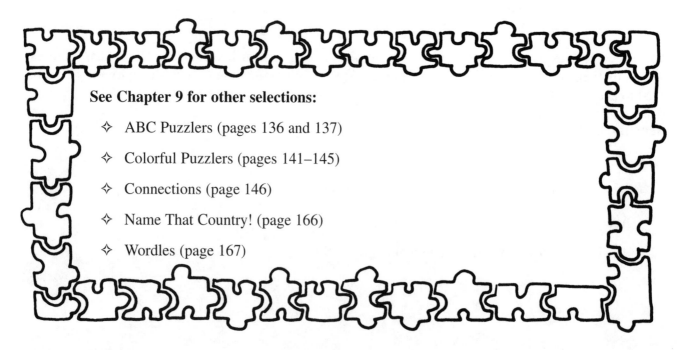

See Chapter 9 for other selections:

"M" Chart

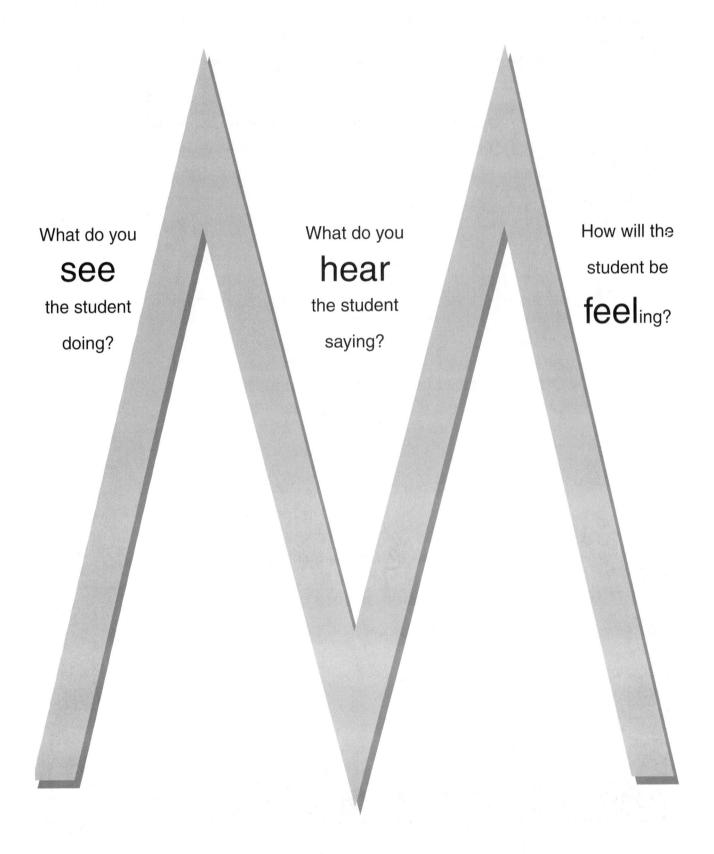

What do you **see** the student doing?

What do you **hear** the student saying?

How will the student be **feel**ing?

Chapter 2: The Questioner
Shawn

Solving brainteasers and reading mysteries delight Shawn. Math is his favorite subject in school, if you don't count the computer lab! Shawn figures things out easily and quickly in his head so abhors laborious paperwork. Charts, timelines, grids, or simple graphic organizers appeal to him as final class products. No written reports! Whether it is a science, social studies or language arts curriculum, Shawn is quick to see patterns and note relationships. Questioning hypotheses or analyzing data seem natural to him because of his excellent logical thinking skills. Financial issues and investments intrigue him so games like *Monopoly®*, *Payday®*, and *Stock Market®* appeal to him, as well as strategy games like *Clue®*, *Battleship®*, or *Mastermind®*. Shawn would like to meet people like Bill Gates, Albert Einstein, Marie Curie, or even Bobby Fisher. He uses a Brainteaser-A-Day Calendar to keep posted. His favorite school field trips included the veterinarian, the school lab, and the bank because he is considering a career in science or finance.

How would you differentiate for Shawn?

Logical/Mathematical Connections

The Questioner

See	Hear
• using calculators	• "Math is my favorite class."
• making lists	• "I love brainteasers."
• figuring math in their heads	• asking questions
• playing *Monopoly*® or *Clue*®	• "May we use the scientific method?"
• loving computers	• "I want to figure this out."
• organizing data	• solving riddles
• hypothesizing	• classifying and categorizing information
• making predictions	• logical problem solving
• preferring financial, scientific jobs	• solving mathematical proofs
• exploring patterns and relationships	
• creating magic squares	
• pursuing financier, mathematician, scientist, physicist, computer, tax auditor careers	

SOS People: Albert Einstein, Bobby Fisher, John Paul Getty, Bill Gates, George Washington Carver, Marie Curie

Warm-Ups: "Valentine Puzzler" (page 18), "Balloon Ride" (page 20)

Games: *Clue*®, *Monopoly*®, *Payday*®, *Challenge 24*®, *Bingo*®, *Quizmo*®, *Mastermind*®, *Battleship*®, *Stratego*®, checkers, *Candyland*®, *Chutes and Ladders*®, *Stock Market*®

Option #	Activity Name	Page #
1.	"What Comes Next?"	22
2.	"Predictions"	25
3.	"What's in the Bag?"	26
4.	"Stacking Categories"	30
5.	"Question the Answers"	34
6.	"Plus, Minus, Interesting"	36
7.	"Array"	38

Valentine Puzzler

Materials

- the 4 x 4 grid below
- 10 game pieces (for example, candy hearts, candy corn, beans, buttons, plastic chips, candy-coated chocolates, etc.)

Directions

Place the 10 game pieces on the grid so that there will only be an even number of pieces going in every direction—vertically, horizontally, and diagonally (from one corner to the other).

See page 19 for possible solutions to this puzzler.

Valentine Puzzler *(cont.)*

Possible Solutions

Balloon Ride

The Hot Air Balloon is coming to town. Free rides will be given to anyone who can cut the last tie rope holding the balloon to the ground. Here are the rules:

- Ten (10) tie ropes hold the balloon to the ground.

- Two (2) people take turns cutting ropes. Each person can cut one (1) or two (2) ropes on a turn.

- Whoever cuts the last rope gets a free ride.

Can you figure out how to get the free ride every time?

Materials (for every two players)

- toothpicks

- "Balloon Ride" game board (page 21)

Directions

Two players make up a team. Each team should set up the game board (page 21) with 10 toothpicks connecting the bottom of the balloon with the ground. Follow the rules listed above. The object is to get a free ride by removing the toothpicks according to a strategy.

Variations

Balloon Ride can be extended by increasing the number of tie ropes and also by increasing the number of ropes each player may cut. For example:

- 21 tie ropes; players may cut 1, 2, or 3 ropes at a time.

- 40 tie ropes; players may cut 1, 2, 3, or 4 ropes at a time.

Would you rather be the first or second player for each of these?

*This is one of the many versions of the ancient Chinese game of NIM.

Math for Girls and Other Problem Solvers. Diane Downie, Twila Slesnick, Jean Kerr Stenmark. EQUALS. Lawrence Hall of Science. University of California. Berkeley, CA 1981. Permission granted by L. Lang (3/16/04). Web site: *www.lawrencehallofscience.org/equals* .

Balloon Ride (cont.)

Game Board

Math for Girls and Other Problem Solvers. Diane Downie, Twila Slesnick, Jean Kerr Stenmark. EQUALS. Lawrence Hall of Science. University of California. Berkeley, CA 1981. Permission granted by L. Lang (3/16/04).
Web site: *www.lawrencehallofscience.org/equals*

What Comes Next?

The following activities are designed to encourage students to find patterns in a group of things. Letters, numbers, shapes, or ideas may be given; and students should categorize and classify them into meaningful groups. Inductive, deductive, and sequential thinking skills are practiced.

Number Patterns

Analyze each of the following patterns. Figure out what the next number in each pattern would be. Hint: Look between the numbers.

Set 1

(5) (10) (15) ( ) (25) (30) (35) ( ) (45)

Set 2

(10) (12) (15) (17) (20) (22) ( ) ( ) ( )

How do these numbers fit together? There is more than one answer; and in some answers, all of the numbers might not be used.

Set 3

(18) (9) (20) (72)

Set 4

(9339) (19091) (747) (3406)

Letter Patterns

What could these letters stand for?

Set 1

(O) (T) (T) (F) (F) (S) ( ) ( ) ( )

Your idea: _____

Set 2

(J) (F) (M) (A) ( ) (J) (J) (A) ( ) (O) ( ) (D)

Your idea: _____

What Comes Next? *(cont.)*

Word Patterns

Find the pattern for each set of words then create your own.

Set 1

(area) (bulb) (critic) (dread) (fluff) (going) (health)

Set 2

(aardvark) (bubble) (raccoon) (daddy) (feed) (gruff) (egg)

Shape Patterns

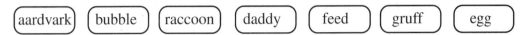

Nature Patterns

(weather systems)   (sun/earth revolution)   (tides)   (fractals)

Historical Patterns

(presidential elections)   (war)   (depressions)

Story Patterns

Silly Milly

Silly Milly likes noodles and spaghetti but does not like pasta.

Silly Milly likes to play chess but not checkers, play the piccolo but not the flute.

Silly Milly reads books but not newspapers or magazines.

Silly Milly has two pets: a parrot and a kitten. She does not have a frog.

What else does she like? _____

Challenge: Can you create other riddles for Silly Milly?

- -

Answers

Number Patterns: Set 1: 20, 40; Set 2: 25, 27, 30 ; Set 3: three numbers are divisible by 9, the digits of three of the numbers add up to odd numbers, etc.; Set 4: three numbers are the same backwards as forwards, etc.

Letter Patterns: Set 1: S, E, N (1st letter of numbers one through nine); Set 2: the months of the year (missing letters are M, S, N)

Word Patterns: Set 1: all words begin and end in same letter; Set 2: all words have double letters

Story Patterns: Milly likes things with double letters.

Patterns

Directions

Look at these patterns carefully. What do you need to add to finish them? Write or draw the missing letters, numbers, or shapes that are needed to complete the patterns.

1. ○○○○○○|○○○○○|○○○○| _____

2. ⊡ ⊡ ⊡ _____

3. △▽|△▽▽|△▽▽▽| _____

4. ○|○○|○○○|○○○○|○○○| _____

5. ACB, JLK, RTS, L _____

6. hear—he, nose—no, meat—me, soak— _____

7. best—state, tenth—thin, into— _____

8. 2349, 5679, 1239, _____

9. foot, ankle, knee, leg, waist, chest, neck, _____

10. ⬜ ⬜ ⬜ ⬜ _____

11. an, ban, can, _____

12. |, +, ✳, _____

13. look, school, book, stoop, w_____

14. noon, afternoon, evening, midnight, _____

15. 154, 253, 352, _____

Rasmussen, Greta. (1989). *Brain Stations. A Center Approach to Thinking Skills.* Stanwood, WA. Permission granted for reprinting by Tin Man Press, P.O. Box 11409, Eugene, OR, 97440. Phone: 800-676-0459 Fax: 888515-1764. Website: *www.tinmanpress.com.*

Suggested answers: 1. ○○○ ; 2. ⊡ ; 3. △▽ ▽ ▽ ; 4. ○○ ; 5. NM; 6. so; 7. took, tooth, toad, etc. (word must begin with last two letters of previous word); 8. 569; 9. head; 10. ⬜ ; 11. Dan; 12. ✳ ; 13. wool or wood; 14. morning; 15. 451

Predictions

Many students enjoy athletic events and competitions. Various thinking skills can be honed with a sports and mathematics connection. An example of a higher order thinking (HOT) skill is prediction.

During basketball, baseball, or football season, offer students the challenge to predict the final scores between two teams in a weekly game. An example might be in football. At the beginning of the week, students are given the names of two teams (including their home team) who will play on the weekend (e.g., Denver Broncos and Miami Dolphins). The variables of the game are analyzed and discussed.

Variables may include the following:

✧ location of game (home stadium, noise, etc.)

✧ weather conditions

✧ personnel playing (injury list, number of superstars, new vs. veteran players, coaching styles, etc.)

✧ history of teams (past records, if teams played each other before, overall team experience)

✧ media hype and pressure

✧ equipment and ground conditions (artificial turf, indoor vs. outdoor)

✧ reliability and validity of referee teams

✧ other factors

Students weigh the evidence and then project the game winner. Predictions are written on a piece of paper then sealed in an envelope. On the Monday after the game, the envelope is opened and the students' predictions are read. Prediction winners may be given rewards such as sports-related candy bars or sports pencils. For added challenge, overall ratings may be projected for the end of a season.

Benefits of "Predictions"

• Makes timely content applications

• Employs versatility and variety of thinking strategies

• Connects with real world

• Adds fun and enjoyment to learning

• Provides option for a learning center

What's in the Bag?

This option may be used as a "hook" to generate intrigue and enthusiasm for beginning a new unit of study. To introduce the topic, the teacher puts a "clue" that connects with the unit in some way in a colorful paper or cloth bag. Students are asked to guess "What's in the Bag?" by asking questions. This activity piggybacks off the game "20 Questions" because the teacher will only give "Yes" or "No" responses. Students work together to guess what's in the bag before 20 questions have been asked.

Sample clues may be:

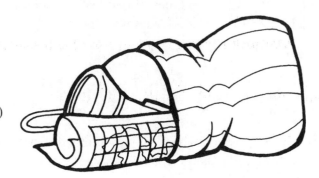

- ✧ battery (study of energy)

- ✧ map (geography study)

- ✧ rubber band (study of tools and/or inventions)

- ✧ balloon (study of transportation)

- ✧ peanut (Black History study)

After the students have guessed the item in the bag, the "Analogy" activity (pages 27–29) is used as a follow-up (for example, how are you like a battery?). This HOT activity generates many creative ideas and meaningful connections. The analogous thinking becomes the most important part of the activity.

Benefits of "What's in the Bag?"

- Promotes discovery learning
- Hooks or grabs the learner
- Reinforces brain research
- Generates HOT: hypotheses, analogy

- Aids the skills of questioning
- Applies to any content area
- Offers fun and delight
- Uses timely or timeless clues

Other applications of this strategy may be "Who Am I?" or "Where Am I?" The teacher holds a card or pretends to be a famous person connected with a study. Students must guess who the person is with the "20 Questions" approach. Or the teacher holds a card naming a specific location (island, mountain range, river, ocean, country, state, etc.). Students follow the same procedure to discover the place. Students may "be" the person or place. Students may work in pairs, teams, or in a large group. After the students have guessed the person or place, then the question (for example, "How are you like Michael Jordan?" or "How are you like Mount McKinley?") is again asked to prompt analogous thinking.

Analogy

An analogy is comparing two items to perceive similarities.

How is _____ like a _____ ?

How are you like a _____ ?

Follow up activity to "What's in the Bag?"

1. Study of energy: (*battery*) I am like a battery because I have positive and negative sides.

2. Study of inventions: (*rubber band*) I am like a rubber band because I can stretch, I can keep things together, and I have a breaking point.

3. Study of plants: (*seed*) I am like a seed because I need water to grow and to blossom.

Follow up activity to "Who am I?"

1. I am like Michael Jordan because I like to play basketball.

2. I am like Sacajawea because I can guide others.

3. I am like Martin Luther King, Jr., because I dream of peace in our world.

Follow up activity to "Where am I?"

1. I am like Mount McKinley because I have to climb high to reach my goals.

2. I am like the Amazon River because ideas flow within me and then surge into action.

3. I am like South Dakota because there are different regions (flat, dry, rugged) to me, just like there are in the state.

Analogy *(cont.)*

An analogy is comparing two items to perceive similarities.

Complete the matrix by thinking of words to complete each category.

Learning is like the color _____ because _____

_____.

Share your ideas with the group.

	Animal	**Color**	**Place**	**Machine**
Learning is like a(n) _____ because . . .				
Creativity is like a(n) _____ because . . .				
Thinking is like a(n) _____ because . . .				
Your idea!				

Analogy *(cont.)*

Use this grid to complete a study using analogies. Here is an example:

If you are studying careers, try this matrix. List careers in the left column. Write the names of objects in the top row. Think about how these things relate to one another.

Careers	flag	door	clock	window
actor				
engineer				
lawyer		a door opens and closes a room, a lawyer opens and closes a case		
author				a window opens the room to fresh air, an author opens a mind to fresh ideas
teacher				
chef				
pilot				

Stacking Categories

Many valuable teaching strategies may be adapted and utilized from television games. "Stacking Categories" is based on *$100,000 Pyramid,* which is an outstanding example of a game show that has direct application into the classroom.

Topics for given areas of study are written on 5 x 7 cards. These cards are placed into individual 8 x 11 plastic photo protectors. The protectors are organized into a pyramid design. Students must give ideas or items that fit into each category. For instance, if the category is "Fruits," students might name a banana, lime, orange, apple, kiwi, or plum. In a competition, students keep naming items until the teammate can name the category. The object is to cover the six areas or categories on the pyramid board in a one-minute time period. In a group setting, one person stands in front of the game board, one person gives the clues, and one person is the time-keeper. The rest of the class observes and practices positive spectator skills during the one-minute competition. Students involved in "Stacking Categories" trade places with other classmates after the one-minute competition.

Examples

Math: decimals, shapes, quadrilaterals, things with numbers, proper fractions, things that measure, Roman numerals, metric terms.

Language Arts: plurals, magazines, words with prefixes, authors, vowels, homonyms

Geography: islands, rivers, states that border the East coast, countries in Africa, kinds of maps, tools used by a navigator

Science: herbivores, inventors, elements on a periodic table, weather terms, spices, machines, bones in the human body, scientists

Benefits of "Stacking Categories"

- Encourages HOT skills: analysis, classify, categorize, inferences

- Provides quick assessment

- Offers healthy competition

- Adds pizzazz and delight to the classroom

- Reinforces positive spectator skills

- Applies to any content area

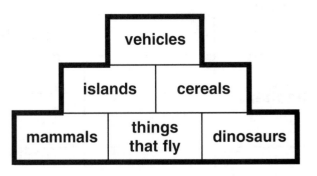

Stacking Categories *(cont.)*

Categories for Game

characters in a book	things you do in the winter	U.S. Presidents
things in a salad	things on a playground	rhyming words
letters of the alphabet	ice cream flavors	vegetables
rivers	parts of a bicycle	holidays
kinds of shoes	candy bars	metric terms
constellations	inventors	cartoonists
relatives	things found in a zoo	paper products

Stacking Categories *(cont.)*

Categories for Game *(cont.)*

human body systems	things that fly	words with prefixes
types of sandwiches	machines	sharp things
cereals	kinds of fruit	mammals
words with double letters	things that measure	things that have teeth
weather instruments	dinosaurs	musical instruments
kinds of boats	fractions	clothing items
things that are green	islands	vehicles

Stacking Categories (cont.)

Categories for Game (cont.)

things on a pizza	sports	things with numbers
things that open and close	mystery books	states and capitals
kinds of houses	things you collect	mountains
insects	computer terms	things found in water
water words	round things	things that are edible
parts of a car	kinds of dogs	energy sources
kinds of trees	months	musical groups

Question the Answers

The television game *Let's Play Jeopardy!* can be an effective teaching/learning tool in any classroom. The students become the knowledge experts on a variety of subjects, learn about the skill of questioning, compete collaboratively with their peers, and have fun learning.

A game board is created on a bulletin board, poster board, or a recycled window shade (a perfect resource because it is very mobile and durable). Six topics or categories are featured at a time. The topics are listed on 5" x 7" cards and clipped at the top of the game board. Four pockets are designated under each topic. Each pocket has points highlighted on the front that range from 10 points to 40 points. In the pocket, the teacher (or students) puts "answers" to the stated topics. The pockets with the higher points have the more difficult answers. The challenge of the game is to have the participant "ask" the question that yields the given answers. If a participant blurts out answers instead of asking a question, he or she receives no points.

The teacher may facilitate the "Question the Answers" game as a review for a test, or students may play the game on their own. Students may also create the answers and questions for the game.

Here is a sample game board:

10	10	10	10	10	10
20	20	20	20	20	20
30	30	30	30	30	30
40	40	40	40	40	40

Question the Answers *(cont.)*

Possible Categories

Presidents	Inventors	Poetry	Relatives	Words That End In "o"	Measurement
Islands	Quotations	Words That Have Double Letters	Gadgets	Explorers	Decimals
Maps	Plurals	Metric Terms	Heroes	States & Capitals	Astronomy
Government	Words That Have a Suffix	Money	Punctuation	Animal Young	Words That Begin With "a"

Sample Answers

Category: Presidents He was the only President who was a bachelor. *(Who was Buchanan?)*	**Category: Money** The value of 5 quarters, 5 dimes, 5 pennies. *(What is $1.80?)*
Category: Quotations He said, "We shall overcome." *(Who is Dr. Martin Luther King, Jr.?)*	**Category: Punctuation** Punctuation found at the end of a declarative sentence. *(What is a period?)*
Category: Measurement This word means 10 years. *(What is decade?)*	**Category: Government** This branch of government makes the laws. *(What is legislative?)*
Category: Plurals The plural of brother-in-law. *(What is brothers-in-law?)*	**Category: Animal Young** Name of a young swan. *(What is a cygnet?)*

Plus, Minus, Interesting

Learning activities that encourage analysis and critical thinking are especially suited for the logical/mathematical learner. Edward de Bono's PMI (plus, minus, interesting) strategy is useful because of its application to any subject area and focus on analytical thinking.

Students must look at an issue, subject, or problem from more than one point of view. The PMI terms help students understand different kinds of thinking. Exercises may include the following:

✧ Students hear a guest speaker on a given topic. After the presentation, students fill out the PMI chart.

> **Plus:** What I liked about the presentation.
>
> **Minus:** What I did not like about the presentation.
>
> **Interesting:** What I learned or found fascinating about the presentation. Questions I have…

✧ Students take the PMI chart on a field trip and record ideas.

✧ Students evaluate different ways of solving a math problem.

✧ Students critique books, movies, art, and inventions with PMI.

✧ Students discuss real-life problems and issues such as school uniforms or year-round school, using the PMI chart.

A Venn diagram may be used as a graphic organizer for analyzing and recording information. In order to stimulate more interaction and group processing, hula hoops may be used for the Venn Diagram structure. Three hula hoops are placed in a chalk tray with PMI labels above the hoops. Students work independently or in small groups to write PMI ideas on different colored sticky notes. These notes are placed inside of the appropriately labeled hula hoop. Students then move around to read the different PMI ideas. As closure, one student may summarize the notes inside each hoop.

Benefits of "PMI"

- Fosters analytical thinking
- Useful in many content areas
- Promotes different points of view
- Application to group process

> **Suggested resource:** Bono, Edward, (1985) *CoRT Thinking Skills*. New York, NY. Pergamon Press.

Plus, Minus, Interesting *(cont.)*

Consider the positive, negative, and interesting aspects of an idea using a single framework.

Plus (+)	Minus (-)	Interesting (!)(?)

Venn Diagram

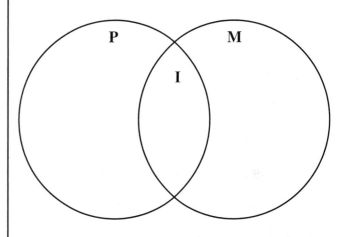

PMI Applications

➥ Evaluate a book, speaker, assembly program, or field trip.

➥ Analyze problem-solving strategies in math or science.

➥ Critique political candidates, a work of art, or a piece of music.

➥ Present an overview of an issue: school uniforms, block scheduling, grading, terms limits, genetic engineering, etc.

➥ Assess your own personal learning.

Ticket-Out-the-Door

Name: _____ Date: _____

Tell something that was **P** (plus), **M** (minus) or **I** (interesting, intriguing) about class today.

_____

_____

_____

_____

_____

Array

The array is a student product especially suited for the logical/mathematical learner. The student first creates a grid that may be four squares by four squares in size or larger. Then the student adds information or data to the grid that fits a certain topic or theme—for example, in each box the student writes the name of an animal. The third step adds the real element of challenge. Within the grid, there is a pattern of letters that spell out a clue or name. The student must determine which information fits the pattern and which information may be deleted. The final step is to solve the clue. In order to solve the final riddle, the student must follow all directions in a specific sequence. Here is an example:

Cross out all words that have a suffix. Then take the first letter of the remaining words and fill in the blanks to name a famous inventor.

event	lately	locale	indent	loveable
watch	friendship	habit	invention	illegal
government	zoology	tonsil	courteous	happiness
nourish	elect	childish	yodel	careful

___ ___ ___   ___ ___ ___ ___ ___ ___ ___

event	~~lately~~	locale	indent	~~loveable~~
watch	~~friendship~~	habit	~~invention~~	illegal
~~government~~	~~zoology~~	tonsil	~~courteous~~	~~happiness~~
nourish	elect	~~childish~~	yodel	~~careful~~

Answer: ELI WHITNEY

Note: Appendix B of Chapter 9 includes other Array puzzles.

Benefits of the "Array"

- Applies to any content area
- Promotes logical thinking
- Practices sequential thinking
- Reinforces following directions
- Varies in degree of difficulty

"M" Chart

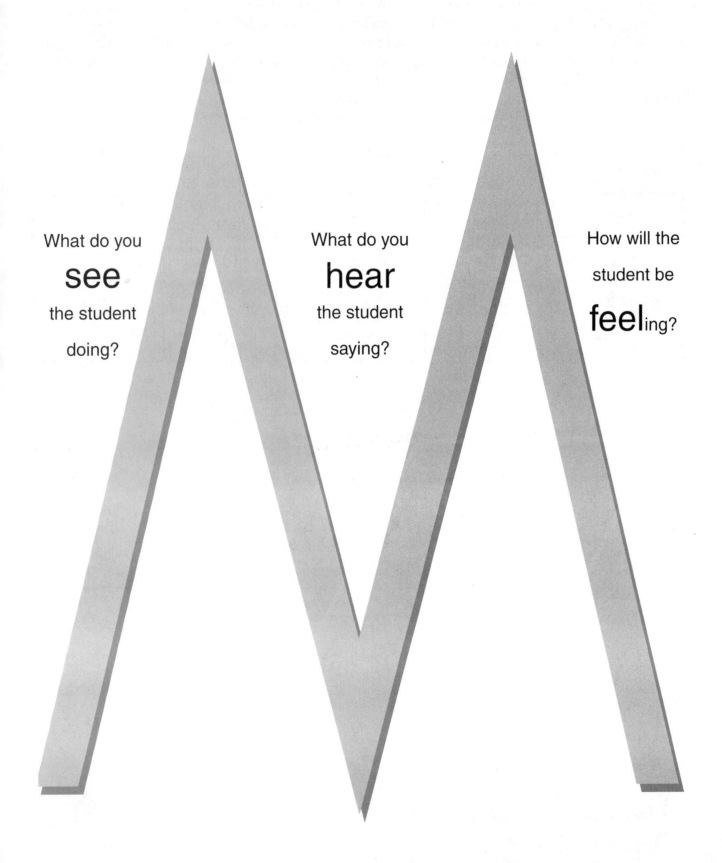

What do you **see** the student doing?

What do you **hear** the student saying?

How will the student be **feel**ing?

Chapter 3: The Visualizer
Sergio

Sergio delights in colors, shapes, designs, images, and unusual ideas; and he would consider a career as a navigator, artist, cartoonist, or inventor. So many options appeal to him! Sergio likes to create collages, storyboards, mobiles, or mind maps to illustrate what he has learned. *Pictionary*® is a favorite game, along with visual strategy games like chess or *Stratego*®. He helps paint the murals for school plays, as well as design the covers for the program handouts. Sergio's hobby is photography, but he also likes to share his own cartoons. In fact, he uses a "Far Side Calendar" for keeping track of dates. People like Garry Trudeau, Thomas Edison, Frank Lloyd Wright, and Georgia O'Keefe intrigue him. Humor is a natural ingredient in his work and life. His playful attitude and nontraditional points-of-view keep his peers laughing or perplexed. Sergio is sensitive to change in the world around him. He always ponders "what if…" or "just suppose…" and imagines new possibilities. Each day poses a new opportunity for Sergio.

How would you differentiate for Sergio?

Visual/Spatial Connections

The Visualizer

See	Hear
• reading picture books	• sharing delight in colors, shapes, and designs
• daydreaming	• "I like the new posters"
• using mindmaps	• comparing facts about artists and architects
• creating collages, storyboards, mobiles	• visualizing scenes from stories, plays, or movies
• playing *Pictionary*®	• explaining different points of view
• wearing bright colors	• sharing photography tips
• drawing and designing	• reading and interpreting maps
• looking at pictures, slides, movies	• using vivid imagery
• sensing changes	• "Do we have to take notes?"
• rotating designs to match example	• "I see you're wearing that red dress again."
• choosing cartographer, cartoonist, painter, navigator, architect, sculptor, inventor careers	

SOS People: Christopher Columbus, Pablo Picasso, Sacajawea, Garry Trudeau, Frank Lloyd Wright, Thomas Edison, Georgia O'Keefe

Warm-Ups: "Four Tangram Puzzle" (page 42), "Toothpick Puzzles" (page 43)

Games: *Pictionary*®, *Jenga*®, chess, *Stratego*®, Rubik's cube, mazes, *Connect Four*®, *Othello*®

Option #	Activity Name	Page #
1.	Visual Interpretations: Symbols	46
2.	Vanity Plates and Floats	48
3.	Droodles	49
4.	Line Design	51
5.	Mind Maps	54
6.	Visualization Activities	55
7.	Illusions	56

The Four Tangram Puzzle

Note: Cut up the puzzle pieces below and place them in an envelope.

Student Directions: Create the number "4" by using the four puzzle pieces below.

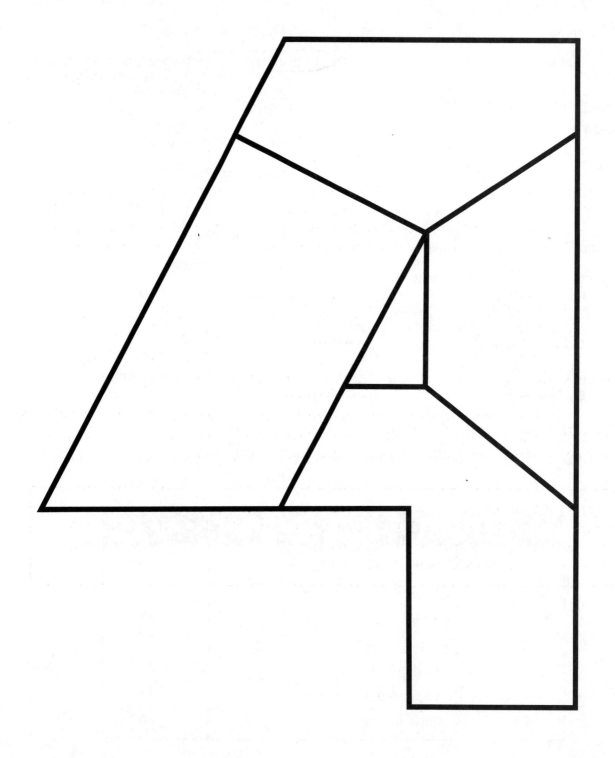

Toothpick Puzzles

Toothpick puzzles abound in mathematics. Usually, a visual image is presented and the problem solver is asked to alter the configuration to produce another by removing or adding a certain number of toothpicks. The breaking of a mind set is frequently necessary. The resulting configuration may look quite different from the original. Students gain confidence by solving simpler puzzles and then tracking more difficult ones.

Materials

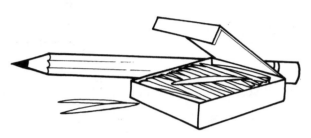

- toothpicks
- buttons
- "Toothpick Puzzles" (page 44)
- pencils

Directions

Divide the class into groups of two. Give each pair of students a pile of toothpicks, a copy of the "Toothpick Puzzles" page, and a pencil. Encourage the students to lay out each configuration with toothpicks and try out many ideas for solving each puzzle. Once a solution is discovered, it can be recorded on the puzzle page. Many of the puzzles have several solutions. You will find a list of possible solutions on page 45.

  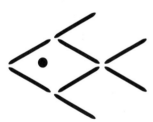

Variations: As students attempt to solve the puzzles provided on the following pages, they are likely to come across interesting configurations of their own. Encourage them to make puzzles of their own. They will be able to create many different puzzles from an initial configuration.

Math for Girls and Other Problem Solvers. Diane Downie, Twila Slesnick, Jean Kerr Stenmark. EQUALS. Lawrence Hall of Science. University of California. Berkeley, CA 1981. Permission granted by L. Lang (3/16/04).
Web site: *www.lawrencehallofscience.org/equals.*

Toothpick Puzzles (cont.)

1. Use 17 toothpicks to construct this figure.

   a. Remove 5 toothpicks and leave 3 squares.

   b. Remove 6 toothpicks and leave 2 squares.

2. Make this figure with 12 toothpicks.

   a. Remove 4 toothpicks and leave 3 triangles.

   b. Move 4 toothpicks and form 3 triangles.

3. With 9 toothpicks, make this figure.

   a. Remove 2 toothpicks and leave 3 triangles.

   b. Remove 3 toothpicks and leave 1 triangle.

   c. Remove 6 toothpicks and get 1 triangle.

   d. Remove 4 toothpicks and get 2 triangles.

   e. Remove 2 toothpicks and get 2 triangles.

4. Use 8 toothpicks and 1 button to form a fish.

   a. Move 3 toothpicks and the button to make this fish swim in the opposite direction.

5. Two farmers have land this shape.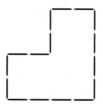

   a. The first farmer wants to divide her land evenly among her three daughters. Add 4 toothpicks to form three parcels of equal size and identical shape.

   b. The second farmer wants to divide her land evenly among her 4 daughters. Use 8 toothpicks to form four parcels of equal size and identical shape.

6. Use 6 toothpicks to form 4 equilateral triangles.

Math for Girls and Other Problem Solvers. Diane Downie, Twila Slesnick, Jean Kerr Stenmark. EQUALS. Lawrence Hall of Science. University of California. Berkeley, CA 1981. Permission granted by L. Lang (3/16/04).

Web site: *www.lawrencehallofscience.org/equals.*

Toothpick Puzzle Solutions

There is an "X" on each toothpick to be removed. In most cases there are several possible solutions. Only one is indicated.

1. a. 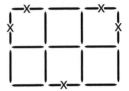 b.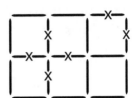

2. a. b.

3. a. b.  c.

   d. e.

4.

5. a. b.

6. Make a 3-dimensional tetrahedron.

Math for Girls and Other Problem Solvers. Diane Downie, Twila Slesnick, Jean Kerr Stenmark. EQUALS. Lawrence Hall of Science. University of California. Berkeley, CA 1981. Permission granted by L. Lang (3/16/04).

Web site: *www.lawrencehallofscience.org/equals.*

Visual Interpretations: Symbols

Students may demonstrate a meaningful understanding of a topic by creating graphic interpretations. Symbols or pictures may be used to design icons, logos, and trademarks. Illustrations, portraits, cartoons, murals, maps, and collages are other examples of HOT thinking (encapsulation) and individual creative expressions.

Symbols may be created for the following:

Science:

 ✧ Food chain

 ✧ Different kinds of research

 ✧ Systems of the human body

History:

 ✧ Branches of government

 ✧ How laws are made

 ✧ Timelines of events

Language Arts:

 ✧ Story elements

 ✧ Storyboards

Math:

 ✧ Story problems

 ✧ Measurement terms

 ✧ Word pictures

PE:

 ✧ Olympic Events

Music:

 ✧ Kinds of instruments

Other:

 ✧ Places in school or school team/group logos

Hieroglyphics

The "Tribal Talk" simulation on the following page and the "Talking Rocks" simulation utilize many visual/spatial thinking skills in communication.

Vernon, Robert F. (1978). *A Simulation on the Origins of Writing.* Talking Rocks. Del Mar, CA

Villalpando, Eleanor. (1984). *Simulations.* Tribal Talk. Phoenix, AZ. Kathy Kolbe Concept, Inc. Web site: *www.kolbe.com.*

Rebus

A rebus puzzle is designed around alphabetical letters, numbers, and visual spatial pictures. Students communicate by incorporating a variety of creative symbols. Here is an example:

More samples of original rebus puzzles have been included in Chapter 9, Appendix B.

Tribal Talk

The "Tribal Talk" simulation is an exercise in communication skills. Any number of people can take part in the simulation. The total number of participants is divided into groups of equal size, numbering from four to eight participants. Groups should work in locations where they cannot overhear or interrupt each other. During the 45-minute time limit, each group decides on a name for its "tribe" and develops an oral language.

It should include the following:

- ✧ a greeting
- ✧ a description of an object or person
- ✧ an evaluative statement

- ✧ two sentences referring to basic needs (food, water, shelter)
- ✧ a farewell

At the end of the 45-minute session, all members of the tribe should be able to "speak" their language. Within each tribe, members number themselves in sequence (1, 2, 3, etc.).

At this stage of the simulation, regrouping takes place. All the 1s from each tribe become a new group. The 2s, 3s, and so on also form new groups.

Within these groups, pairs are formed and each member of the pair must teach his/her new tribal language to the other, using no English or other recognizable language.

The diagram below will clarify the grouping and regrouping.

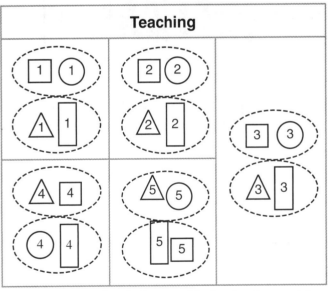

Twenty minutes should be adequate for the teaching session. This simulation could also be done with real languages using predetermined phrases. Tribes should then return to original groups to discuss reactions to teaching sessions.

Group discussion might include the following:

- What did this experience illustrate about communication?
- What were your feelings during the simulation?
- How does the simulation relate to real live situations?

Villalpando, Eleanor. (1984). *Simulations.* Tribal Talk. Phoenix, AZ. Kathy Kolbe Concept, Inc. Web site: *www.kolbe.com.*

Vanity Plates and Floats

Vanity Plates

Students may create a vanity plate as a visual/spatial product. Vanity plates challenge students to encapsulate information into an abbreviated space. Letters, numbers, and symbols may be used for the product.

Here are some sample vanity plates:

(Excuse me!)

(Accentuate the positive!)

(I am one to excel!)

(What are you up to?)

Vanity plates may be designed for explorers, scientists, mathematicians, authors, Olympians, cartoonists, presidents, songs, students in the classroom, etc.

Floats

Floats may be used as another visual/spatial product. Floats may be designed to honor states, countries, heroes, animals, careers, or any other content topic. Students find an empty box; cover the box with butcher paper; and then decorate with fringe, markers, etc. Selected artifacts or visual aids are displayed on the float to demonstrate pertinent connections to the topic. Wheels are added to the float product. Floats are hands-on products that may be displayed in the classroom, media center, or hallways.

Benefits of Visual/Spatial Products

- Elicits creative thinking (elaboration, originality)
- Provides avenue for individual self-expression
- Reinforces HOT: encapsulation, decision-making
- Adds challenge and delight to the classroom
- Provides unique form assessment
- Adapts to independent or group projects, as well as many other content areas

Droodles

Droodles are artistic interpretations of brainteasers. Students create pictures or illustrations to present information. Word clues may be used to tease the reader. Additional Droodles are located in Chapter 9, Appendix B.

Droodle... What could it be? _____ _____	Droodle... What could it be? _____ _____
Droodle... What could it be? _____ _____	Droodle... What could it be? _____ _____
Droodle... What could it be? _____ _____	Droodle... What could it be? _____ _____

Benefits of "Droodles"

- Encourages individual expression
- Promotes creative thinking
- Combines verbal and visual skills
- Uses right brain-and left-brain thinking
- Adapts to any curriculum area
- Adds fun and enjoyment to classroom activities
- Allows for humor in the classroom

"If you think of..." Parts 1 and 2 (pages 156–159 in Chapter 9, Appendix B) offer other visual problem-solving and flexible-thinking activities.

Rasmussen, Greta. (1989) *Brain Stations. A Center Approach to Thinking Skills.* Stanwood, WA. Tin Man Press. Permission granted by Tin Man Press, P.O. Box 11409 Eugene, OR 97440. Phone: 800-676-0459. Web site: *www.tinmanpress.com*

Droodles (cont.)

Droodles are artistic interpretations of brainteasers. Pictures or illustrations are used to present information. Symbols may represent different things depending on the context. Word clues may be added.

What could this droodle be? Write your ideas below.

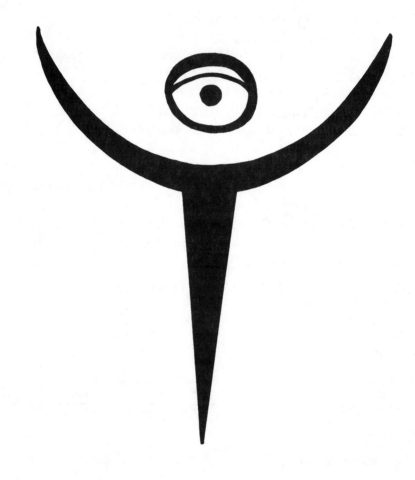

_____

_____

_____

Line Design

Line Design is a unique way to offer students a means of self-expression and to encourage creativity. Students are given a paper with a line design on it and are asked to convert or create the design into something else. There are no wrong answers. Line Design generates the HOT skills of elaboration and originality. The Line Design becomes an easy differentiation activity because it offers options for various levels of difficulty. When you use the Line Design in the classroom it is easy to note the students who demonstrate originality and elaborative thinking. See the next page for an example of a Line Design. *Invisible Unicorn* (see publishing information below) is an excellent resource of line-design starters.

Students are asked to draw a picture using only numerical and mathematical symbols in the drawing. Parallel lines become windows or doors, the number "7" becomes a bird in the sky, the number 11 becomes the trunk of a tree, an equilateral triangle may be the top of a tower, etc. This activity allows a quick assessment of the quantity and quality of mathematical symbols. In this activity, students may work individually or in teams to construct the drawing.

Variation

A three-person drawing can be a positive spin-off of "Line Design." See page 53 for a sample format. Students work in trios to complete a drawing within a time-designated period. Students take turns drawing the picture, but no discussion is allowed beforehand and no talking is allowed during the drawing. Students may draw lines curved or shaped in any way. After the time for the "quiet" work session is over, the trio selects a name for the drawing. The trio evaluates their collaborative product and cooperative work environment.

Benefits of "Line Design"

- Encourages self-expression

- Nurtures artistic intelligence

- Useful for any grade level

- Provides quick assessment in elaborative and original creative thinking

- Promotes positive interaction

Suggested resource: Gold-Vukson, Michael and Marji. (1989). *Invisible Unicorn.* Mobile, AL. GCT, Inc.

Sample Line Design

Three-Person Line Design

Begin here ➡

Directions:

• Without talking, take turns in drawing a group picture. Do not decide beforehand what the picture will be.

• Each person should not draw a line that would exceed this length: _____ .
The lines can be curved or shaped in any way.

Mind Maps

A mind map is a creative pattern of connected ideas and a useful organizing tool of visual/spatial learners. The students use lines, symbols, color, and words to represent information. The steps to making mind maps are as follows:

1. Start with a topic and enclose it in the center of the paper.

2. Add branches to hold key sub-topics.

3. Add details to the branches.

4. Personalize it for the right brain with symbols, pictures, colors, and shapes.

Mind maps may be used in any subject area. Activities may include the following:

✧ Mind map your school day or school week.

✧ Mind map the life of yourself or a VIP.

✧ Mind map the research study of an animal, country, cause, etc.

✧ Mind map the elements of a story.

✧ Mind map branches of government, human body systems, solar system, etc.

✧ Mind map a plan for an event.

Benefits of "Mind Maps"

• Provides framework for organization and prioritization

• Utilizes right side of the brain

• Summarizes information on one page

• Lends itself to brain research practices

• Offers challenge and variety in the classroom

From Mapping Inner Space: Learning and Teaching Mind Mapping by Nancy Margulies. Copyright© 1991. Permission to publish granted by Zephyr Press, P.O. Box 66066, Tucson, AZ 85728-6006. Web site: *www.zephyrpress.com.*

Visualization Activities

Learning activities that cause the students to form mental images of something that is not actually present are called visualization activities. These activities enable the student to activate function of the right side of the brain. Attention to detail and elaborative description is reinforced. Students are allowed to express their own POV (point-of-view) in visualization activities.

Visualization activities may include the following:

✧ Picture in your mind the character of the story. Describe him/her.

✧ Picture in your mind the setting for this story. Describe the scene.

✧ Pretend you were a participant at this historical event. How did it feel?

✧ What if you could be [any VIP] for a day, how would your life be different?

✧ Think through and picture the steps in solving a math problem.

Visualization activities are useful for planning (visualize what things I need to take on a field trip), honing organizational skills, and providing an integral step in problem solving.

Benefits of "Visualization Activities"

• Encourages the ability to imagine

• Promotes creative thinking

• Emphasizes right-brain thinking

• Helps in problem solving

Here are some more useful visualization activities:

✧ In your mind picture your own bedroom. How would you change the room arrangement?

✧ In your mind retrace your trip to school today. Share some landmarks you recall.

✧ You are going to create a travel poster. Visualize in your mind how the poster will look.

✧ Visualize what you will look like 20 years from now. What will you be doing?

✧ Discuss the value of visualization skills to athletes. Does it help football players, skaters, gymnasts, divers, etc., to visualize their routines before they execute them?

✧ John Nasbitt stated in his book *Megatrends* that students who graduate today will have three career changes and 10 different jobs in their lifetime. Visualize some careers of the future.

✧ Picture yourself as a famous person of the past or the future. Write a journal or role play what you are doing and what you are thinking.

✧ Think of an object you used yesterday. Visualize the object from the top, the bottom, and from a side view. Draw the objects from different views.

Illusions

Illusions, or visual puns, challenge the imagination and sometimes confound one's sense of logic. Illusions are two-fold expressions of an image. As a teaching aid, teachers will be amazed at the way students get involved in the discovery process. As a learning aid, students will be excited at the way perception skills are enhanced. Illusions can be a fun way to invite discussion and expression.

Take a good look at this picture . . .

Can you find both the old woman and the young woman?

Suggested Resources:

- Kay, Keith. (1991) *The Little Giant Book of Optical Illusions.* New York, NY. Sterling Publishing Co., Inc.

- Okaes, Bill. *Illusions.* Kingston, NH. Acorn Press, Inc.

- Permission granted for above picture, "My Wife and My Mother-in-law," by the University of Illinois Press. From the *American Journal of Psychology,* Volume 42, page 444, Copyright 1930 by the Board of Trustees of the University of Illinois.

"M" Chart

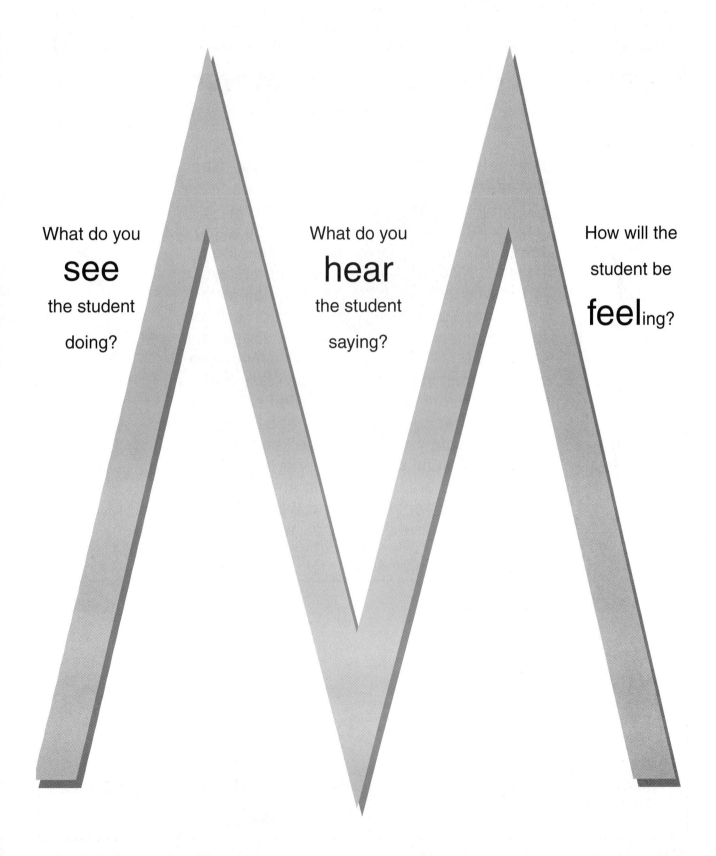

What do you **see** the student doing?

What do you **hear** the student saying?

How will the student be **feel**ing?

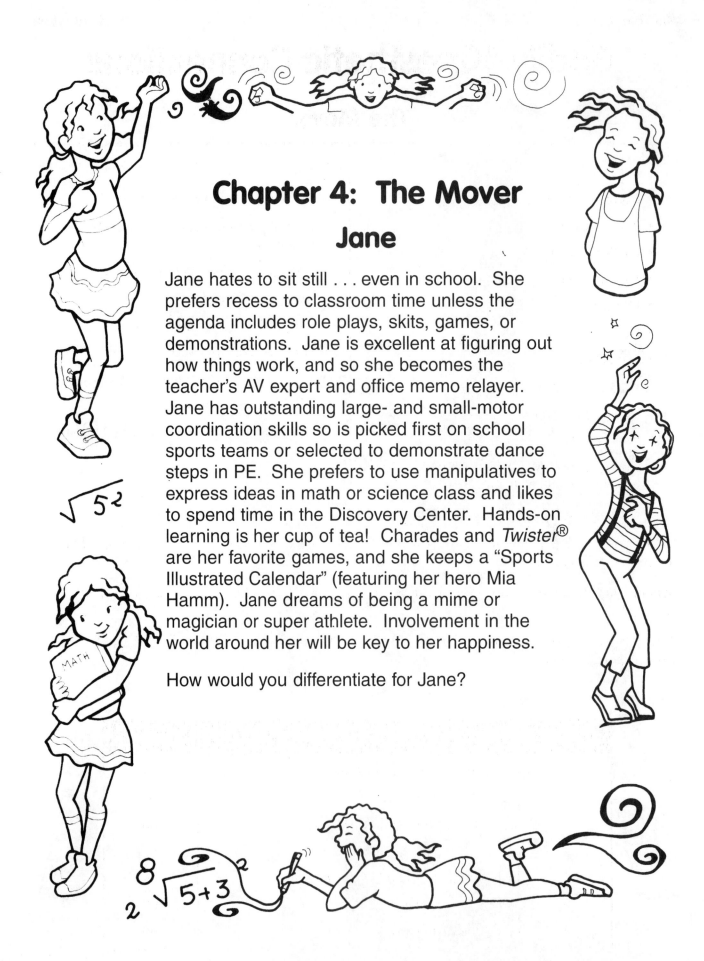

Chapter 4: The Mover

Jane

Jane hates to sit still . . . even in school. She prefers recess to classroom time unless the agenda includes role plays, skits, games, or demonstrations. Jane is excellent at figuring out how things work, and so she becomes the teacher's AV expert and office memo relayer. Jane has outstanding large- and small-motor coordination skills so is picked first on school sports teams or selected to demonstrate dance steps in PE. She prefers to use manipulatives to express ideas in math or science class and likes to spend time in the Discovery Center. Hands-on learning is her cup of tea! Charades and *Twister*® are her favorite games, and she keeps a "Sports Illustrated Calendar" (featuring her hero Mia Hamm). Jane dreams of being a mime or magician or super athlete. Involvement in the world around her will be key to her happiness.

How would you differentiate for Jane?

Bodily/Kinesthetic Connections

The Mover

See	Hear
• expressive gestures	• "When is it time for recess?"
• playing Charades	• processing knowledge through body sensations
• touching things	• new ideas for the Discovery Center
• moving around	• steps for a new dance
• role plays	• rehearsals for plays and skits
• demonstrations	• "May we play Twister?"
• simulations	• cues for nonverbal communication
• involvement in sports	• involvement in various crafts
• able to fix things	• enjoying fitness programs and conditioning
• pantomimes	
• choosing careers of a dancer, mime, surgeon, juggler, magician, athlete	

SOS People: Michael Jordan, Martha Graham, Marcel Marceau, Jackie Joyner Kersee, Maya Lyn, Tiger Woods, Mia Hamm

Warm-Ups: Move your arms in many different ways, play "Simon Says", do "Pencils" activity (page 60)

Games: *Jenga*®, *Twister*®, *Cootie*®, Pick-up sticks, Charades, *Legos*®, "Simon Says," clay, *Play-Dough*®, *Connect Four*®

Option #	Activity Name	Page #
1.	Nonverbal Communication	61
2.	Body Machines	62
3.	Human Graphs and Taking Sides	63
4.	Simulations	64
5.	Manipulatives and Hands-On Activities	64
6.	Dot-to-Dot Stories	65
7.	Build-A-Monument	66

The Pencil Problem

Time Limit

- 10 minutes

Materials

- six pencils (or similar objects, such as stir sticks or straws)

Directions

- Using six pencils, make four equal triangles.

Rule

- The angles of the triangle must be formed by the ends of the pencils, not the intersection of the pencils. See the pictures below.

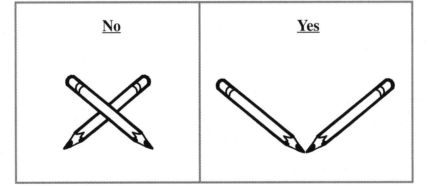

Nonverbal Communication

Charades

Charades, a game where students "act out" ideas, gives students the opportunity to express knowledge and understanding through bodily/kinesthetic intelligence. For instance, students may be given lists of vocabulary words in any content area and challenged to "define" the word through active demonstration. Vocabulary words may vary in degree of difficulty.

Example: Select one word from the following list. Pronounce the word. Then, act out the vocabulary word so that the class members understand the meaning.

- ✧ desist (to cease; stop)

- ✧ gambol (to skip around joyfully; frolic)

- ✧ ichthyology (study of fish)

- ✧ imperious (domineering; overbearing)

- ✧ salvo (loss of strength; bodily weakness)

- ✧ vociferous (noisy; loud)

- ✧ pule (whine; whimper)

- ✧ asthenia (slowing down gradually)

Names of books, films, music, magazines, famous people, places, etc. may be used as topics. Students may work individually or cooperatively in groups when playing charades.

Gestures

Studying gestures helps students to understand the value and power of nonverbal communication. Challenge students to brainstorm ways we communicate without the use of the spoken word. Students may research gestures used in various countries and cultures.

Benefits of "Nonverbal Communication"

- Utilizes different kinds of intelligence

- Adapts to any content area

- Provides humor

- Helps ESL students

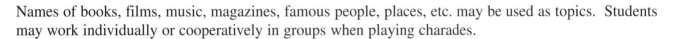

Body Machines

An interactive and cooperative learning experience may be the creation of body machines. Students work together in small or large groups to construct machines. Each student becomes a vital part or piece of a bigger gadget or machine.

For Primary Grades

In primary grades, students may create popcorn poppers, toasters, or telephones in the study of machines or inventions. Learning how to tell time may be reinforced by having the students create body clocks: students actually become the minute hands that move from number to number. In math, bodies may be used to illustrate math concepts in problem solving or used to interpret math commutative or associative laws.

For Upper Grades

Student in upper grades may find body machines helpful in understanding different systems of the body or scientific theories of such historical figures as Copernicus and Ptolemy. Human body sentences may be composed in language arts. Individual students become the nouns, verbs, adjectives, adverbs, etc., and then work cooperatively to construct meaningful sentences. Geometric concepts may be illustrated with body machines—for instance, examples of quadrilaterals (squares, rectangles, parallelograms, rhombuses, diamonds, etc.) may be demonstrated.

Benefits of "Body Machines"

- Employs different ways to express self

- Fosters cooperative learning

- Adds pizzazz to the classroom

- Applies to any content area

- Reinforces HOT thinking: interpretation, decision-making

Human Graphs and Taking Sides

Human Graphs

Students may create human body graphs to demonstrate analysis of data. Students line up in a grid created to present data collection then data analysis. For instance, human graphs may illustrate the following information:

✧ months of students' birthdays (students cluster signs of January, February, March, April, etc.)

✧ kinds of pets students own

✧ number of languages students speak

✧ favorite types of books students read

In discussion of specific issues, human graphs offer students the option to "move" to a specific location to signal their point-of-view on a certain topic. Display around the room the following signs, which offer a continuum or a range of feelings about an issue:

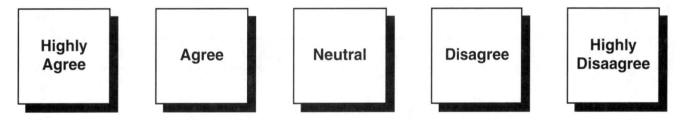

Students move to the spot that best signifies their point of view, listen to others, then contribute to the discussion. If there is not room for the signs to be displayed, students may hold the signs. This activity encourages greater risk-taking because students personally and visibly express opinions.

Taking Sides

"Taking Sides" is a group activity that lends itself to bodily/kinesthetic intelligence. All students stand on a line in the classroom. The teacher reads a statement. If the students agree with the statement, they move to the left side; if they disagree with the statement, they move to the right side. Students must justify their opinions when they move off the line. Students who stay on the line and have no opinion may not talk.

Topics may include the following:

✧ Year-round school is a necessity in this new millennium.

✧ All athletes should be tested for drugs (urinalysis).

✧ The Alaska Wilderness areas should be open to further oil development.

Benefits of "Human Graphs" and "Taking Sides"

• Promotes the analysis of information

• Encourages POV (points-of-view) and risk-taking

• Adapts to various content areas and age groups

Simulations

Simulations offer the students opportunities to participate in real-life experiences. Court simulations or mock trials may be useful in government, literature, and science studies.

Here are some ideas for simulations:

✧ re-staging the *Mayflower's* journey

✧ re-enacting "Goldilocks and the Three Bears" from a legal point of view (breaking-and-entering)

✧ replaying different theories, such as Copernicus' (sun-centered universe) vs. Ptolemy's (earth-centered universe)

✧ reproducing historical events, such as the Continental Congress writing the U.S. Constitution.

These simulations help students to better understand the significance of an event. Participating in a land-use planning panel affords students opportunities for realistic problem-solving scenarios.

The book *Simulations* by Eleanor Villalpando is an excellent resource for the classroom.

Benefits of "Simulations"

• Promotes HOT thinking   • Connects to real life issues

• Adapts to various content areas

Villalpando, Eleanor. (1984). *Simulations.* Phoenix, AZ. Kathy Kolbe Concept, Inc.

Manipulatives and Hands-On Activities

Visual aids and manipulatives are very effective in helping students to understand concepts. Legos®, tinker toys, clays, play dough, toothpicks, and sugar cubes may be useful creative resources. A menu of product options may include the following:

✧ build models   ✧ put together puzzles

✧ design games   ✧ construct scavenger hunts

✧ create mobiles   ✧ produce videotapes or films

✧ perform skits or plays   ✧ use animation

✧ make kites   ✧ construct floats

Brain Gloves

In her book *Mapping Inner Space*, Nancy Margulies provides a rich learning activity for understanding the brain. Students learn about the brain by using pictures, symbols, and parts of the body. Brain gloves are created as a final product to demonstrate the learning.

From *Mapping Inner Space: Learning and Teaching Mind Mapping* by Nancy Margulies. Copyright 1991. Permission to publish granted by Zephyr Press, P.O. Box 66006, Tucson, AZ 85728-6006. Web site: *www.zephyrpress.com*.

Dot-to-Dot Stories

Creating Dot-to-Dot Stories, presented by Nancy Johnson in her book *The Best Teacher "Stuff"* is an effective teaching strategy to help students work collaboratively to create stories. The teacher uses self-stick colored dots in several colors. The students place a dot on the back of one hand. Then the students are put into groups—trios if three colors are used, quartets if four colors are used, quintets if five colors are used.

The teacher gives these verbal instructions:

"Don't say anything out loud. Just think about my directions. All the blue dots (one in each group) think of a name for a character. It could be a character from a book, a TV character, historical character, or one you make up. An example could be 'Christopher Columbus.'

"Don't say anything out loud. Just think about it. All red dots (one in each group) think of a place. It can be a city, a country, in a cave, over the rainbow, or any place you think of. An example would be 'Disneyland.'

"Don't say anything out loud. Just think about it. All green dots (one in each group) think of a problem or situation. It can be a simple, ordinary problem that happens in everyday life or it can be an imaginative problem. An example of a problem would be 'Sour Milk.'"

After some think time the teacher says,

"The group members share with each other the name of the character, place, and problem. Create a story that includes that character, place, and problem. After five minutes, a spokesperson from each group will share your story with the rest of the class."

Later, after stories have been shared, the teacher says,

"Remember what character, place, and problem you are. That does not change. Keep the same dot. Now all the blue dot people move to a different group. When the blue dot gets to the new group, the red and green dots tell their story. The blue dot then adds a new character to the story and all three continue the story."

The teacher asks each group to retell the story. The stories become longer and more involved. The pattern of switching one dot, adding to the story, then telling the story again with new changes, is repeated several times. At some point, direct the students to return to their seats and write the story. They may work alone or with partners.

Repeat this activity several times, changing the premise or adding more dots each time. Other colors may be added: yellow may be time or seasons of the year; pink may be used for emotions or feelings. Another color may be used to represent careers.

Used by permission. Pieces of Learning© 1-800-729-5137. *The Best Teacher "Stuff"* by Nancy Johnson. Pages 72-73.

Build-A-Monument

Challenge students to build a monument to demonstrate understanding of a given topic or concept. Students work cooperatively in teams of four or five. Each group is given the same supply of generic resources. The teams must use the materials to create a meaningful monument around the designated topic or concept.

Resources may include the following:

- crepe paper
- rubber band
- string
- straws

- markers
- tape
- twist ties
- plastic sticks

- newspaper
- shopping bags
- balloons

Monument challenges may include the following:

✧ systems of the body (respiratory, digestive, skeletal, etc.)

✧ various kinds of research (historical, descriptive, casual-comparative, etc.)

✧ planets of the solar system

✧ endangered animals

✧ different kinds of smarts or multiple intelligences

✧ heroes

Benefits of "Build-A-Monument"

- Builds cooperative learning skills
- Promotes flexibility and originality in creative thinking skills
- Provides different medium of resources
- Ties into any curriculum area
- Offers "hands-on" learning

"M" Chart

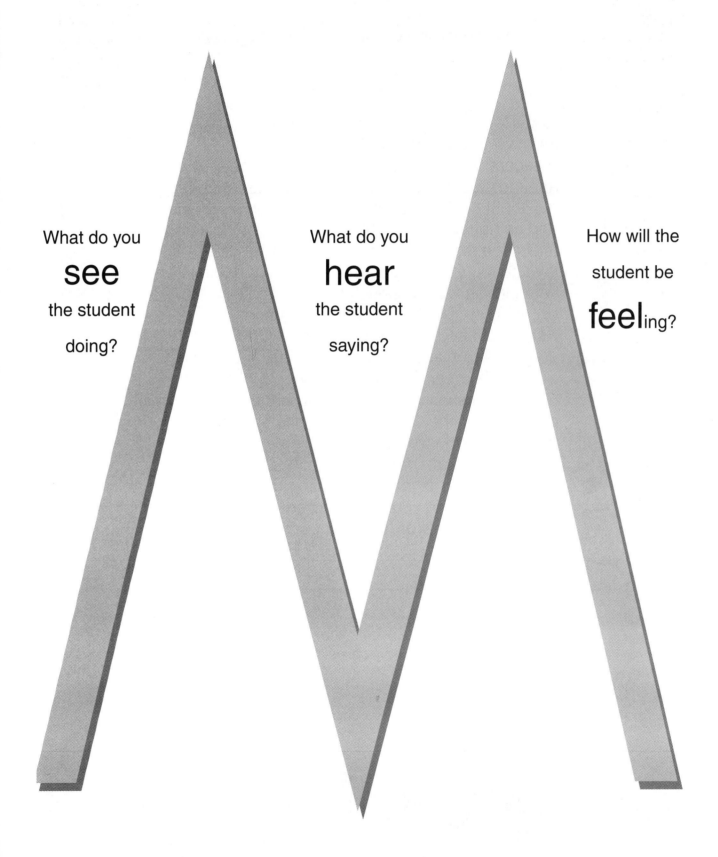

What do you **see** the student doing?

What do you **hear** the student saying?

How will the student be **feel**ing?

Chapter 5: The Observer
Roberto

Roberto's classroom is the real world around him, 24 hours a day! He is fascinated with the outdoors and can identify flora and fauna that abound. Field trips to the zoo or ocean or caves delight him. Roberto learns best by doing things and being involved in the real world. Binoculars, telescope, compass, microscope, or ropes are his favorite tools. Shadowing a forester or botanist or veterinarian would constitute a terrific field experience. The Texas Space Camp for Astronauts and Jacque Cousteau's lab ship *Calypso* are places he wants to visit. Roberto is a keen observer and can readily note his observations with descriptive journal entries or detailed sketches. He likes real-life experiments and becoming involved in real-life ecological campaigns. Letter writing to politicians is a hobby. He has enjoyed designing blindfold hikes or I Spy treks for younger children, as well as "how-to" manuals or field guides for older kids. Roberto's heroes include Teddy Roosevelt, Henry Thoreau, Rachel Carson, and Jane Goodall, but he is also inspired by nature artwork and prose.

How would you differentiate for Roberto?

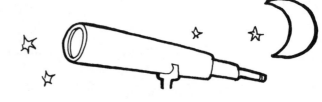

Naturalist Connections

The Observer

See	Hear
• involvement in the outdoors	• observations of the natural world
• collecting rocks, shells	• understanding cause and effect
• using microscope or telescope	• "big picture" ideas
• creating models	• questioning
• keeping a log of observations	• "May we take a field trip to the zoo?"
• visiting natural parks	• explanation of the ecosystem
• planning for field trips	• analysis of new field guides
• exploring	• identification of constellations
• working with manipulatives	• hands-on learning experimentation
• choosing careers of a forester, naturalist, ecologist, farmer, botanist, or astronomer	• building models
	• "Look at my butterfly collection!"

SOS People: Rachel Carson, Teddy Roosevelt, Charles Darwin, Henry Thoreau, Jane Goodall, Jacques Cousteau

Warm-Ups: Make a list of natural things and manmade things.

Games: Scavenger Hunts, I Spy, blindfold walks and games, charades of animal creatures

Option #	Activity Name	Page #
1	Collections	70
2	Observations of . . .	71
3	Cube It!	73
4	Rescue	77
5	Simulations	78
6	Talking It Up!	79
7	Incredible Edibles	80
8	Puzzlers	80

Additional activities ("Hidden Animals," "If True…Do," and "Name that Country") are located in Chapter 9, Appendix B.

Collections

A positive learning activity that enriches any content area and allows for the development of individual student passion is sharing collections students have generated. This activity is especially meaningful to the naturalist learner who enjoys collecting various natural specimens such as rocks, seashells, pine cones, or even animal clues (teeth, antlers, skulls, porcupine quills, snake skins, etc.). Students' collections may be used to enhance the study in many content areas—coin collections in math, stamp collections in cultural studies, unique music boxes in music, comic books in language arts, baseball cards in physical education class, antique dolls or toys in history class, etc. Graphic organizers may be designed or big questions developed to challenge students as they view the collections of classmates.

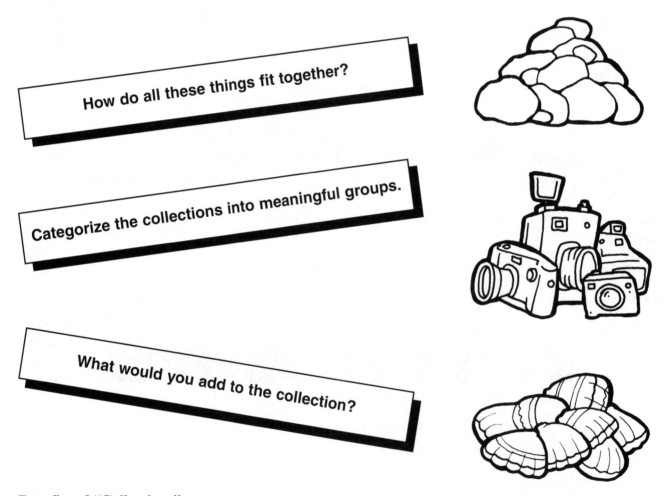

How do all these things fit together?

Categorize the collections into meaningful groups.

What would you add to the collection?

Benefits of "Collections"

- Shares passion and expertise in subject areas

- Provides avenue for further study

- Provides means for alternative assessment

- Adds interest to classroom visual décor

- Challenges students to pursue new interests

- Supplements timely resources for study

Observations of...

In order to become a good thinker, one has to first become a good observer. To be a good observer, one has to look at things differently and from a different point of view. This HOT thinking skill can be honed in a variety of ways and is a fun learning activity for any classroom.

1. Select any everyday object to observe using different senses. Giving the students a cracker or edible object adds appeal and creates intrigue. Begin the observation visually, and then observe and analyze an object using different senses:

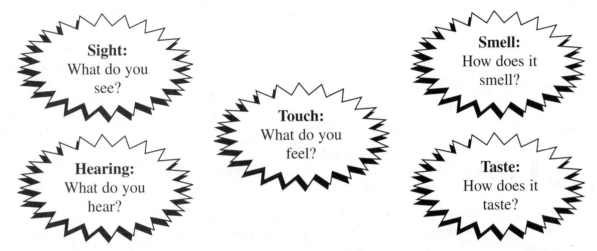

Sight: What do you see?

Touch: What do you feel?

Smell: How does it smell?

Hearing: What do you hear?

Taste: How does it taste?

Students write their observations down and record findings for each sense. This activity forces the student to be a flexible thinker in observing things from more than one perspective.

2. Have the students observe something they think they are familiar with and know well. "Observe your thumb" has been a successful activity. Students are given a time period to observe their thumbs. Use the prompt: Observe your thumb with more than one of your senses. Raise the degree of challenge by telling the students (1) you want at least 15 observations or (b) they must keep observing and writing until they note the observation the teacher is looking for. The teacher may select a more complex observation that requires critical thinking. Examples in observing the thumb might be: "hair on my thumb," "connected to my hand," "has a hinge joint," etc. Various discussions can piggyback from many of the observations.

3. Give each student a piece of string. Take the string outdoors to encircle a specific area on the playground to observe. Students are encouraged to record their observations. Challenging students to think beyond "I see grass!" will be invigorating. Use the fluency, flexibility, originality, and elaboration categories in creative thinking to analyze the record of observations.

4. Witness activity can be used anytime to reinforce observation skills. During a class meeting, study hall, or assembly, have a person come into the room and talk to the teacher or give something to the teacher. Later, ask the students to describe the individual that appeared. Discuss the value of being a credible "witness" and when these skills would be useful.

5. First-hand accounts or diaries may be written by students who have role played or "observed" moments in history. Students may create personal observations with words, pictures, sounds, feelings, etc., to make the historical moment come alive. These observations may be videotaped for further presentations and study.

Observations of... *(cont.)*

6. The book *The Private Eye* is a wonderful resource for utilizing observation skills in nature. Students use loupes in some of the observation activities. Journal recordings, artistic interpretations, and creative writings are student products.

> Reuf, Kerry. (1992) *The Private Eye.* Seattle, WA. The Private Eye Project

7. Various graphic organizers may be used to facilitate greater thinking during observation skill activities. Resources for graphic organizers are as follows:

> Bellanaca, James. (1990) *The Cooperative Think Tank.* Palantine, IL. Skylight Publishing.
>
> Black, Howard and Sandra Black. (1990) *Organizing Thinking.* Pacific Grove, CA. Midwest Publications.
>
> Epley, Thelma M. (1982) *Models for Thinking: Activities to Enhance Modes of Thought.* Ventura, CA. Ventura Country Superintendent of Schools Office.
>
> Hyerle, David. (1996) *Visual Tools for Constructing Knowledge.* Alexandria, VA. ASCD

8. Everyday observation activities may be selected from a variety of resources:

> Johnson, Dee and Kathy Kolbe. (1980) *Options & Observations.* Phoenix, AZ. Think Ink Publications.
>
> Johnson, Nancy. (1996) *Look Closer.* Beavercreek, OH. Pieces of Learning Consultants, Inc.

Other Observation Activities:

1. Display a common object used at home or at school. Observe the object from different angles and perspectives. Draw what you see.

2. Use a magnifying glass to look at things up close and personal.

3. Bring photographs of a person at different ages. Observe changes.

4. Give children mirrors. Observe own images. Discuss what makes them special.

5. Take a field trip to a museum. Keep a journal of observations.

6. Observe the classroom for geometric terms (rectangle, parallel lines, perpendicular lines, congruent shapes, etc.).

7. Use posters such as "Illusions" (page 56) to observe different points of view.

8. Use a microscope to study tiny things up close and personal.

9. Play a tape with various sounds. Observe with your ears. Identify the source of the sounds.

10. Observe a familiar object in the room. Describe the object to another person. Have the other person draw the object after listening to observations or descriptions.

See Chapter 9, Appendix A for more information on these HOT thinking strategies.

Cube It!

Cubing is a strategy designed to help students think about a topic or idea from many different angles. Cubes help students avoid "flat" thinking—thinking that is one-dimensional and lacks elaboration.

A cube includes six commands—one on each of its six faces—followed by a prompt that describes the task the student should do that is related to the command. There are many different thinking commands that can go on a cube. Here is an example:

Command: Describe

Prompt: Describe the rainforest; use as much information as you can and involve as many of your senses as possible in your description.

Cubes can be used to differentiate activities on the basis of student readiness. Prompts can be modified so there are different levels of difficulty. Cubing is also a way to differentiate an activity based on student interest or learning profile. Various products may be highlighted—make a limerick, create a pun, tell a story, write a song, draw a sketch, make a model, present an argument—that relate to a student's interest or talent.

Cubing models used to demonstrate Bloom's Taxonomy (page 74), Edward de Bono's *Six Thinking Hats* (page 75), and Elements of a Story (page 76) are found on the following pages.

Other applications may be:

❖ taxonomy of animals (mammals, birds, reptiles, amphibians, insects, etc.)

❖ cues for oral reports

❖ assessment tool

Benefits of "Cubing"

• Encourages critical thinking

• Adapts to any curriculum area

• Promotes different points of view

• Facilitates thinking with a "hands on" visual tool

• Useful with many grade levels

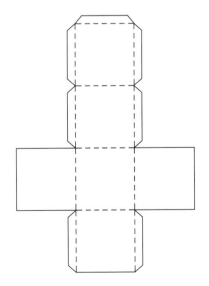

Suggested resource: de Bono, Edward. (1985) *Six Thinking Hats.* New York, NY. Penguin Books.

Cube It! *(cont.)*

Bloom's Taxonomy

Use the cube below to learn more about a topic study. Cut on the solid lines, and fold on the dotted lines. Tape the sides, then use the cube as a prompt for recording information.

A   describe it

B   associate it with something else, reminds me of…?

C   apply it, tell how to use it

D   analyze it, look at the parts

E   create something new with it

F   evaluate it, argue for or against it

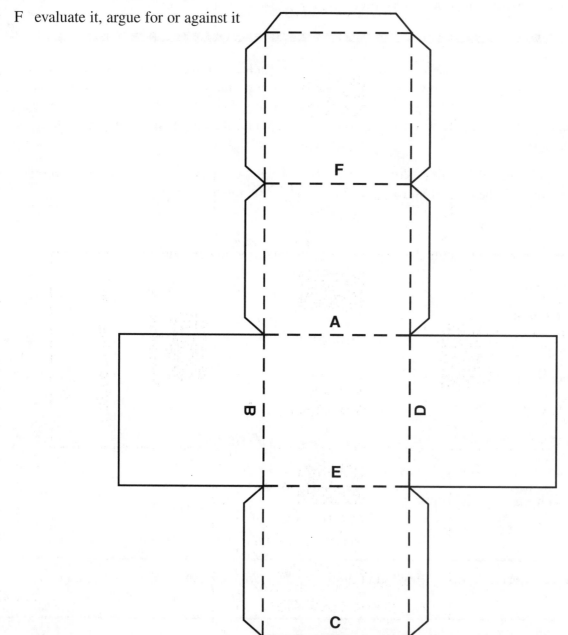

Cube It! *(cont.)*

Six Thinking Hats

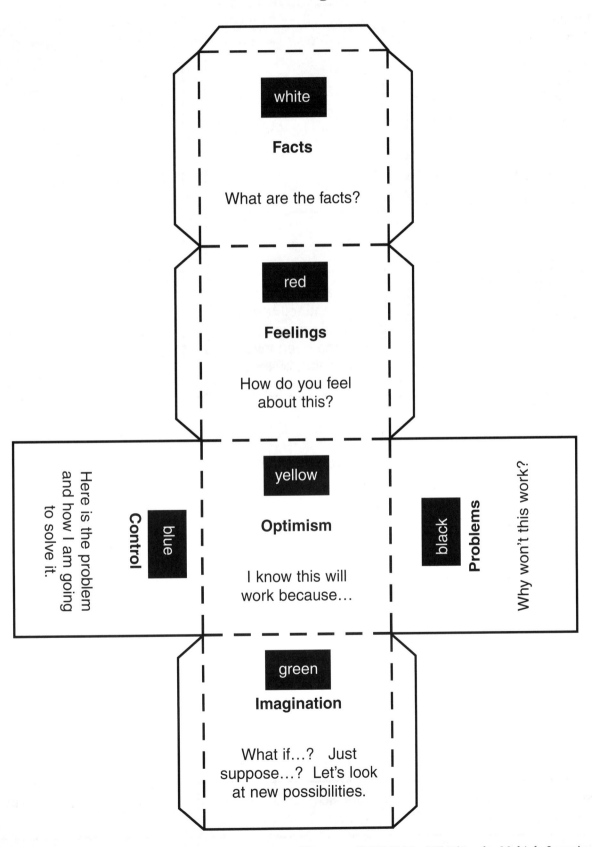

white

Facts

What are the facts?

red

Feelings

How do you feel about this?

yellow

Optimism

I know this will work because…

blue

Control

Here is the problem and how I am going to solve it.

black

Problems

Why won't this work?

green

Imagination

What if…? Just suppose…? Let's look at new possibilities.

Cube It! *(cont.)*

Elements of a Story

Directions

- Cut on all solid lines.
- Fold and crease on all broken lines.

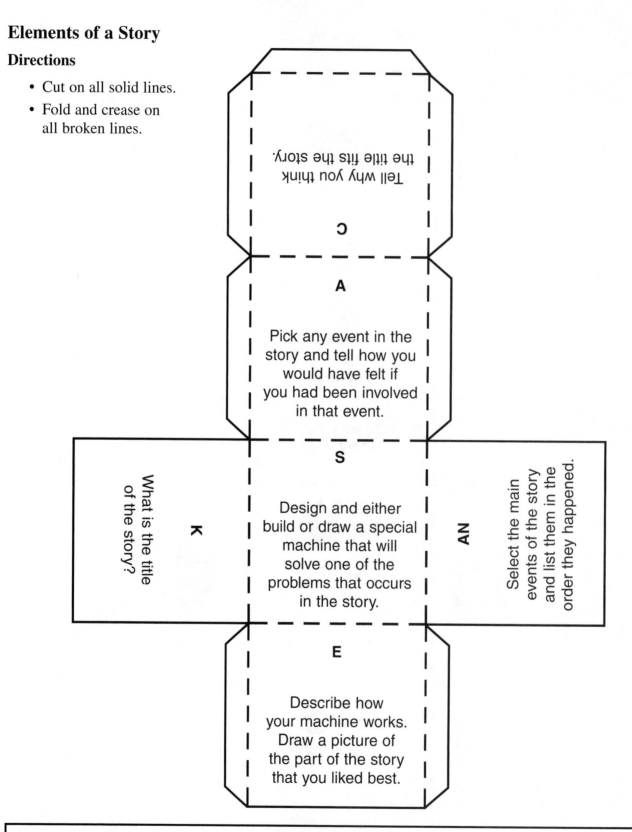

C

Tell why you think the title fits the story.

A

Pick any event in the story and tell how you would have felt if you had been involved in that event.

K

What is the title of the story?

S

Design and either build or draw a special machine that will solve one of the problems that occurs in the story.

AN

Select the main events of the story and list them in the order they happened.

E

Describe how your machine works. Draw a picture of the part of the story that you liked best.

Used by permission. Pieces of Learning© 1-800-729-5137. *Questioning Makes the Difference* by Nancy Johnson.

Rescue

"Rescue" provides a learning experience where students utilize group problem-solving skills. Students are divided into small groups. Each group is given a situation card with several resource cards. Students must create rescue plans for these real-life situations.

Procedures for "Rescue" are as follows:

1. Divide the class into groups of six to eight students.

2. Place packs of situation cards and rescue cards on a table.

3. Each group sends a member to the table to draw one situation card and five resource cards.

4. The person returns to his group. Teacher signals a 10-minute think-tank period where the students create resource plans.

5. After a given time limit, each group reports back what the situation was, resources available, and rescue plan recommended.

Sample Scenarios

- While playing hide-and-seek in your urban neighborhood, you and your friends are accidentally locked in an abandoned warehouse. What can you do?

- Your class takes a field trip to the New York Empire State Building. During a power failure one group gets caught in an elevator between floors. What can you do?

- You are enjoying the day at King's Dominion Amusement park. You are on the Cyclone Roller Coaster when the power fails. What can you do?

- You are attending a World Series game in California when an earthquake occurs. Chaos breaks out. What can you do?

- Your family is on a vacation in the West. During a drive through a vast desert, the car runs out of gas. What can you do?

- Your class takes a trip to the zoo. The class is divided into groups. Your group is accidentally locked in the zoo after hours. What can you do?

Sample Resources

❖ bicycle	❖ four quarters	❖ box of paperclips	❖ hat
❖ strip of velcro	❖ 12 donuts	❖ rubber bands	❖ duct tape
❖ adhesive bandages	❖ rope	❖ matches	❖ compass
❖ hatchet	❖ watch	❖ belt	❖ aluminum foil
❖ lighter	❖ hula hoop	❖ basketball	❖ ladder
❖ trumpet	❖ candle	❖ sack of walnuts	❖ knife
❖ bottle of soda	❖ magazine	❖ clothesline	❖ parachute
❖ hammer	❖ pillowcase	❖ pie tin	❖ silly putty
❖ coconut	❖ transistor radio	❖ lantern	

Extra Extension: Give each group of students a "bag" of resources to design or create a tool that could be used in the rescue.

❖ twist tie	❖ rubber band	❖ plastic wrap	❖ foil
❖ paper plate	❖ cardboard tube	❖ pencil	❖ tape
❖ paper clips	❖ straw		

Simulations

Simulations are real-life situations enacted for practical problem-solving skills. Current issues are presented for cooperative and collaborative groups. Simulations that apply to outdoor concerns make an appropriate connection to the naturalist learner.

Students are organized into groups. Each group may be given the situation or various issues and asked to solve the problem by acting it out. It is important that all students are involved in the problem solving activity.

Examples might be as follows:

- Proposed park land in city—simulation of city council debate of pros and cons

- Increased bag limit for hunting specific game

- Adding a new species to endangered list—develop criteria for list

- Recommending alternative energy sources for everyday use (solar, radiant, wind, water, steam, etc.)

- Opening rain forest areas for eco-tourism

Benefits of "Simulations"

- Promotes group problem-solving skills

- Gives realistic applications to everyday life situations

- Honors positive group processes

- Integrates many thinking processes

- The world becomes the classroom

- Makes learning come alive in the classroom

Suggested resources:

Slattery, Britt Eckhardt. (1991) *WOW: The Wonder of Wetlands.* St. Michaels, MD. Environmental Concern, Inc.

Villalpando, Eleanor. (1984) *Simulations.* Phoenix, AZ. Kathy Kolbe Concept, Inc. Web site: *www.kolbe.com.*

Talking It Up!

This activity offers students practice in communication, problem-solving, and cooperative-learning skills. The teacher builds a model out of building blocks or toys. Students cannot watch the teacher build this model, and the model should be hidden from classroom view. Student groups of five to six are seated at tables. In each group, students are assigned different roles. The students work cooperatively in their assigned roles to solve the problem of constructing a new model.

The roles are as follows:

➥ **Observer**

There is one observer for each group (perhaps designate the person with the longest first name). The observer looks at the teacher-model, carefully observes details and specifics, then tells the runner his/her observations. The observer does not see the builders at work.

➥ **Runner**

There is one runner in each group (perhaps the person with the shortest first name). The runner listens to the observer's descriptions, then runs to the builders to relay or report the information. The runner is the "go-between" person on the team. The runner may not see the original model. The runner may not build.

➥ **Builder**

There are several builders on a team. The builders listen to the runner's report, then construct the model following the directions. They may ask questions of the runner who also may ask questions of the observer. The builders are the only ones to "touch" the building.

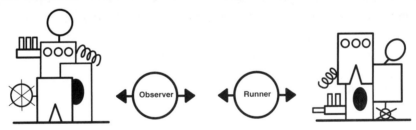

The groups are given a designated amount of time to work cooperatively to build a new model. When the time is up, the original model is displayed. Groups compare their versions to the original. Evaluation follows on which person (Observer, Runner, Builders) had the most difficult job.

Extension: The activity can be used in other content areas by having students create an artistic interpretation instead of building a model. The roles would be Observer, Runner, and Designer. Materials would include butcher paper and markers for the final product. Again, comparisons and evaluation would follow the activity.

Benefits of "Talking It Up"

- Fosters collaborative and cooperative skills

- Employs many thinking strategies

- Adds spark and fun to the classroom

Villalpando, Eleanor. (1984) *Simulations*. Phoenix, AZ. Kathy Kolbe Concept, Inc. 27-28. Permission granted for reprinting by Kolbe Corp. and Kathy Kolbe, Web site: *www.kolbe.com*.

Incredible Edibles

An exciting edible product for students is the creation of "Incredible Edibles". This project would be especially timely for nutrition studies or cultural research. Students are asked to create an object, animal, or person out of real foods. Students are given a large paper plate and access to general ingredients that may include the following: marshmallows, spaghetti, cereals, licorice, peanut butter, pretzels, etc. Students have a designated time to create and name their Incredible Edible. The products are displayed in the classroom. (**Safety Note:** Be sure to check for allergies before allowing students to eat anything in your classroom.) Here is a useful recipe for Peanut Butter Clay:

Peanut Butter Clay

- Measure equal parts of peanut butter, corn syrup or honey, dry milk, and powdered sugar.

- Warm peanut butter in double boiler for easy mixing.

- Add enough corn syrup to get a stirring consistency.

- Add equal parts of non-fat dry milk and powdered sugar to get a workable consistency.

As a variation, students may create "Incredible Edibles" by using magazine pictures to create artistic interpretations. Each student is given poster paper, glue, scissors, and various magazines to select pictures for the project. Teacher may voice the expectation that all food groups must be represented. The size of the incredible edibles may vary—they may be full-sized incredibles! Students may work in groups. Students give their creations appropriate titles or names.

Benefits of using "Incredible Edibles"

- Provides option for individual creative thinking
- Utilizes decision-making skills

- Gives access to different levels of resources
- Generates originality in self expression

Puzzlers

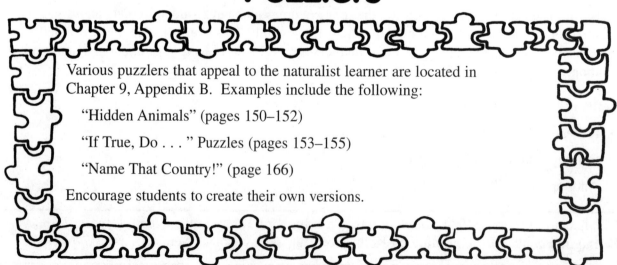

Various puzzlers that appeal to the naturalist learner are located in Chapter 9, Appendix B. Examples include the following:

"Hidden Animals" (pages 150–152)

"If True, Do . . ." Puzzles (pages 153–155)

"Name That Country!" (page 166)

Encourage students to create their own versions.

"M" Chart

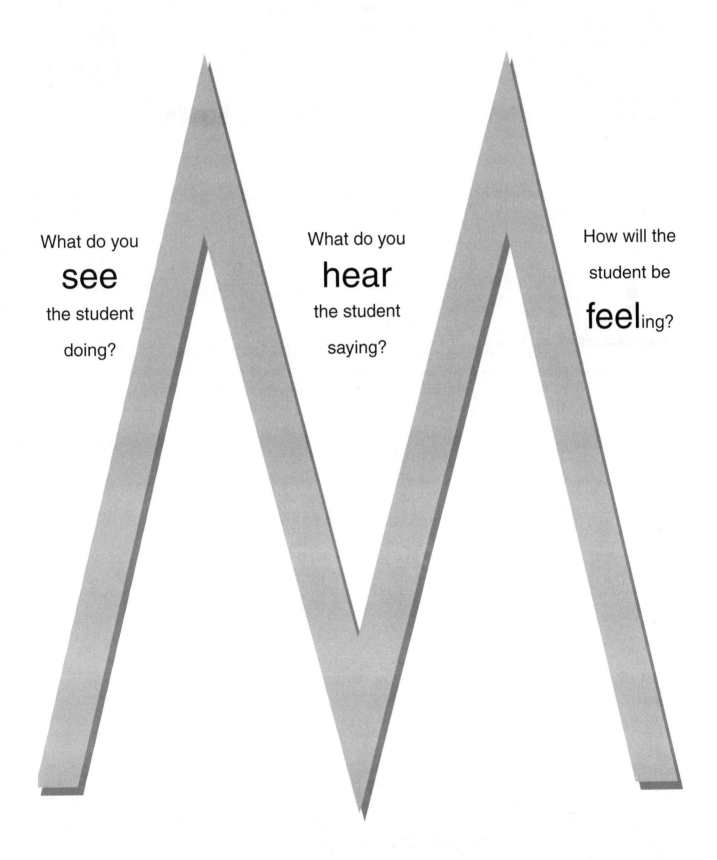

What do you **see** the student doing?

What do you **hear** the student saying?

How will the student be **feel**ing?

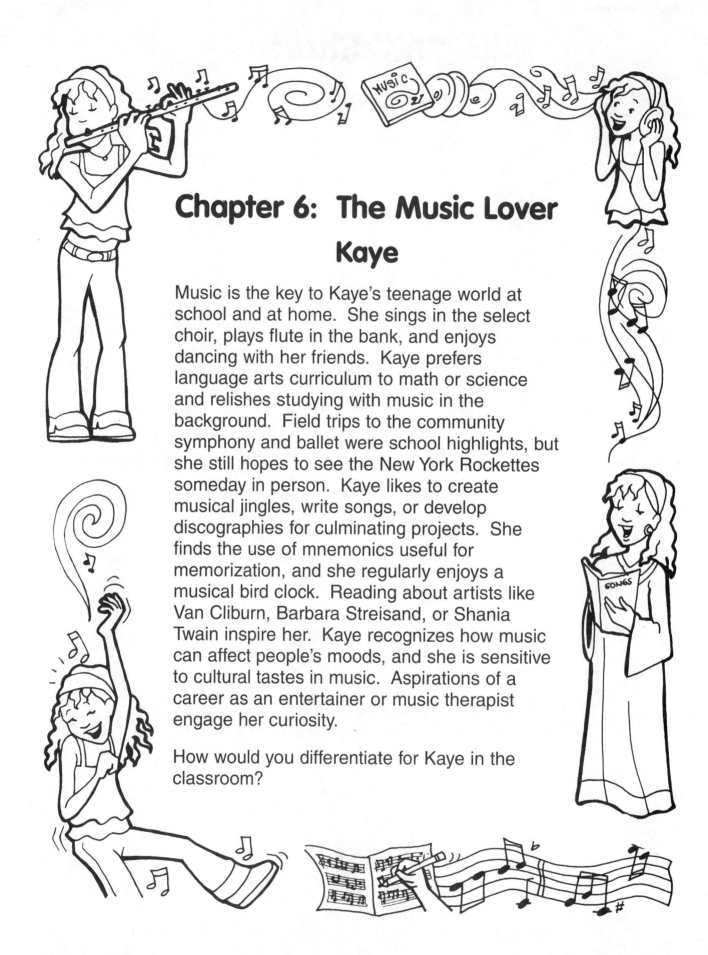

Chapter 6: The Music Lover
Kaye

Music is the key to Kaye's teenage world at school and at home. She sings in the select choir, plays flute in the bank, and enjoys dancing with her friends. Kaye prefers language arts curriculum to math or science and relishes studying with music in the background. Field trips to the community symphony and ballet were school highlights, but she still hopes to see the New York Rockettes someday in person. Kaye likes to create musical jingles, write songs, or develop discographies for culminating projects. She finds the use of mnemonics useful for memorization, and she regularly enjoys a musical bird clock. Reading about artists like Van Cliburn, Barbara Streisand, or Shania Twain inspire her. Kaye recognizes how music can affect people's moods, and she is sensitive to cultural tastes in music. Aspirations of a career as an entertainer or music therapist engage her curiosity.

How would you differentiate for Kaye in the classroom?

Musical Connections

The Music Lover

See	Hear
• listening to music	• remembering melodies
• playing instruments	• "May we play music while we work?"
• responding to music	• creating raps, chants, jingles
• singing in a choir	• using mnemonics for memorization
• attending cultural festivals	• humming while at work
• studying with earphones	• rhythmic tapping
• attending concerts	• identifying sounds in nature
• noticing musical tones, patterns	• using music to alter moods
• selecting careers as an entertainer, composer, conductor, violinist, musical therapist	• impersonations of entertainers
	• "That song keeps playing in my head."
	• composing music

SOS People: Mozart, Barbara Streisand, Ella Fitzgerald, Johann Sebastian Bach, Elvis Presley, Elton John, John Lennon

Warm-Ups:

- Create a sound
- List sounds you hear right now
- Name songs with geographical places in the title
- Name songs with numbers in the title
- Name songs with careers in the title

Games: *Music Bingo, Name That Tune, Simon, Trivial Pursuit*

Option #	Activity Name	Page #
1.	Play Music	84
2.	Musical Punctuation	84
3.	Video Pen Pals	85
4.	Listening Maps	85
5.	Music and Content Connection	86
6.	Music and Mnemonics	87
7.	Music Note Words	88

Play Music

Play music before, during, and after class. Recent research applauds the use of music in the classroom. Music played at the beginning of class may help to create an atmosphere for learning and can be used as a management tool. When music is played as students come into a classroom, the environment is friendlier and more inviting. Music may be played as students go to their work stations. When the music stops, students must be in their places. Music played during work time may provide a centering focus for students and drown out other distractions. Music played at the end of class may be a management tool for orderly dismissal or help transfer learning.

Music is a complementary tool for studying content areas. Music may be helpful to research certain decades of time (20s, 40s, 60s, etc.) or periods of history (Renaissance, Baroque, etc.). Music may also be used to study geographical areas (Stephen Foster of the South or John Denver of the West) and culture (Spanish, German, etc.). Music helps children see and value differences.

Music has a direct connection to cognitive skills as well. Playing classical music causes a "priming" condition for students to think better. Students who take tests have been found to perform better if classical music (Mozart) is used to introduce the class.

Suggested resources:

Black, Susan. (1997) *The American School Board Journal.* "The Musical Mind." 20-22.
Synder, Neal. (1995) *Teaching Music.* "Frances Rauscher: Music and Reasoning."
Viadero, Debra. (1998) *Teacher Magazine.* "Bach to Basics."

Musical Punctuation

Victor Borge's talent for combining music and punctuation has produced an entertaining and effective means for enhancing communication skills. First, the class lists specific punctuation marks on the board that are used most often in writing: period, question mark, exclamation point, comma, quotation marks, etc. Then musical cues are assigned and agreed upon for each punctuation mark. The list of marks and cues are posted on the board. As students proofread or edit their written work, the musical punctuation cues are used. This activity offers some humor, originality, and great transfer to the writing process. Here are some sample cues:

Punctuation Mark	Sound
period (.)	"pling" (singing voice)
exclamation (!)	"Whee!" (exciting voice, high-to-low range)
comma (,)	"Sh" (say sh!)
quotation marks (" ")	"click-click" (click with tongue and snap fingers)
question mark (?)	"bop" (say with lips)

Benefits of "Musical Punctuation"

- Offers creative evaluation in the writing process
- Stimulates critical thinking
- Incorporates musical intelligence into the classroom
- Enhances enjoyment and humor in the classroom

Video Pen Pals

Students enjoy working together to produce original video projects. Establishing video pen pals between schools in two different locations may offer excitement, as well as application of many skills. Students in Colorado and New York collaborated over a school year to generate monthly videos, and they became pen pals. Each month, a specific class in the school was responsible for the video production including script, sound, visuals, etc. All students in that class participated in the project. After the video was sent to the pen pals, students eagerly anticipated their response.

When the Denver Broncos played the New York Giants in the Super Bowl one year, Colorado students prepared cheers and other video PR to send to their New York pen pals before the game. After the game, New York students created a rap eulogy video to send to their Colorado pen pals in honor of the Broncos' crushing loss.

Other musical products may include raps, jingles, songs, rhymes, rhythms, beats, patterns, creation of musical instruments, etc.

Benefits of "Video Pen Pals"

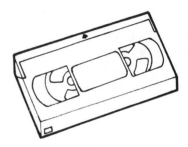

- Promotes positive communication skills
- Encourages productive cooperative group skills
- Integrates musical intelligences
- Addresses holistic content areas

Listening Maps

Playing music for students in the classroom exposes them to a wide range of music, creates various connections to cultural studies, and offers opportunities to hone specific thinking skills. To perfect listening skills and observation skills, students may listen to CDs such as Peter, Paul and Mary's *Peter, Paul and Mommy*, which contains such entertaining, descriptive songs as "That Marvelous Toy," "I'm Being Swallowed by a Boa Constrictor," or "Going to the Zoo Tomorrow." Students must illustrate the song with a drawing. The song may be played several times to elicit more details in elaborative thinking.

A reflective thinking activity can be implemented by encouraging the students to create "listening maps." Students use line and color to create a "map" that expresses the thoughts and feelings that emerge as they listen to the music. The vividness of color, broadness or bigness of the lines, as well as the movement of lines (straight, squiggly, broken, etc.) help to depict individual expression.

Benefits of "Listening Maps"

- Integrates music intelligence into the curriculum
- Hones listening and observation skills
- Nurtures creative expression
- Perfects visualization skills

Peter, Paul & Mary. *Peter, Paul and Mommy*. Los Angeles, CA. Warner Brothers, 1969.

Music and Content Connection

Recent research in Rhode Island public elementary schools produced strong evidence that sequential, skill-building instruction in art and music integrated with the rest of the curriculum can greatly improve children's performance in reading and math. Learning art skills forces mental stretching, which can be useful to other areas of learning.

> Gardiner, Martin, Alan Fox, Faith Knowles, and Donna Jeffrey. (1996) *Nature.* "Learning Improved by Arts Training"
>
> Viadero, Debra. (1998) *Teacher Magazine.* "Bach to Basics."

In his book *To Open Minds,* Howard Gardner noted that music and dance share some of the rigorous notational potential of mathematical symbol systems because features of each art form can be expressed in notation.

Researchers in California and Wisconsin have concluded that early training in piano seems to hone some of the reasoning skills children will use to do well in science and math. Piano training is even better than computer training at building spatial-temporal skills, which are used to detect patterns in space and time and to form mental images from physical objects. Spatial-temporal skills are critical to understanding principles such as proportions and geometry.

> Virginia Journal of Education. (1977) "Piano Training May Boost Reasoning Skills, Math, Science Ability."

Frances Rauscher has demonstrated that learning experiences developed around math and music improve reasoning skills. All other things being equal, if you look at two kids—one who studies music and one who doesn't—the child who studies music will have enhanced spatial reasoning. Rauscher suggests that music might be considered a pre-language which, while children are very young, excites inherent brain patterns and promotes their use in complex reasoning tasks. She predicts that music training at an early age provides exercise for higher brain functions.

> Synder, Neal (1995) *Teaching Music.* "Frances Rauscher: Music and Reasoning."

Here are some options for math-music connections:

- estimate the number of people attending popular music concerts
- estimate financial and energy costs related to a music concert
- compare the patterns in music with the patterns in numbers
- analyze "note" values in whole and fractional numbers (half note, whole note, eighth notes, etc.)
- research and rank salaries and fees of musicians and entertainers with other careers
- determine prices of musical instruments, consider discount coupons
- research then create time lines of famous composers
- construct attribute charts for instruments

> Allen, Steve. "How to Think." Sewell, NY. Meadowlane Music, Inc.
>
> O'Neal, Kate. *Effective Schools.* Vol. 13 No.1. Research Abstracts. 1998-1999 Series. Citation.
>
> Kelstrom, Joyce J. (1998) NASSP Bulletin 82, 597. "The Untapped Power of Music: Its Role in the Curriculum and Its Effect on Academic Achievement." 34-43.

Music and Mnemonics

Music plays a powerful role in learning and remembering. The letters of the alphabet, multiplication facts, states and capitals, and the bones of the body can all be learned with a song. Combining conceptual information with a song embeds the learning faster and on a deeper level.

Chants

➥ 1, 2 button my shoes

    3, 4 shut the door

    5, 6 pick up sticks

Rhymes

➥ "Thirty Days Hath September" (months of the year)

➥ Letter I before E except after C…

Rhythms

➥ clap number of syllables in words

Patterns

➥ number and arrangement of musical notes

Poems

➥ Shel Silverstein books

Songs

➥ "I'm Being Swallowed by a Boa Constrictor"

➥ "Dry Bones"

➥ "Hokey Pokey"

➥ "Did you ever see a tooth brush, a tooth brush? Did you ever see a tooth brush? Now you tell me one." (Compound words)

Benefits of "Mnemonics"

• Adds humor and delight to the classroom

• Adapts to any content or curriculum area

• Awakens musical intelligence in individuals

• Eases memorization and understanding of difficult concepts

Suggested Resource: Sousa, David. (1995) *How the Brain Learns*. Reston, VA. NASSP

Music Note Words

Students can have fun creating note words as a different kind of communicative product. Students use the letters (A, B, C, D, E, F, G) on the musical scale to create the words. The words may be placed on the chalkboard as an early-bird riddle warm-up, or the class can make riddle posters as a large-group activity. Challenge the students to make the largest word possible with musical notes. Words can be tied into specific content areas—nutrition (egg), measurement (decade), travel (baggage)—or used randomly.

As an extension, students may create stories using note words. These stories may be shared with other students at different grade levels. See page 89 for a list of words that can be made from musical notes and page 90 for an example of a musical-note story. More musical-note stories are provided in Chapter 9 on pages 160–165.

To decode musical-note stories, students will need to know the names of the notes. Use this graphic as a guide:

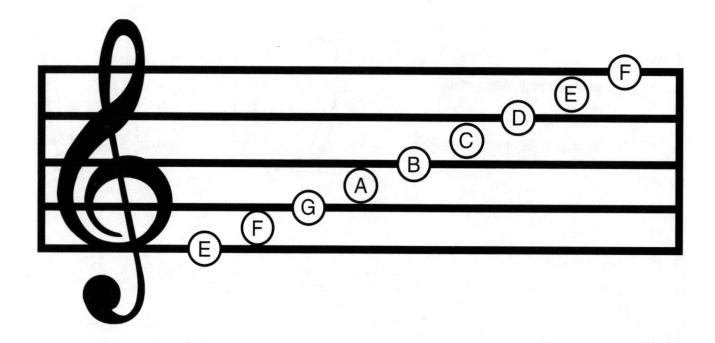

Benefits of "Music Note Words"

- Combines music and verbal intelligence for communication
- Provides a challenge
- Adapts to various curriculum areas
- Offers a unique product for assessment

Music Note Words *(cont.)*

Here are some words that can be made from musical notes:

deaf	feed	ace
bead	bee	badge
cabbage	deed	decade
egged	bad	Abe
cage	fed	dead
face	age	fade
bagged	egg	baggage
café	gabbed	façade
begged	bade	ABBA
cab	bag	fab

Music Note Words *(cont.)*

Here is an example of a note story. See other note stories in Appendix B on pages 160–165.

"M" Chart

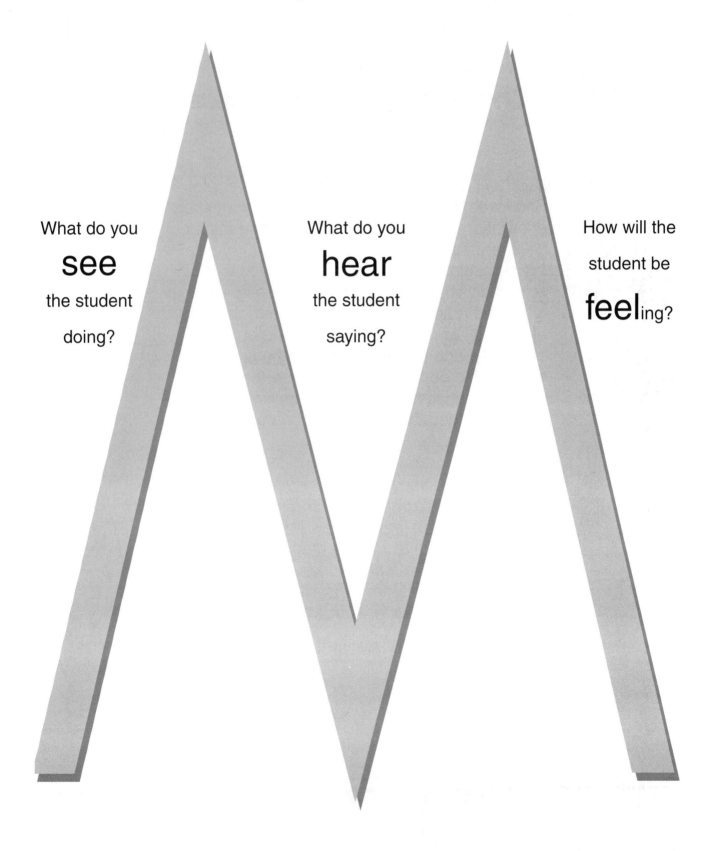

What do you
see
the student
doing?

What do you
hear
the student
saying?

How will the
student be
feeling?

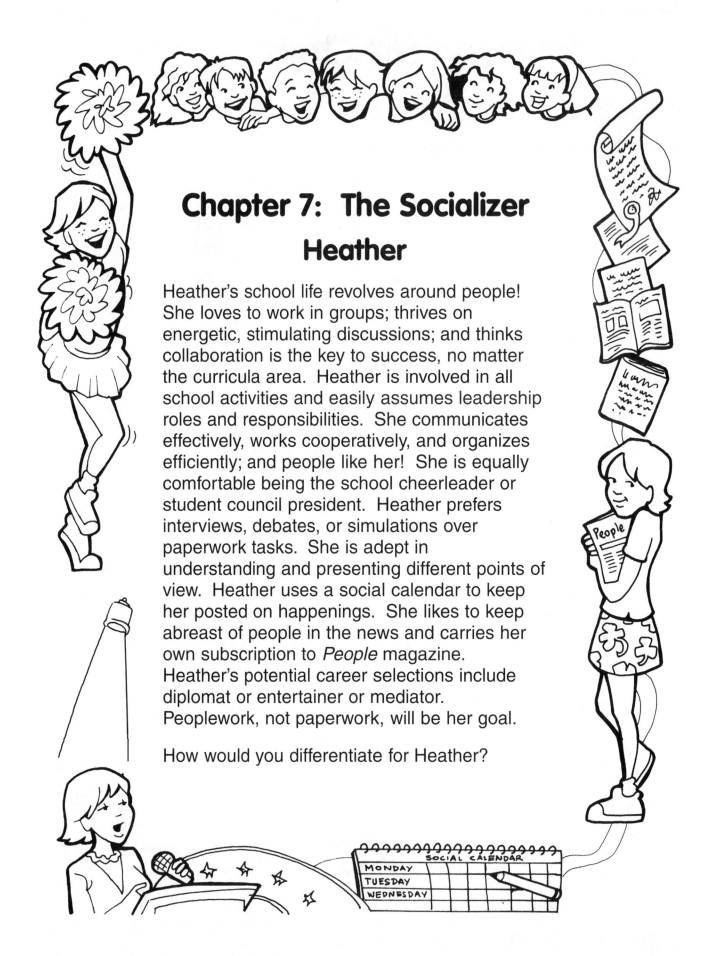

Chapter 7: The Socializer
Heather

Heather's school life revolves around people! She loves to work in groups; thrives on energetic, stimulating discussions; and thinks collaboration is the key to success, no matter the curricula area. Heather is involved in all school activities and easily assumes leadership roles and responsibilities. She communicates effectively, works cooperatively, and organizes efficiently; and people like her! She is equally comfortable being the school cheerleader or student council president. Heather prefers interviews, debates, or simulations over paperwork tasks. She is adept in understanding and presenting different points of view. Heather uses a social calendar to keep her posted on happenings. She likes to keep abreast of people in the news and carries her own subscription to *People* magazine. Heather's potential career selections include diplomat or entertainer or mediator. Peoplework, not paperwork, will be her goal.

How would you differentiate for Heather?

Interpersonal Connections

The Socializer

See	Hear
• many friendships	• organizing
• working in different groups	• collaborative talks
• socializing	• interviews and discussions
• street smart	• conversing, sharing
• cooperative learning	• relating personal views
• effective people skills	• positive communication
• competition meets	• ways to work together
• playing various games	• "I have some party ideas!"
• manipulation of adults	• active listening
• full social calendars	• open-ended questioning
• selecting careers of a politician, diplomat, entertainer, comedian, mediator, teacher, minister	• creating group games
	• "May we work together?"

SOS People: Billy Graham, Oprah Winfrey, Bill Cosby, Martin Luther King, Jr.

Warm-Ups: "Write-in Activity" (page 94), "International Scavenger Hunt" (page 95)

- Name instances when two heads are better than one.
- Name different ways for people to line up.
- Name favorite games.

Games: *Around the World, Jeopardy, Trivial Pursuit, Bingo, Charades, Twister, Scruples*

Option #	Activity Name	Page #
1.	Flexible Grouping	96
2.	Point-of-View	97
3.	Communicate	101
4.	Everything I Needed to Know	103
5.	How Do They Fit Together?	104
6.	The News Bowl	107
7.	Games	108

See Chapter 9, Appendix B for examples of thought<u>full</u> games.

Write-in Activity

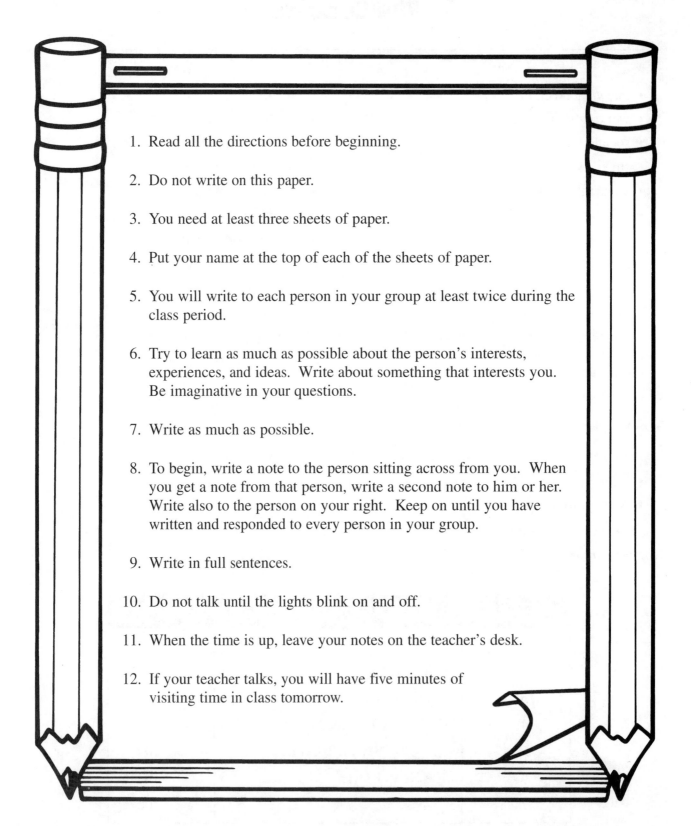

1. Read all the directions before beginning.

2. Do not write on this paper.

3. You need at least three sheets of paper.

4. Put your name at the top of each of the sheets of paper.

5. You will write to each person in your group at least twice during the class period.

6. Try to learn as much as possible about the person's interests, experiences, and ideas. Write about something that interests you. Be imaginative in your questions.

7. Write as much as possible.

8. To begin, write a note to the person sitting across from you. When you get a note from that person, write a second note to him or her. Write also to the person on your right. Keep on until you have written and responded to every person in your group.

9. Write in full sentences.

10. Do not talk until the lights blink on and off.

11. When the time is up, leave your notes on the teacher's desk.

12. If your teacher talks, you will have five minutes of visiting time in class tomorrow.

International Scavenger Hunt

Directions: Move around the room and interview different people. Write the names of the people who meet the following criteria. Try to find a different person for each number.

1 person who has traveled to another country Name: _____ When: _____ Country: _____	**2** person who can name a sports star from another country Name: _____ Star: _____ Country: _____	**3** person who can name a music group from another country Name: _____ Group: _____ Country: _____
4 person who has a family car from another country Name: _____ Car: _____ Country: _____	**5** person who can speak a language from another country Name: _____ Language: _____ Country: _____	**6** person who hosted guests from another country Name: _____ When: _____ Country: _____
7 person who is wearing clothing from another country Name: _____ Clothing: _____ Country: _____	**8** person who can name a movie star from another country Name: _____ Star: _____ Country: _____	**9** person who has seen a foreign film Name: _____ Film: _____ Country: _____
10 person who has a relative living in another country Name: _____ Relative: _____ Country: _____	**11** person who can name a leader from another country Name: _____ Leader: _____ Country: _____	**12** person who can name the capital of another country Name: _____ Capital: _____ Country: _____

Flexible Grouping

Promoting flexible grouping options in the classroom is an effective differentiation strategy. Students live in a world of others, and so giving them opportunities to work with many different kinds of groups is important. Writer Carol Tomlinson says flexible grouping gives students the opportunity to audition for life. Students may be grouped for instruction in many ways such as by age, skill, interest, random-selection, or self-selected. Sometimes students may be grouped with their chronological peers, other times with their intellectual peers. Discussion groups, cross-age tutoring, and partner-buddy work are other grouping strategies. It is important to expose children to a variety of different groups.

Cooperative learning groups may be effective if used properly. Johnson and Johnson books (see below) guide the organization and implementation of cooperative groups. One recommendation from their work suggests that students spend an hour block grouped in this way:

- 15 minutes—large group activity
- 15 minutes—independent activity
- 30 minutes—cooperative group activity

Benefits of "Flexible Grouping"

- Exposes students to real world situation: working with different groups
- Adds variety to the classroom
- Gives students the opportunity to be with intellectual peers some of the time
- Avoids tracking issues
- Allows for creative scheduling
- Creates meaningful options for differentiation in instruction

Suggested resources:

Johnson, David W. and Roger T. Johnson. (1984) *Cooperation in the Classroom.* Edina, MN. Interaction Book Company.

Tomlinson, Carol Ann. (1995) *How to Differentiate Instruction in Mixed-Ability Classrooms.* Alexandria, VA. ASCD.

Point-of-View

Edward de Bono's thinking strategy point-of-view (POV) is useful in productive problem solving. The POV skill teaches students how to look at problems and situations from different perspectives. POV has applications to all content areas:

Art:

❧ Draw an object from three different points of view (top, bottom, side view).

Math:

❧ Solve the problem in three different ways.

Language Arts:

❧ Write a journal entry or create a play backdrop depicting a certain POV.

Science:

❧ Draw a food chain from a bird's POV.

Social Studies:

❧ Role play an opinion or create an editorial representing a current issue.

The poem of "The Blind Men and the Elephant" (see page 98 for complete poem) presents an example of how many points of view give a more accurate picture. Each blind man touches a specific part of the elephant and imagines what the animal looks like. If all the men worked together, a full image would have emerged. Synergy can result from sharing different perspectives and POVs.

Point-of-View cards have been a long-lasting successful teaching tool. Please note specifics for this activity on the following pages.

Benefits of "Point-of-View"

• Adapts to any curriculum area

• Transfers as a life skill: expression of an opinion

• Reinforces critical thinking

• Adds challenge and enjoyment to discussions

• Allows for all students to contribute "safely" to discussion

---

Suggested resources:

de Bono, Edward. (1985) *CoRT Thinking Skills.* New York, NY. Pergamon Press.

Fogarity, Robin. (1990) *Keep Them Thinking.* Palantine, IL. Skylight Publication.

Saxe, John G. *Anthology of Children's Literature.* Modern Fables. "The Blind Men and the Elephant."

Point-of-View (cont.)

The Blind Men and the Elephant

by John G. Saxe
(1816–1887)

It was six men of Indostan
To learning much inclined,
Who went to see the Elephant
(Though all of them were blind),
That each by observation
Might satisfy his mind.

The First approached the Elephant,
And happening to fall
Against his broad and sturdy side,
At once began to bawl:
"God bless me! But the Elephant,
Is very like a wall!"

The Second, feeling of the tusk,
Cried, "Ho! What have we here
So very round and smooth and sharp?
To me 'tis mighty clear
This wonder of an Elephant
Is very like a spear!"

The Third approached the animal,
And happening to take
The squirming trunk within his hands,
Then boldly up and spake:
"I see," quoth he, "the Elephant
Is very like a snake!"

The Fourth reached out his eager hand,
And felt about the knee.
"What most this wondrous beast is like
Is mighty plain," quoth he;

"I'm clear enough the Elephant
Is very like a tree!"

The Fifth, who chanced to touch the ear,
Said, "E'en the blindest man
Can tell what this resembles most;
Deny the fact who can
This marvel of an Elephant
Is very like a fan!"

The Sixth no sooner had begun
About the beast to grope
Than, seizing on the swinging tail
That fell within his scope,
"I see," quoth he, "the Elephant
Is very like a rope!"

And so these men of Indostan
Disputed loud and long,
Each in his own opinion
Exceeding stiff and strong,
Though each was partly in the right,
And all were in the wrong!

Point-of-View (cont.)

Follow these steps to analyze how different people look at the same situation.

POV Applications

1. Draw an object from the top, bottom, side, inside, etc.
2. Tell how to solve a math problem from your point of view.
3. Role play different characters in a story or historical event.
4. Discuss current events from different perspectives.
5. Illustrate a cartoon showing your opinion.
6. Gauge the emotional climate with a barometer check.

   (On a scale of 1-10, today I am _____ because _____.)
7. Assess your own personal learning.

Point-of-View (POV) Cards

Directions: Select the names of famous people. Write names on recipe cards. Circulate the cards among class participants. Encourage the VIP's POV on a given topic.

Suggested categories of people

Actors	Cartoon Characters	Leaders	Poets
Artists	Explorers	Musicians	Politicians
Athletes	Family Members	Olympians	Presidents
Authors	Inventors	Philosophers	Scientists

Possible VIPs for POV Cards

William Shakespeare	Sally Ride	Big Bird	Mahatma Gandhi
Sandra Day O'Connor	Jacques Cousteau	Marco Polo	Mark Twain
Orville Wright	Cinderella	Helen Keller	Galileo Galilei
Albert Einstein	Tiger Woods	Madonna	Amy Tan
Charlie Brown	Lance Armstrong	Maya Angelou	Clara Barton
Columbus	Ponce de Leon	Ludwig van Beethoven	Abraham Lincoln
Sacagawea	Popeye	Ben Franklin	Maya Lin

Ideas for using POV cards

- Name the VIP's favorite book.
- What is the VIP's favorite number? Why?
- Tell about the VIP's summer vacation.
- What would the VIP like for a birthday gift?
- Which Olympic event would the VIP like to enter? Why?
- Tell about the VIP's favorite toy.
- What advice would the VIP give to a 10-year-old today?
- What is a question this VIP would ask the teacher on the first day of school?
- What music would the VIP prefer?
- What would be the VIP's favorite holiday? Why?
- What place would the VIP like to explore? Why?
- Describe the VIP's favorite lunch.
- How would the VIP dress for Halloween?

Point-of-View (cont.)

The following are sample questions that can be posed with the POV Cards:

➡ (*math*) What is _____'s favorite number? Why?

Example for Tiger Woods: "1," because he wants a hole-in-one in golf.

➡ (*government/leadership*) Name some problems _____ faced. How did _____ solve the problems?

Example for Abe Lincoln: He used collaboration in dealing with war issues.

➡ (*calendar reference*) What would _____ like for Thanksgiving dinner?

Example for Popeye: He would like spinach.

➡ (*teaching/counseling*) What advice would _____ give a 16-year-old today?

Example for Thomas Edison: "Play with ideas." "Don't give up."

➡ (*current events*) If _____ was in charge of the United States budget, how would he or she allocate funds?

Example for Helen Keller: She would support monies for disabled people around the world.

➡ (*social studies or government*) Describe the characteristics _____ would like in a president.

Example for Dr. Martin Luther King, Jr.: He would like fairness and tolerance.

➡ (*science*) Name a machine or invention that helped _____ be successful.

Example for Ben Franklin: a kite

➡ (*science*) What change in science would surprise _____ today?

Example for Sacajawea: She would be amazed at the Global Positioning Systems in cars.

➡ (*government, leadership*) Who would be _____'s hero? Why?

Example for Dr. Martin Luther King, Jr.: Gandhi would be his hero because of his love of peace.

➡ (*arts, astronomy*) What cartoon or comic would be preferred by _____? Why?

Example for Sally Ride: She would like Buck Rogers' space adventures.

Communicate

"Communicate" is a simulation activity, played in pairs, that focuses on the direction-giving, processing, and follow-through skills of both players.

Materials

- shapes (page 102)

- scissors

Directions

Each person cuts out specific shapes (see page 102). Together they agree on color and design for each shape so the sets are identical. When the shapes are ready, the players sit back-to-back with pieces laid out in front of each player so neither set can be seen by the other player. Players take turns as instructor and listener. The instructor arranges shapes into a design, then communicates the location and placement of each shape as the design takes form. The listener's task is to process directions and duplicate the instructor's design. As an option, the listener may not ask questions or peek at the design until the instructor is finished with directions. When all shapes have been placed, designs are compared. The instructor and listener discuss differences, problems, and challenges. Then the roles are reversed and the simulation repeated.

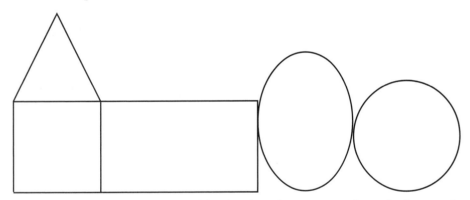

As an option, a similar activity can be conducted by having the partners draw designs rather than create them with geometric shapes. Pencils, markers, or crayons and drawing paper may be used.

Benefits of "Communicate"

- Promotes interactive communication

- Offers hands-on learning activity

- Provides teacher with a quick assessment during class activity

- Reinforces mathematical concepts

- Allows for creative thinking in design

- Practices skills of following directions

Villalpando, Eleanor. (1984) *Simulations*. Phoenix, AZ Kathy Kolbe Concept, Inc. 31-32. Permission granted for reprinting by Kolbe Corp. and Kathy Kolbe. Web site: *www.kolbe.com.*

Communicate (cont.)

Cut out each shape carefully. With your partner, agree on how each piece will be identified. They can be colored or patterned, lettered, or left as they are!

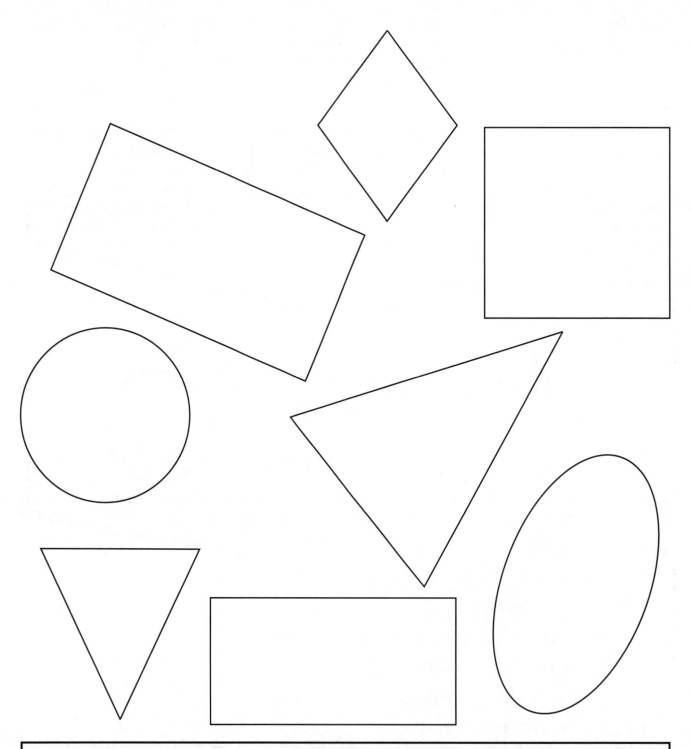

Everything I Needed To Know

Students work together in a large group writing facts about a given topic. All the facts are recorded on the chalkboard or poster paper. After a given amount of time, students are then asked to reread the paragraph of information. Students (one at a time or in small groups) then use colored markers to cross out all unnecessary words. A final task is to underline or circle the *five* key words that are left. These key words should be the essence of the paragraph. This activity reinforces the HOT skill of encapsulation, promotes group discussion, and offers insight into personal POVs (points of view).

Topics may include:

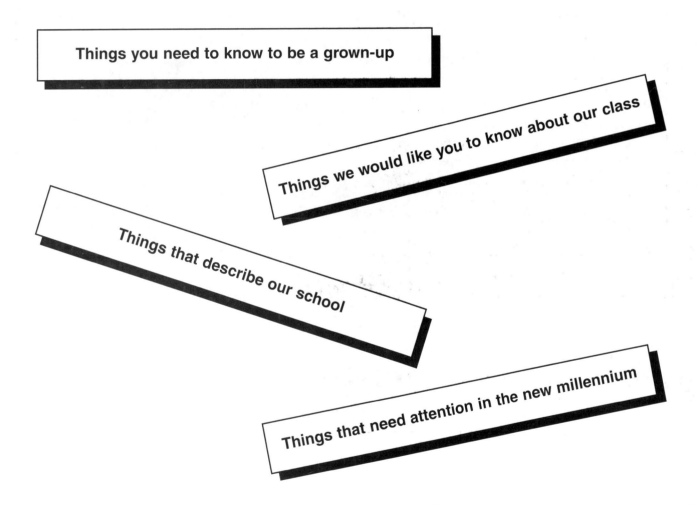

Things you need to know to be a grown-up

Things we would like you to know about our class

Things that describe our school

Things that need attention in the new millennium

Benefits of "Everything I Needed to Know"

- Provides option for large group discussion

- Encourages different points of view

- Offers practice in encapsulation in a directly visible way

- Gives teacher or facilitator additional insight into class dynamics and knowledge

- Adds interest and challenge to classroom

How Do They Fit Together?

The brain naturally makes sense out of things. It is important to give students many opportunities to work with a given set of objects and determine how the objects fit together. Instead of the teachers making the connections between objects, it is more powerful and meaningful to have the students generate the connecting patterns and relationships.

This activity offers practice in the skill of "making connections" and is very teacher-friendly. The guidelines are as follows:

- Collect several random articles/objects and place them in a basket.

- Each student selects an object from the basket.

- Each object is observed carefully to note its attributes and characteristics.

- Each student takes his or her object and walks around the room to make a connection with another object someone else has selected (same color, size, use, where found, number of pieces, texture, etc.).

- Students make as many connections as they can with one object (one person) or try to connect with several or all objects.

- Students move to the next person for new connections.

The final goal is that students will see that *all* things are connected and interrelated.

Using an analogy grid as a graphic organizer helps students record the various connections. The grid helps students compare two items in order to perceive similarities. Creative thinking (originality, flexibility, risk-taking) is a positive benefit of this activity. This activity is a great warm-up before doing writing that uses metaphorical thinking.

See the sample analogy grid on page 105 and the blank grid on page 106.

Benefits of "How Do They Fit Together?"

- Offers hands-on learning experience

- Encourages open-ended thinking ("no wrong answers")

- Allows for social interaction and mobility among students

- Adds spark and intrigue to the classroom

- Gives teacher quick assessment

How Do They Fit Together? *(cont.)*
Sample Analogy Grid

Use this grid to complete a study using analogies.

Directions: Each student selects an object and observes that object carefully. Then the student looks at objects other students have selected and seeks connections between the various objects. The final goal is for students to link all objects together in a meaningful way. (There are no wrong answers!)

Objects	book	shoe	cup	protractor
pencil	A book and a pencil can be used to communicate ideas			
hat		A shoe and a hat are both containers; both items can be worn.		
watch				A watch can measure time, a protractor can measure degrees in an angle.

How Do They Fit Together? *(cont.)*
Blank Analogy Grid

Use this grid to complete a study using analogies.

Directions: Each student selects an object and observes that object carefully. Then the student looks at objects other students have selected and seeks connections between the various objects. The final goal is for students to link all objects together in a meaningful way. (There are no wrong answers!)

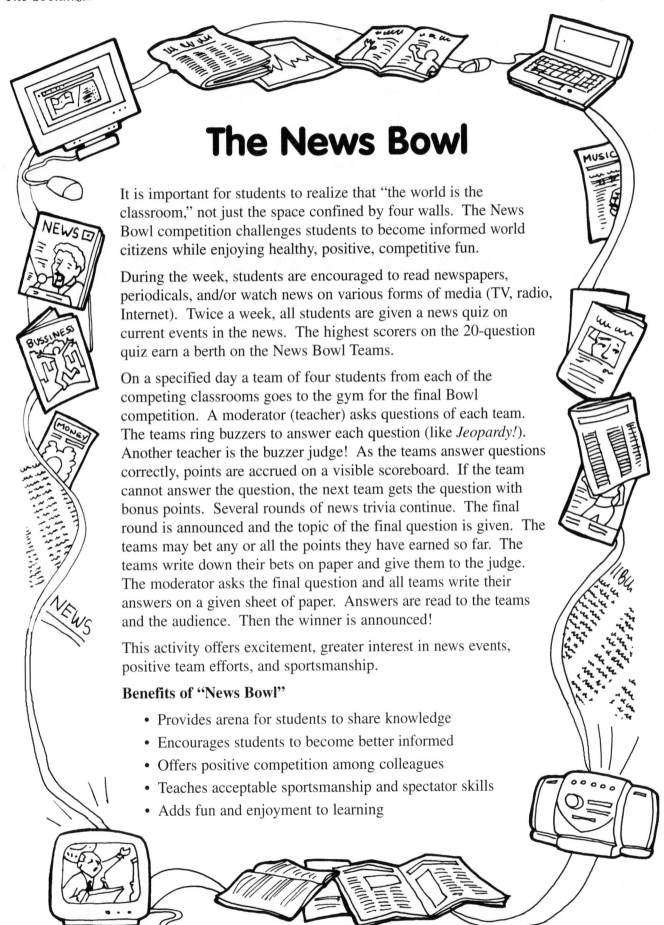

The News Bowl

It is important for students to realize that "the world is the classroom," not just the space confined by four walls. The News Bowl competition challenges students to become informed world citizens while enjoying healthy, positive, competitive fun.

During the week, students are encouraged to read newspapers, periodicals, and/or watch news on various forms of media (TV, radio, Internet). Twice a week, all students are given a news quiz on current events in the news. The highest scorers on the 20-question quiz earn a berth on the News Bowl Teams.

On a specified day a team of four students from each of the competing classrooms goes to the gym for the final Bowl competition. A moderator (teacher) asks questions of each team. The teams ring buzzers to answer each question (like *Jeopardy!*). Another teacher is the buzzer judge! As the teams answer questions correctly, points are accrued on a visible scoreboard. If the team cannot answer the question, the next team gets the question with bonus points. Several rounds of news trivia continue. The final round is announced and the topic of the final question is given. The teams may bet any or all the points they have earned so far. The teams write down their bets on paper and give them to the judge. The moderator asks the final question and all teams write their answers on a given sheet of paper. Answers are read to the teams and the audience. Then the winner is announced!

This activity offers excitement, greater interest in news events, positive team efforts, and sportsmanship.

Benefits of "News Bowl"

• Provides arena for students to share knowledge

• Encourages students to become better informed

• Offers positive competition among colleagues

• Teaches acceptable sportsmanship and spectator skills

• Adds fun and enjoyment to learning

Games

Many games lend themselves to the development of positive interpersonal skills. Games can be connected to any curriculum area. A suggested roster of games for each multiple intelligence has been noted on the T-chart at the beginning of each chapter. See the next page for lists of various board and computer games.

Creating original games is a challenging, intriguing and enjoyable task for students. This book includes many samples of original, thoughtful games.

Benefits of Games

- Provides medium for teaching many interpersonal skills

- Adapts to various curriculum areas

- Reinforces content connections

- Adds fun and excitement to classroom learning

- Nurtures creative thinking (game products)

- Offers means for review and summary work

Games *(cont.)*

Verbal/Linguistic ("The Word Player")
Word Smart

Boggle   Hangman
Scrabble   Balderdash
Trivial Pursuit   *World Library*
Connect Four   *Just Grandma and Me*
Spill and Spell   *Missing Links*
Scattergories   *Mavis Beacon Teaches*
                                    Typing

Logical/Mathematical ("The Questioner")
Number Smart

Challenge 24   Bingo, Quizmo
Jeopardy   Mind Trap
Battleship   Checkers
Mastermind   *Math Blaster*
Monopoly   *King's Rule*
Clue   *Science Tool Kits*
Aggravation   *Lemonade Stand*

Visual/Spatial ("The Visualizer")
Art Smart

Pictionary   *Dazzle Draw*
Mazes   *Chessmaster*
Chess   *Tetris*
Stratego   *Living Jigsaws*
Rubricks cube   *New Print Shop*
Etch-A-Sketch   *Sensei's Geometry*
Young Artist's Tool Box

Musical/Rhythmic ("The Music Lover")
Music Smart

Simon   *Exploration*
Musical Bingo   *Music Studio*

Bodily/Kinesthetic ("The Mover")
Body Smart

Jenga   Play Dough
Charades   Simon Says
Twister   *Flight Simulator*
Statue   *Dactyl Nightmare*
Follow the Leader   *Shufflepack Café*
Lego, the Leader   *Lego to Logo*

Naturalist ("The Observer")
World Smart

Scavenger Hunts   Geoscope
I Spy   *The Oregon Trail*
Invention/Convention   *Where in the World Is*
                                    Carmen San Diego?

Interpersonal ("The Socializer")
People Smart

Around the World   Board Games
Team Games   *Kidsnet*
Card Games   *Sim City*
Sports Games

Intrapersonal ("The Individualist")
Self Smart

Ungame   *Decisions, Decisions*
Scruples   *The Perfect Career*
Computer Games

Italicized titles = computer games

"M" Chart

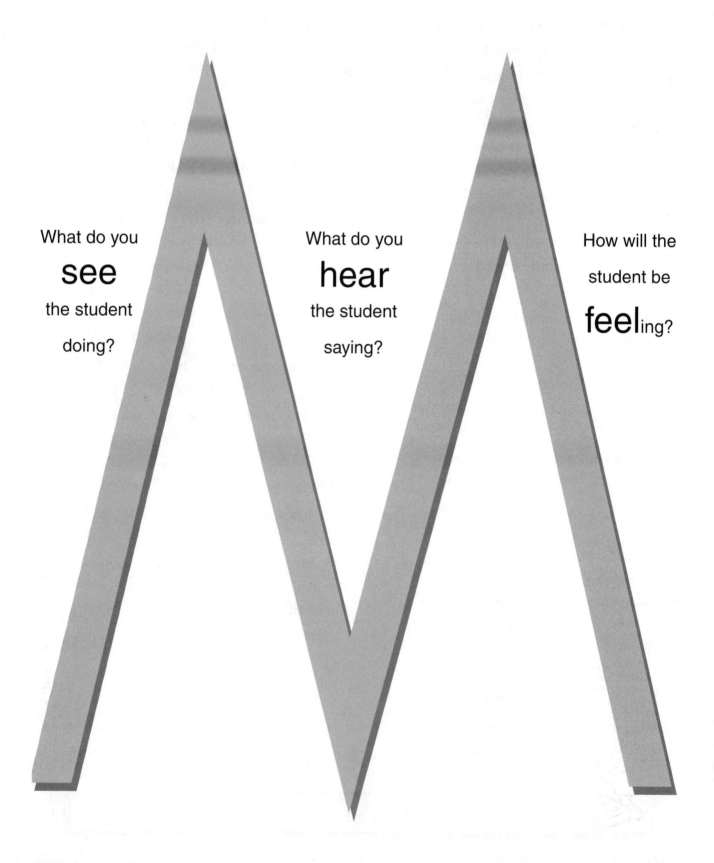

What do you
see
the student
doing?

What do you
hear
the student
saying?

How will the
student be
feeling?

Chapter 8: The Individualist

Peggy

Self-motivated Peggy has a focused concentration on school and is goal-oriented. Learning comes easy for her because she has autonomous skills and does not need hand-holding. Persistence and tenacity describe Peggy. She is not a follower but is content to be herself and is welcome in any group because of her fairness and diplomacy. Peggy is a reflective and insightful thinker who is comfortable writing essays, keeping journals, or assessing situations. Peggy prefers self-assessment projects rather than involvement in flashy grandstand productions. Peggy likes reading philosophy and enjoys computer games. Biographies of Mahatma Gandhi, Helen Keller, Anne Frank, Tiger Woods, and Ralph Nader have inspired her. She contemplates a career as a counselor or advisor.

How would you differentiate for Peggy?

Intrapersonal Connections

The Individualist

See	Hear
• pursuing own interests	• reflective thinking on feelings, dreams
• keeping a diary or journal	• assessing strengths and weaknesses
• following instincts	• self-motivation
• individuality	• metacognition
• persistence	• mature self understanding
• being original	• "I like quiet time."
• working alone	• self talk
• reading meditation calendars	• sharing an insight
• relaxing	• thinking about thinking
• careers: therapist, counselor, activist, philosopher	• "I have outlined my goals for next year."

SOS People: Ralph Nader, Margaret Mead, Gandhi, Helen Keller, Anne Frank, Tiger Woods

Warm-Ups: "Four Square" (page 113), "Reflections" (page 114), "What's Significant About Your Name?" (page 115)

Games: *Ungame®*, *Draw-Me-a-Picture®*, *Concentration®*, computer games

Option #	Activity Name	Page #
1	Journals Writing/Goal Writing	116
2	Ticket-Out-the-Door	117
3	Barometer Check	120
4	MI Report Card	120
5	Me-Box	122
6	Personal-I-Tie	124
7	Glyphs	124

Four Square

Directions: Write the answers to the following cues in the box.

1. Write one thing you are good at.

2. Name one thing that makes you happy.

3. Name your greatest achievement to date.

4. Name one thing you would like to achieve in the next four years.

1	**2**
3	**4**

Now, you can share your information with others.

Reflections

Directions: Try this metacognitive thinking exercise. Fill in the boxes to describe yourself.

I am like . . .

the animal _____ because . . .	the plant _____ because . . .
the machine _____ because . . .	the color _____ because . . .

Reflections *(cont.)*

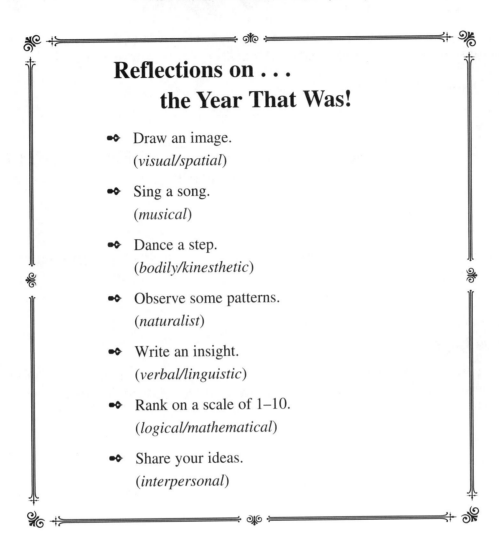

**Reflections on . . .
the Year That Was!**

- Draw an image.
  (*visual/spatial*)

- Sing a song.
  (*musical*)

- Dance a step.
  (*bodily/kinesthetic*)

- Observe some patterns.
  (*naturalist*)

- Write an insight.
  (*verbal/linguistic*)

- Rank on a scale of 1–10.
  (*logical/mathematical*)

- Share your ideas.
  (*interpersonal*)

What's Significant About Your Name?

Answer the following questions:

1. How did you get your name?_____

   _____

2. Describe family history connected with your name._____

   _____

3. Do you like/dislike your name? Why?_____

   _____

4. Share an interesting experience associated with your name. _____

   _____

Journal Writing/Goal Writing

There are many ways to nurture the self-smart in a student. Giving students ownership, responsibility and accountability for their own learning is key. Students plan for their own success.

Some specific strategies are as follows:

✦ Goal Writing

Students write down goals for the year, goals for a week, goals for a unit of study, goals for behavior and performance. A decisions/outcomes chart may be used to list goals then record resulting outcomes.

✦ Journal Recording

A specific time is designated each day for students to write their feelings, thoughts, reflections in a journal. Journals may be used to plan further study, set goals, analyze performance, and monitor growth. The journals may become part of a student's portfolio of work for assessment and evaluation.

✦ Progress Logs

As students proceed through compacted studies, individual logs are kept to keep track of progress and to organize new work. Each day, the students record work accomplished then determine what needs to happen next. The logs are a management tool for teachers and students.

Benefits of "Journal Writing/Goal Writing"

- Makes student responsible and accountable
- Provides means of assessment
- Offers insight into student thought and behavior
- Promotes skills of metacognition
- Provides positive management tool

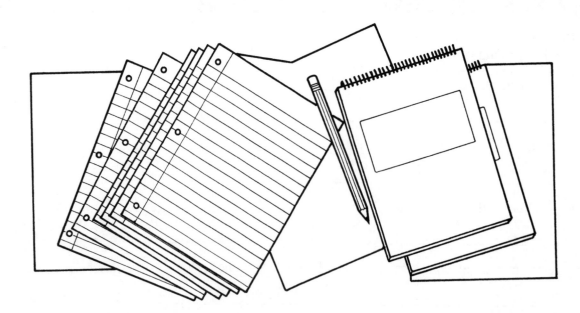

Ticket-Out-the-Door

An effective classroom management tool and student self-assessment device is Ticket-Out-the-Door. The tickets become viable tools for metacognition, which means students evaluate their own thinking and performance. Before the students leave the classroom, each student must individually complete a ticket and give it to the teacher. These tickets are filed for further interpretation, analysis, and discussion.

The tickets are constructed as follows:

1. Create a 3" x 5" recipe card form on white paper (4–6 to a page)

2. At the top of the card write "Date" and "Name," and add a line after each.

3. Write a question for the student to answer relating to study. Questions may integrate various thinking strategies: brainstorming, analysis, evaluation, elaboration, critique, interpretation, etc.

4. Copy different tickets on different colored paper and cut them out.

5. Students fill out the forms and give them to the teacher before leaving class.

6. Tickets are read by the teacher and filed in a recipe box.

7. Tickets may be shared at conferences.

Ticket samples follow on the next few pages.

Benefits of "Ticket-Out-the-Door"

- Makes student responsible for assessing personal work

- Practices metacognition skills

- Offers positive management tool for class departures

- Applies to any subject area or grade level

- Provides another assessment tool for parent conferences

Date: _____
Name: _____
On a scale of 1–5 rating (5 being high),
I would give myself a _____
because _____
_____
_____

Ticket-Out-the-Door *(cont.)*

Directions: Students fill out a self-assessment "ticket" before they leave the classroom. The tickets are collected by the teacher and kept for further discussion/reflection. Ticket content may include a thinking strategy.

Date: _____ Name: _____ Something I learned today: _____ _____ _____	Date: _____ Name: _____ Something that was **P** (plus), **M** (minus), or **I** (interesting) about class today: _____ _____ _____
Date: _____ Name: _____ Some recommendations I would make for this class: _____ _____ _____	Date: _____ Name: _____ On a scale of 1–5 rating (5 being high), I would give myself a _____ because _____ _____ _____
Date: _____ Name: _____ I feel _____ because _____ _____ _____	Date: _____ Name: _____ I would like to visit _____ because _____ _____

Ticket-Out-the-Door *(cont.)*

Date: _____ Name: _____ Today I discovered _____ _____ _____ _____ _____	Date: _____ Name: _____ What would happen if…? _____ _____ _____ _____	Date: _____ Name: _____ I like to read about _____ _____ _____ _____
Date: _____ Name: _____ I get my best ideas when _____ _____ _____	Date: _____ Name: _____ I prefer _____ because _____ _____ _____	Date: _____ Name: _____ A question I have is _____ _____ _____ _____
Date: _____ Name: _____ My favorite place in school is _____ because _____ _____	Date: _____ Name: _____ What would _____ mean _____ from the viewpoint of _____ _____ _____	Date: _____ Name: _____ I would like to change because _____ _____ _____
Date: _____ Name: _____ Today I learned about the strategy_____ I can use this when _____ _____	Date: _____ Name: _____ How else can you solve the problem? _____ _____ _____	Date: _____ Name: _____ I am surprised that _____ _____ _____ _____

Barometer Check

Barometer Check is a helpful strategy for beginning a class or for sharing and assessing student responses during a class. The teacher instructs the class to think of a number on a scale from 1–10: the rating of the scale is graduated and interpreted as follows (you may make up your own interpretations):

10 = terrific!	7 = pretty good	5 = so-so	1 = "the pits"

At the beginning of a school day, ask the kids: "How are you doing?" or "How are you feeling?" Then tell the kids to put up fingers to show their response. Students do not shout out the answer but show their response non-verbally. Each student is then invited to tell (verbal) why he or she feels that way. The teacher notes which students gave low ratings and which students say nothing. During the day, the teacher visits with the student one-on-one to understand the student's point-of-view. This activity helps gain insight into the student's real life or other things happening in the student's life.

The Barometer Check has equal merit for teachers. The teacher can show the students at the beginning of the day his/her reading. Teachers are not robots or machines; and consequently, they have emotional changes, too. Letting students know ahead of time that the teacher has a (2) reading or a (9) reading can have positive effects for the whole class.

Benefits of "Barometer Check"

- Addresses affective area
- Provides additional insight into the whole person
- Adapts to various size and age groups
- Encourages self-assessment

"MI" Report Card

Various report cards may be designed to record student growth, performance, and progress. The MI (multiple intelligence) report card helps students become aware that they are smart in different ways. See pages 121 for an example.

The student is given a MI card and asked to complete the different categories. Using words and graphics helps to make the MI card user-friendly for different ages.

Benefits of "MI Report Card"

- Provides tools for self-realization
- Encourages positive self-assessment
- Fosters positive self-esteem: "We are smart in different ways."
- Practices skills of meta-cognition
- Adds to depth of knowledge
- Enhances appreciation and respect for diversity

Suggested Resources: Chapman, Carolyn. (1993) *If the Show Fits…how to Develop Multiple Intelligences in the Classroom.* Palantine, IL. IRI/Skylight Publishing, Inc.

Lazer, David. (1991) *Seven Ways of Teaching.* Palatine, IL. IRI/Skylight Publishing, Inc.

"MI" Report Card *(cont.)*

Your Name: _____

Write the title of a book you read recently.	Observe some patterns in your life.
What do you do for personal renewal?	Draw a feeling you had today.
Name your favorite kind of music or artist.	Rank yourself on a scale of 1–10 on your math ability (1-2-3-4-5-6-7-8-9-10)
Name a physical feat you have mastered.	Now, share this information with another person.

Me-Box

To help build self-esteem, it is important for students to honor and celebrate what makes them special. Giving students the opportunity to create projects (logos, symbols, collages, murals, floats, etc.) that represent them and their individuality is very beneficial. The Me-Box is a sample project that incorporates HOT skills along with self-expression. Directions for the Me-Box are given below.

Benefits of "Me-Box"

- Encourages self-expression
- Builds self-esteem
- Gives option for the creation of different kinds of products
- Allows the use of variety of resources
- Provides insight
- Increases interest and intrigue
- Adds enjoyment to learning

Me-Box for Valentines

Objectives: to create a "personalized" container for valentines; to review many HOT thinking skills

Materials: empty cereal or laundry box, construction paper, yarn, magazines, old greeting cards, fabric, stickers, glue, markers, scissors, other

Directions: Students bring empty cereal or laundry boxes to class, cover it with colored butcher paper, and then design/decorate the outside of the box according to the following criteria:

1. **Cereal Title:** Use student's first name and add descriptive phrases using alliteration. *Example:* Karen's Krunchy Krispies.

   HOT skill: POV (point-of-view) elaboration

2. **Cereal Company:** Use the student's last name. *Example:* Streeter and Co.

   HOT skill: POV (point-of-view)

3. **Cereal Box:** Decorate the box with a collage of pictures (drawn or cut our from magazines or cards) that describe the person. The collage should include family, hobbies, favorite things, pets, places lived or visited, career goals, etc.

   HOT skill: mind mapping, elaboration

4. **Ingredients:** One side of the cereal box should list ingredients that make up the qualities of that person, such as helpfulness, patience, strength, humor, wit, dependability, responsibility, etc. Students must list percentage amounts for each ingredient. The final sum of ingredients must equal 100%. Ingredients can be positive, negative, or interesting attributes.

   HOT skill: analysis, PMI (plus, minus, interesting), POV (point-of-view)

5. **Coupon:** One side of cereal box features a coupon offer from this person. *For example:*

   - This coupon entitles you to one day of smiles and cheerfulness, compliments of _____.
   - This coupon entitles you to one free joke as told by _____.
   - This coupon entitles you to travel to _____ with _____ and photographs by _____.

   HOT skill: fluency, flexibility, originality, elaboration

Me-Box *(cont.)*

6. **Back of Box:** This should include a game or puzzle designed by the student. Rebus, crossword, dot-to-dot, magic squares, maze…any variety of original puzzle encouraged.

   HOT skill: originality

7. **Top of Box:** This must have an opening for valentines and offer a recipe that the student creates.

   Example: ⅓ cup being yourself

   ⅓ cup accepting others as they are

   ⅓ cup Golden Rule (treat others as you want them to treat you)

   HOT skill: originality, analogy, decisions & outcomes

8. **Cereal Cost:** Students may use conventional monetary values or create imaginary ones

   HOT skill: originality, flexibility, POV (point-of-view)

9. **Cereal Weight:** Students may use conventional weights and measurements or create new ones

   HOT skill: originality, flexibility, POV (point-of-view)

10. **Pizzazz:** The extra sparkle and spunk added to make the Me-Box unique. **Example:** sound effects, gadgetry, movable parts, color and design, etc.

    HOT skill: originality, encapsulation, flexibility

Added notes:

Students may evaluate the Me-Boxes. An evaluation form was created with the 10 criteria listed. Students used a rating scale of 1 (low) to 4 (high) to assess each criterion. If a student forgot one of the criteria, he or she receives zero points. If a student demonstrated a superb effort on a specific criterion, he or she receives 4 points. The point system may be used to determine grades. Additional comments could be added by the evaluator. Students draw names randomly to see which Me-Box he or she will evaluate. Use this form for the evaluations:

Me-Box Evaluation by _____

Directions: Please use the following rating scale to judge each criterion.

0	1	2	3	4
none	poor	average	above average	outstanding

Criteria:

Title	
Company	
Collage	
Ingredients	
Coupon	
Game or Puzzle	
Recipe	
Cost	
Weight	
Pizzazz	
Total:	

Comments on back (attractiveness, completeness, neatness, creativity, etc.)

Personal-I-Tie

The Personal-I-Tie is a unique product that encourages self-expression and creative thinking by the student. Students are prompted to create a Personal-I-Tie that encapsulates their personality and being.

Directions: Think about your own personality and what makes you special. Consider your strengths, hobbies, and favorite people, places, and things. You will use these ideas to create your own Personal-I-Tie. Begin with an old necktie then add "hands-on" information that best represents you. Share your Personal-I-Tie with others.

Suggested Materials

- necktie
- labels
- needle/thread
- pins
- stickers
- cloth
- tie-tacks
- paints
- miniatures
- badges
- cards
- jewelry
- buttons
- hot glue gun

The Personal-I-Ties may be displayed in the classroom on mug racks and used for discussion starters.

As an extension activity, students may create Personal-I-Ties for famous people.

Benefits of the "Personal-I-Tie"

- Encourages self expression
- Promotes creative thinking
- Uses a variety of unique resources
- Adapts to a variety of uses in the classroom
- Creates a colorful, thought-provoking display for school

Glyphs

Some of the earliest forms of writing are glyphs. These writing symbols are visual-spatial interpretations of concepts or data. Students may use various shapes, sizes, colors, and designs to present glyphs, an encapsulation of information. Glyphs adapt well to math concepts and problem solving.

Bio-glyphs are intriguing and creative projects for students to learn more about themselves and each other. The student draws a figure that represents himself/herself) using descriptive, colorful features for greater self-expression. See page 125 for specific bio-glyph directions.

Benefits of "Glyphs"

- Offers unique product idea
- Encourages self-expression
- Provides a colorful, meaningful school display
- Honors individual uniqueness and specialty
- Adds to self-realization and appreciation of others

Let's Create a Bio-glyph!

Face Shape

◯ male

◑ female

Hair

One hair for each book you read over the summer

| fiction

ξ non-fiction

Mouth

Favorite subject at school

⊓ math

⊔ science

⌣ language arts

👄 social studies

Ears

left	Ɛ	brother
right	Ʒ	sister
One	●	on the correct ear for each brother or sister

Collar

born in a U.S. state

born in Washington, D.C.

born outside of the U.S.

Hat

Add a hat if you are happy to be back in school.

Eye Shape

How you came to school

◇ van	◇ walk
○ truck	○ bike
△ car	△ bus

Eye Color

Where you spent your summer vacation

Lake = blue

Beach = brown

Desert = orange

Cruise = purple

Mountains = green

Out of the U.S. = red

Stayed close to home = black

Eyebrows

Favorite activity outside of school

⌒ ⌒ playing competitive sports

ᴍᴍ doing fine or performing arts

⋇⋇ playing outside in the neighborhood

⌃⌃ reading

⌁⌁ using the computer or playing video games

⸳⸳⸳ organized group activities (scouts, youth groups, clubs, etc.)

◠◠ other

Nose

Select only one to show your pet

⌓ none	ꞷ fish
△ dog	ʊ bird
○ cat	▱ other

"M" Chart

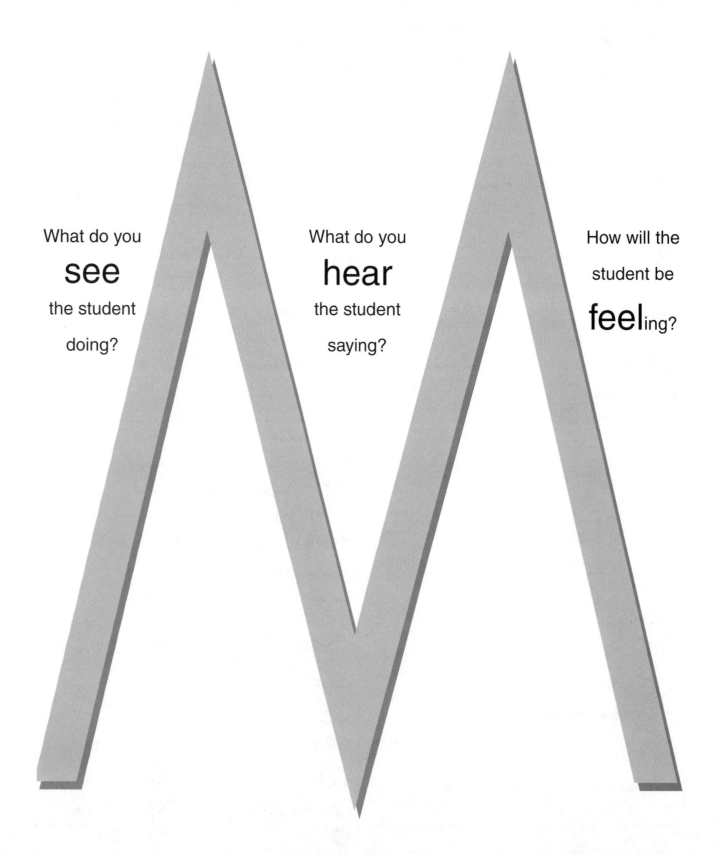

What do you
see
the student
doing?

What do you
hear
the student
saying?

How will the
student be
feeling?

Table of Contents

HOT (Higher-Order-Thinking) Strategies

Definitions

Analogy: comparing two items in order to perceive the similarities; a relation of likeness between two things

Brainstorming: divergent thinking; spontaneously contributing ideas

Fluency: expressing many ideas and possibilities, listing ideas

Flexibility: producing different ideas; grouping and organizing ideas

Elaboration: re-combining ideas; adding detail to existing ideas; "piggy-backing"; modifying ideas

Originality: creating new ideas; using unique thinking

Decisions and Outcomes: understanding that choosing from alternatives affects the events which follow

Encapsulation: stating ideas in a precise and concise form

Metacognition: thinking about thinking; invisible talking

Evaluation: examining carefully; appraising; assessing

Prediction: anticipating; foretelling

Reflection: pondering; mental consideration or contemplation

Mind Mapping: recording information with supporting ideas and examples branching out from the main idea; a creative pattern of connected ideas

Observation: inspecting; taking notice; watching; paying attention

Plus, Minus, Interesting: considering the positive, negative, and interesting aspects of an idea using a single framework

Point-of-View: analyzing how different people look at the same situation

Visualization: forming mental images of something that is not actually present to the senses

Graphic Organizers and Visuals

Analogy

Analogy involves comparing two items in order to perceive the similarities.

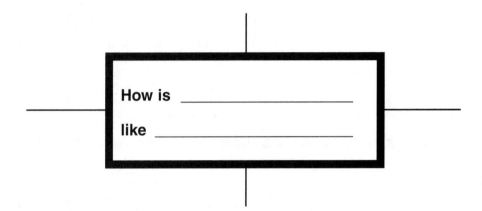

How is _____

like _____

Brainstorming

Brainstorming involves . . .

divergent thinking

spontaneously contributing ideas

expressing many ideas and possibilities

producing different ideas

grouping and categorizing ideas

Graphic Organizers and Visuals (cont.)

Brainstorming (cont.)

Fluency

How many?	a bunch
one	a few
oodles	lots

Flexibility

variety	different
detour	change
adapt	re-direct
alternative	

Elaboration

embellish	build
stretch	enrich
enlarge	embroider
expand upon	add on

Originality

unusual	new
clever	novel
unique	

Graphic Organizers and Visuals *(cont.)*

Professor Rodent's Rules for Brainstorming

Record all ideas
(Write your ideas down.)

Offbeat/original
(Think out-of-the-box.)

Defer judgment
(Do not evaluate or critique.)

Elaborate or "piggy-back"
(Add on to ideas.)

Numerous ideas
(Think of as many ideas as you can.)

Time limit
(Work within a specified time period.)

Graphic Organizers and Visuals (cont.)

Decisions and Outcomes

Decisions and Outcomes means understanding that choosing from alternatives affects the events that follow.

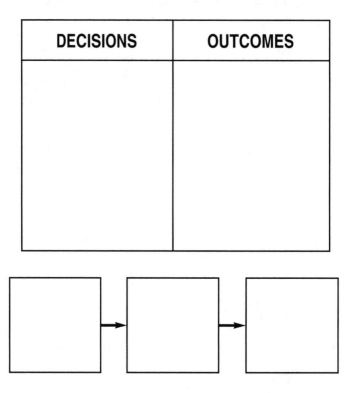

Encapsulation

Encapsulation is stating ideas in a precise and concise form.

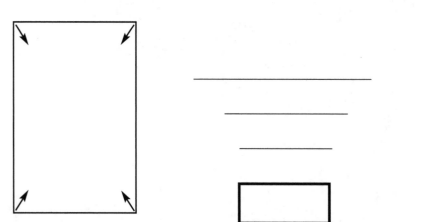

Graphic Organizers and Visuals (cont.)

Metacognition

Metacognition is thinking about thinking.

Mind Mapping

Mind Mapping is recording information with supporting ideas and examples branching out from the main idea.

Thought Tree

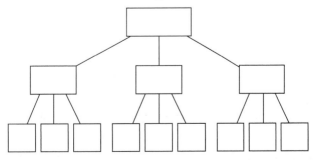

Graphic Organizers and Visuals *(cont.)*

Observation

Observation is inspecting, taking notice, watching, and paying attention.

List Observations

1. _____

2. _____

3. _____

4. _____

5. _____

6. _____

7. _____

Draw Observations

Plus, Minus, Interesting

Plus, Minus, Interesting involves considering the positive, negative, and interesting aspects of an idea, using a single framework.

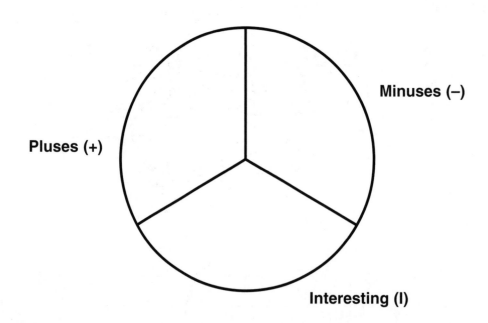

Minuses (–)

Pluses (+)

Interesting (I)

Graphic Organizers and Visuals *(cont.)*

Point of View

Point of View involves analyzing how different people look at the same situation.

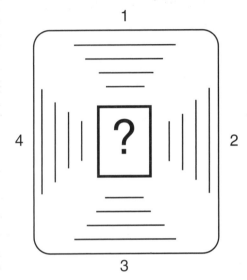

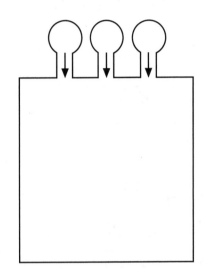

Visualization

Visualization is forming mental images of something that is not actually present to the senses.

ABC Puzzlers

Each equation below contains the initials of words that will make the statement correct. Find the missing words. A few examples have been given.

Examples:

9 P in the SS = _nine planets in the solar system_

3 BM, SHTR = _three blind mice, see how they run_

5 D in a ZC = _five digits in a zip code_

1. 26 L in the A _____

2. 52 W in a Y _____

3. TE invented the LB _____

4. A 4LC means GL _____

5. 52 C in a D of C _____

6. 4Q in a D _____

7. 3 sides on a T, but 4 sides on a S _____

8. 7 C on the planet E _____

9. An I has 6 L, but a S has 8 L _____

10. At 32 D, water F _____

11. GW was the first P _____

12. 360 D in a C _____

13. 64 S on a CB _____

14. 4 S on a V, but 6 S on a G _____

15. A U has 1 W, but a B has 2 W _____

ABC Puzzlers *(cont.)*

Answer Key

1. 26 letters in the alphabet

2. 52 weeks in a year

3. Thomas Edison invented the light bulb

4. a four leaf clover means good luck

5. 52 cards in a deck of cards

6. four quarters in a dollar

7. three sides on a triangle, but four sides on a square

8. seven continents on the planet Earth

9. an insect has six legs, but a spider has eight legs

10. at 32 degrees, water freezes

11. George Washington was the first president

12. 360 degrees in a circle

13. 64 squares on a chess board

14. four strings on a violin, but six strings on a guitar

15. a unicycle has one wheel, but a bicycle has two wheels

Array Grid

Directions: Read each word in the boxes below. If the word has two syllables in it, cross the word out. Then take the first letter of each word that is not crossed out and write the letter in the blanks below the box. You will spell the name of a famous woman.

symbolic	future	frequent	anticipate	auction
location	lever	moisten	legal	loyal
target	litigation	breakfast	youth	routine
representative	independent	defer	dominate	eligible

___ ___ ___ ___ ___ ___ ___ ___ ___

- -

Fold this section under before copying.

Answer: Sally Ride

Another Array Grid

Directions: Read each word in the boxes below. Cross out any word that is a number word. Take the first letter of each word that is left and write the letters in order in the blanks below the box. The letters will spell a famous scientist.

twenty	five	million	greater	hundredth
hundred	area	sixteen	dozen	trillion
length	century	decade	seventy	tenth
invert	fifty	zero	four	thirty
less	fifteen	equal	billion	thousand
seven	sixty	one-half	order	twelve

___ ___ ___ ___ ___ ___ ___

- -

Fold this section under before copying.

Answer: Galileo

Aunt Birdie Fish

Aunt Birdie Fish likes things that follow a rule. Can you figure out the rules to the following statements? The answers are given below.

Riddle #1

Aunt Birdie Fish likes balloons and banners for celebrations, but not flags or candles.

She eats pizza and spaghetti but does not like ice cream.

Her favorite sports are soccer, tennis, and football but she does not like rugby.

Aunt Birdie Fish has two pets: a parrot named Polly and a kitten called Puff.

Aunt Birdie Fish will read books but not any newspapers or magazines.

What is the rule? _____

Riddle #2

Aunt Birdie Fish is unusual.

She likes weasels but not squirrels.

She eats charcoal-broiled foods but not roasted, and cooks with oils, not butter.

Aunt Birdie Fish prefers pastel clothes not plaids, and wears canvas shoes not loafers.

Aunt Birdie Fish prefers to live in Pennsylvania, not Alabama.

She reads paperback books, not hardbacks.

What is the rule? _____

Challenge: Create your own Aunt Birdie Fish stories.

- -

Fold this section under before copying.

Answers: Riddle #1—Aunt Birdie Fish likes words with double letters.

           Riddle #2—Aunt Birdie Fish likes words with artist supplies hidden in them.

Colorful Puzzlers

Match the colorful phrases with the appropriate descriptors. Can you make up your own colorful versions?

White

_____ 1. termite   A. white chocolate

_____ 2. a Disney character   B. white flag

_____ 3. chocolate of a different color   C. Snow White

_____ 4. signal of surrender   D. white ant

_____ 5. polar mammal   E. White House

_____ 6. fib   F. white bear

_____ 7. home of the U.S. President   G. white lie

Black

_____ 1. hockey team   A. black and blue

_____ 2. a space place   B. black-eyed peas

_____ 3. book about a horse   C. *Black Stallion*

_____ 4. beaten up   D. black hole

_____ 5. place to play games   E. blacktop

_____ 6. vegetable   F. Black Hawks

_____ 7. no electricity   G. blackouts

Colorful Puzzlers *(cont.)*

Red

_____ 1. really tall tree

_____ 2. care facility

_____ 3. "caught in the act"

_____ 4. mad

_____ 5. nursery rhyme

_____ 6. fruit

_____ 7. "hot" vegetable

A. red chili pepper

B. red in the face

C. red apple

D. red-handed

E. redwood

F. "Little Red Riding Hood"

G. Red Cross

Pink

_____ 1. flower

_____ 2. beverage

_____ 3. Grammy-winning artist

_____ 4. disease

_____ 5. movie about a detective

_____ 6. fish

_____ 7. a notice of dismissal

A. pink eye

B. *Pink Panther*

C. pink slip

D. pink carnation

E. pink lemonade

F. pink salmon

G. Pink

Colorful Puzzlers *(cont.)*

Blue

_____ 1.	a joke	A. "Blue Suede Shoes"
_____ 2.	hockey team	B. blue blood
_____ 3.	Elvis Presley song	C. "Little Boy Blue"
_____ 4.	nursery rhyme	D. blue cheese
_____ 5.	salad dressing	E. bluebells
_____ 6.	noble or aristocratic family	F. "blooper"
_____ 7.	flowers	G. Blue Jackets

Green

_____ 1.	someone who grows plants well	A. Greenland
_____ 2.	jealous	B. greenhouse
_____ 3.	inexperienced person	C. green light
_____ 4.	structure for growing plants	D. green-eyed
_____ 5.	name of a country	E. greenhorn
_____ 6.	nickname for Vermont	F. green thumb
_____ 7.	proceed ahead	G. Green Mountain State

Colorful Puzzlers *(cont.)*

Yellow

_____	1. disease	A.	yellow streak
_____	2. phone book	B.	yellow brick road
_____	3. coward	C.	yellow fever
_____	4. place in Wizard of Oz	D.	yellow pages
_____	5. type of bee	E.	yellow metal
_____	6. gold	F.	yellow card
_____	7. warning in soccer	G.	yellow jacket

Brown

_____	1. a dessert	A.	brownstone
_____	2. football team	B.	Brownies
_____	3. dimming of lights	C.	Brown Swiss
_____	4. Girl Scout division	D.	Brown Betty
_____	5. hearty breed of dairy cattle	E.	brown sugar
_____	6. sandstone used for building	F.	brownout
_____	7. cookie ingredient	G.	Browns

Colorful Puzzlers *(cont.)*

Answer Key

White

1. D
2. C
3. A
4. B
5. F
6. G
7. E

Black

1. F
2. D
3. C
4. A
5. E
6. B
7. G

Red

1. E
2. G
3. D
4. B
5. F
6. C
7. A

Pink

1. D
2. E
3. G
4. A
5. B
6. F
7. C

Blue

1. F
2. G
3. A
4. C
5. D
6. B
7. E

Green

1. F
2. D
3. E
4. B
5. A
6. G
7. C

Yellow

1. C
2. D
3. A
4. B
5. G
6. E
7. F

Brown

1. D
2. G
3. F
4. B
5. C
6. A
7. E

Connections

Directions: Think of a word that could be used with each term to make a compound word or phrase. An example has been provided.

Example:

| foot | game | snow | __ball__ |

1. opera   box   hand   _____

2. head   Easter   fried   _____

3. Christmas   flies   Magazine   _____

4. whipped   sour   cheese   _____

5. shelter   atomic   time   _____

6. book   garbage   pipe   _____

7. light   cards   back   _____

8. go   wheel   shopping   _____

9. moon   night   year   _____

10. city   way   mark   _____

11. Adam's   tree   core   _____

12. ballpoint   pal   pig   _____

13. power   shoe   race   _____

14. birds   sick   puppy   _____

15. ball   lid   pink   _____

- -

Fold this section under before copying.

Answers: 1. soap; 2. egg; 3. time; 4. cream; 5. bomb; 6. bag; 7. flash; 8. cart; 9. light;
         10. hall; 11. apple; 12. pen; 13. horse; 14. love; 15. eye

Droodles

Droodles are artistic interpretations of brainteasers. Pictures or illustrations are used to present information. Symbols may represent different things depending on the context. Word clues may be added.

What could these droodles be?

Droodle #1

What could it be? _____

Droodle #2

What could it be? _____

Droodle #3

What could it be? _____

Droodle #4

What could it be? _____

Droodle #5

What could it be? _____

Droodle #6

What could it be? _____

Droodles *(cont.)*

Droodle #1	Droodle #2
	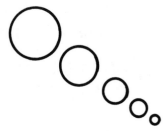
What could it be? _____	What could it be? _____
Droodle #3	**Droodle #4**
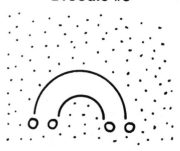	
What could it be? _____	What could it be? _____
Droodle #5	**Droodle #6**
	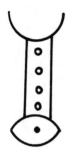
What could it be? _____	What could it be? _____

Droodles *(cont.)*

Droodle #1 What could it be? _____	**Droodle #2** What could it be? _____
Droodle #3 What could it be? _____	**Droodle #4** What could it be? _____
Droodle #5 What could it be? _____	**Droodle #6** What could it be? _____

Hidden Animals

The name of an animal is hidden in each sentence. It is not one of the obvious animal names used and may be hidden inside one or several words. Can you find each one? The first one has been done for you.

1. We li<u>ke e</u>lephants. _____ eel _____

2. Bob catches a ball at every game. _____

3. Sara and I went to the movies but Katie came late. _____

4. In the crosstown race, Emily ran with awkward strides. _____

5. After the movie, my mother came and picked me up. _____

6. Mom called, "Catch Marc at the grocery store. Hurry!" _____

7. "Joe, we better head back," I said. _____

8. I milked the cow last night at the farm. _____

9. Julio, Nate, and Josh went to the store. _____

10. The crowd was huge at the carnival. _____

- -

Fold this section under before copying.

Answers: 1. eel; 2. bobcat; 3. camel; 4. hawk; 5. moth; 6. cat; 7. ewe; 8. owl; 9. lion; 10. crow

Hidden Animals (cont.)

11. Jim was painting a picture._____

12. The car I bought yesterday is shiny and beautiful._____

13. Mary took a picture of a panther in a cage. _____

14. All amazing tricks are fascinating. _____

15. Ramon keys into more projects than other kids. _____

16. My new neighbor, Mo, uses peppers on his pizza. _____

17. To and fro, Gary pushed his sister on the swing._____

18. Jennifer ate three pieces of fudge._____

19. The wagon of oxen pulled the people. _____

20. The new car glimmered in the light._____

- -

Fold this section under before copying.

Answers: 11. asp; 12. caribou; 13. ant; 14. llama; 15. monkey; 16. mouse; 17. frog;
18. rat; 19. fox; 20. hen

Hidden Animals *(cont.)*

21. The small ambulance blared its siren. _____

22. The small crab bit my arm._____

23. Randolf is happy because he just got a new dog. _____

24. Cathy likes to eat carrots._____

25. She said, "Hush, Arkansas boy!" _____

26. Do George and Anne like pizza? _____

27. My friend's cargo at the dock was lost. _____

28. Racquel knit a sweater for Gabe._____

29. Either Zach or Seth should be named captain of the team. _____

30. On the box it said: Diet Kit, ten short steps. _____

- -

Fold this section under before copying.

Answers: 21. lamb; 22. rabbit; 23. fish; 24. cat; 25. shark; 26. dog; 27. goat; 28. elk;
        29. horse; 30. kitten

"If True, Do..." Puzzles

To solve the puzzle and find the hidden word, read the sentences below the puzzle. If the statement is true, color in the numbered puzzle spaces as directed.

5	2	7	6	4	7
					2
	9		3	9	5
9	3 1 6	5			8
7	8	4	2	4	1

If 3 x 9 = 27, color the #1 spaces.

If 13 − 9 = 5, color the #2 spaces.

If 5 x 9 = 54, color the #3 spaces.

If 8 x 4 = 16 x 2, color the #4 spaces.

If 5^2 = 25 x 2, color the #5 spaces.

If 7 + 3 + 8 + 2 = 21, color the #6 spaces.

If 6 x 0 = 0 x 6, color the #7 spaces.

If 100 − 41 = 50 + 8, color the #8 spaces.

If 10 x 10 x 10 = 1,000, color the #9 spaces.

What word did you find? _____

"If True, Do..." Puzzles *(cont.)*

To solve the puzzle and find the hidden word, read the sentences below. If the statement is true, color the numbered puzzle spaces as directed.

11	7	8	10	2	4	1	13
4	14	5	6	12	15	12	14	4	16
12	1	3	13	8	11	8	16	5	15
9	6	5	2		3	9	13	10	1

If cows give milk, color the #1 spaces.

If whales swim, color the #2 spaces.

If birds have scales, color the #3 spaces.

If worms have feet, color the #4 spaces.

If lions have stripes, color the #5 spaces.

If camels have humps, color the #6 spaces.

If pigs "oink," color the #7 spaces.

If snakes are mammals, color the #8 spaces.

If squirrels eat nuts, color the #9 spaces.

If elephants have trunks, color the #10 spaces.

If a zebra has stripes, color the #11 spaces.

If chickens "quack," color the #12 spaces.

If spiders spin webs, color the #13 spaces.

If cats have fur, color the #14 spaces.

If an ant is an insect, color the #15 spaces.

If eagles have feathers, color the #16 spaces.

What word did you find? _____

"If True, Do..." Puzzles *(cont.)*

To solve the puzzle and find the hidden word, read the sentences below. If the statement is true, color the numbered puzzle spaces as directed.

2	9	12	2	5	13	10 / 3	6 / 5	2	14 / 1	9
14 / 4	11	14	8	6	10	11 / 13	1 / 9	12 / 6	4 / 9	6
12	1	2	12	6	5	10	6	14	2	9
8	4	14	9	13	3	5 / 8	7	5	12	7
14	2	8	11	3	10	1 / 4	11	9	14	

If Mississippi is an ocean, color the #1 spaces blue.

If Tennessee is a state, color the #2 spaces red.

If Hawaii is a state, color the #3 spaces blue.

If Mexico is a country, color the #4 spaces red

If Michigan is a country, color the #5 spaces red.

If Florida is a river, color the #6 spaces blue.

If Kentucky is in South America, color the #7 spaces red.

If Canada is a country, color the #8 spaces red.

If England is a continent, color the #9 spaces blue.

If Washington is a state, color the #10 spaces blue.

If Ohio is an island, color the #11 spaces blue.

If New York is a city, color the #12 spaces red.

If California borders an ocean, color the #13 spaces blue.

If Australia is an island, color the #14 spaces red.

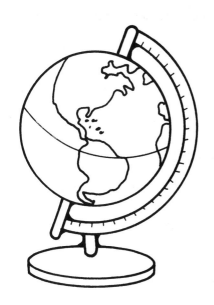

What word did you find? _____

If You Think of...

Part I

The emphasis of this activity is on flexible thinking. The idea that the same symbol can represent different things depending on the context is not an easy premise, but once children make the connection, they'll be off and running.

Materials

- nine note cards
- tagboard
- page 157

Directions (for teachers)

Copy the drawings below onto note cards and glue them to a piece of tagboard.

1	2	3
(two circles)	(one circle)	(V shape)
4	**5**	**6**
(grid of rectangles)	(two vertical lines)	(wavy S line)
7	**8**	**9**
(arc)	(T shape)	(rows of vertical lines)

Note: Remember to be flexible when you evaluate the answers. For example, if a child thinks the "hair" in Question 4 looks something like a profile, why argue?

- -

Suggested answers: 1. hammer; 2. ball; 3. icicle; 4. hair; 5. eyelashes; 6. anthill; 7. light bulb; 8. road; 9. moon; 10. child; 11. fence; 12. cone; 13. balloon; 14. leaves

Rasmussen, Greta. (1989) *Brain Stations. A Center Approach to Thinking Skills.* Stanwood, WA. Tin Man Press. Permission granted for reprinting by Tin Man Press, P.O. Box 11409. Eugene, OR 97440 800-676-0459 FAX 888-515-1764 Website: *www.tinmanpress.com.*

If You Think of . . . (cont.)

Part I (cont.)

Student Directions: Number your paper 1–14 and answer these questions.

If you think of . . .

1. Number 3 as a nail, what could Number 8 be?

2. Number 4 as a net, what could Number 2 be?

3. Number 1 as snow, what could Number 3 be?

4. Number 7 as a head, what could Number 6 be?

5. Number 1 as eyes, what could Number 9 be?

6. Number 2 as an ant, what could Number 7 be?

7. Number 8 as a lamp, what could Number 2 be?

8. Number 2 as a car, what could Number 5 be?

9. Number 7 as the sun, what could Number 2 be?

10. Number 1 as parents, what could Number 2 be?

11. Number 9 as cows, what could Number 4 be?

12. Number 2 as ice cream, what could Number 3 be?

13. Number 6 as string, what could Number 2 be?

14. Number 5 as a tree, what could Number 9 be?

If You Think of...

Part II

Materials

- nine note cards
- tagboard
- page 159

Directions (for teachers)

Copy the drawings below onto note cards and glue them to a piece of tagboard.

1	2	3
4	5	6
7	8	9

Note: Remember to be flexible when you evaluate the answers. We've thrown a couple of curveballs here. The suggested answer for Number 15 is "sun" because it takes the sun to make a rainbow. However, "raindrop" would be an acceptable answer. Also, number 13 is a question where the clue is totally conceptual. See how they handle it.

- -

Suggested answers: 1. string; 2. window; 3. bug; 4. smile; 5. cloud; 6. uncooked;
7. egg white; 8. needle; 9. smoke; 10. popcorn kernel; 11. town; 12. glass;
13. quiet or silence; 14. pot or pan; 15. sun; 16. eyebrow;

Rasmussen, Greta. (1989) *Brain Stations. A Center Approach to Thinking Skills.* Stanwood, WA. Tin Man Press. Permission granted for reprinting by Tin Man Press, P.O. Box 11409. Eugene, OR 97440 800-676-0459 FAX 888-515-1764 Website: *www.tinmanpress.com.*

If You Think of . . . *(cont.)*

Part II *(cont.)*

Student Directions: Number 1–16 on your own paper, look at the drawings and then get ready for some fun thinking!

If you think of . . .

1. Number 5 as a yo-yo, what could Number 1 be?

2. Number 2 as a door, what could Number 3 be?

3. Number 4 as a bird, what could Number 9 be?

4. Number 8 as a frown, what could Number 4 be?

5. Number 7 as wind, what could Number 6 be?

6. Number 7 as cooked spaghetti, what could Number 1 be?

7. Number 5 as an egg yolk, what could Number 6 be?

8. Number 7 as thread, what could Number 1 be?

9. Number 2 as a chimney, what could Number 7 be?

10. Number 6 as popcorn, what could Number 9 be?

11. Number 5 as a city, what could Number 9 be?

12. Number 1 as a straw, what could Number 2 be?

13. Number 7 as noise, what could Number 1 be?

14. Number 3 as a stove, what could Number 9 be?

15. Number 8 as a rainbow, what could Number 5 be?

16. Number 5 as an eye, what could Number 8 be?

Musical Note Stories

Decipher the puzzle stories by interpreting the musical scale notes: A, B, C, D, E, F, G. Use this diagram to help you learn your notes.

Musical Staff

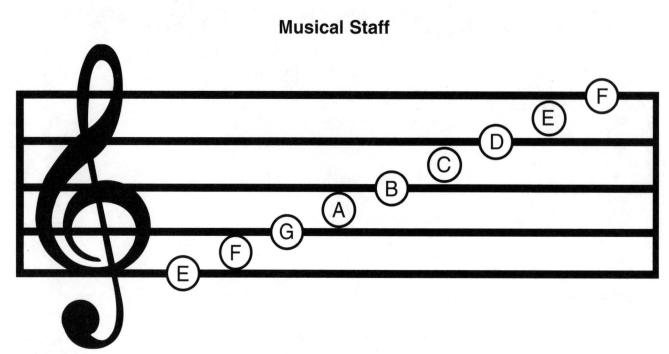

━━━━━━━━━━ **Music Story #1** ━━━━━━━━━━

Four friends named [music notes] ,

[music notes] , [music notes] , and [music notes]

took a hike. They found a bird [music notes]

and a [music notes] frog.

Musical Note Stories (cont.)

Music Story #1 *(cont.)*

They saw a

buzzing near a flower.

They  a baby rabbit

and put it safely in a  .

The friends had happy  s.

Musical Note Stories *(cont.)*

Music Story #2

My friend , who is one

 old, took a trip. He

rode in a taxi  to a

 where he ate

and  and listened to  .

Musical Note Stories (cont.)

His  was lost.  felt

but a man with a  found

his 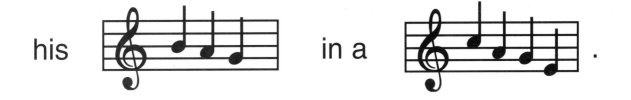 in a 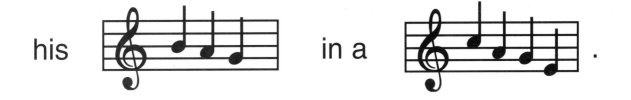 .

 's  was glad!

Musical Note Stories *(cont.)*

Music Story #3

Two friends,  and

took a hike with  and .

They 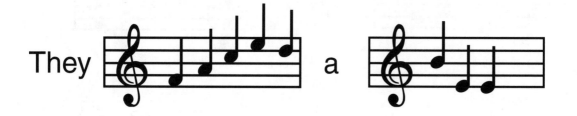 a

buzzing near a flower.

Musical Note Stories (cont.)

Music Story #3 *(cont.)*

They were sad to see

a  bird near a tree.

They found an empty

and searched for the rabbit.

Name That Country!

Directions: Read the statements below. Fill in the blank with a name of a country.

1. Wow! In track _____ 24 miles this week.

2. I got _____ all over my shirt when I was frying chicken.

3. You must _____ sick person to the hospital.

4. We ate _____ and ham sandwiches for lunch today.

5. The sheep like to graze on _____.

6. Mother has pottery plates as well as fancy _____ dishes.

7. My _____ pig likes to eat lettuce and spinach.

8. The pilot was flying to the North _____ back again.

9. During the winter it is _____outside.

10. I want a _____'s good pizza for lunch!

Now, write one of your own. Underline the name of the country in your sentence.

_____

_____

- -

Fold this section under before copying.

Suggested Answers: 1. Iran; 2. Greece; 3. Russia; 4. Turkey; 5. Greenland; 6. China;
7. New Guinea; 8. Poland; 9. Chile; 10. Panama

Wordles

The object of Wordles is to create a familiar word, phrase, saying, or name from each arrangement of letters and/or symbols in the boxes. Try to solve the following. Use the clues to help you.

1. sec/ond

   Clue: small amount of time _____

2. world, world, world, world

   Clue: sporting event _____

3. mustickd

   Clue: a boring person _____

4. fiddler
   roof

   Clue: a musical play/movie _____

5. BIRD

   Clue: He's yellow. _____

6. T
   O
   U
   C
   H

   Clue: 6 points _____

7. surelifence

   Clue: just in case . . . _____

8. S S
   S S
   S S
   S S
   S S

   Clue: court sport _____

- -

Fold this section under before copying.

Answers: 1. split second; 2. World Series; 3. stick in the mud; 4. Fiddler on the Roof;
5. Big Bird; 6. touchdown; 7. life insurance; 8. tennis

Sports Stumpers I

Find the name of the football, basketball, baseball, or hockey team that fits each clue. Choose your answer from the list below.

1. Tool used to help fishermen _____

2. Nickname for people up North _____

3. New York opera house _____

4. Young horses _____

5. Endangered birds _____

6. Razor cuts? _____

7. Part of a car _____

8. Big fish _____

9. Style of music _____

10. Queens' spouses _____

11. Scissors _____

12. Bold and courageous _____

Teams List

Braves	Jazz	Mets
Clippers	Kings	Nets
Colts	Knicks	Pistons
Eagles	Marlins	Vikings

- -

Fold this section under before copying.

Answers: 1. Nets; 2. Vikings; 3. Mets; 4. Colts; 5. Eagles; 6. Knicks; 7. Pistons; 8. Marlins; 9. Jazz; 10. Kings; 11. Clippers; 12. Braves

Sports Stumpers II

Find the name of the football, basketball, baseball, or hockey team that fits each clue. Choose your answer from the list below.

1. This team is proud to be American _____

2. This team looks like itself. _____

3. This team travels in packs. _____

4. This team can bury you alive. _____

5. This team is always well behaved. _____

6. This team is hard to hit. _____

7. You can feel this team circling. _____

8. This team might have cubs. _____

9. Each year, this team runs through the streets of Spain. _____

10. This team is friends with thunder. _____

11. This team gets good grades. _____

12. This team is always looking for gold. _____

Teams List

A's	Dodgers	Saints
Avalanche	49ers	Sharks
Bears	Lightning	Timberwolves
Bulls	Patriots	Twins

- -

Fold this section under before copying.

Answers: 1. Patriots; 2. Twins; 3. Timberwolves; 4. Avalanche; 5. Saints; 6. Dodgers;
7. Sharks; 8. Bears; 9. Bulls; 10. Lightning; 11. A's; 12. 49ers

Concentration

Concentration is a memory game adapted from the classic television game show of the same name. The game can be used to review or learn a variety of math concepts while at the same time enhancing memory skills.

- **Topics Involved:** memory skills, variety of math concepts
- **Grades:** all grades
- **Materials:** two-inch construction paper squares
- **Type of Activity:** small group/whole class game

The Idea

Each student is given small two-inch colored squares of construction paper onto which they write equivalent pairs of math concepts. The math concepts can either be around a specific theme, such as addition facts, or around a variety of concepts. Some examples are shown on page 171.

Before playing the game, give each student 12 squares of the same color. Have students write six pairs of math concepts on the cards. When they are done, have them mix up the cards and turn the cards facedown on their desks. Working individually, students should turn over one card and try to find its match by turning over one other card. If a match is made, the cards are picked up. If a match is not made, the cards are returned facedown to their original spot. The game continues until all cards are matched. After playing this solitaire version, have the students play with partners. The game now includes 24 cards so the challenge level has increased. Students take turns and follow the same procedure, trying to match the pairs. If a match is made, the player gets an additional turn. The student with the most cards at the end of the game is the winner.

Extensions

- Allow students to make up their own cards on whatever math subject they choose.

- Create Concentration tournaments. Each time a winner advances to the next round, add another set of 12 cards.

Concentration *(cont.)*

Sample Cards

Addition Facts

4 + 5

9

Multiplication Facts

8 x 7

56

Roman Numerals

L

50

Equivalent

$^5/_{15}$

$^1/_3$

Geometrical Shapes

octagon

Time

10 years

1 decade

Money

4 dimes
2 pennies

42¢

Exponents

4^2

16

Corral

Corral is a creative variation of the classic "Make-a-Square" game in which players try to make the most squares on dot paper. In this version, the winner is the player with the most points, not the most squares. The game helps students develop their spatial sense as they anticipate and visualize future moves.

Topics Involved: problem solving

Grades: third and up

Materials: game board on page 173

Type of Activity: two-person game

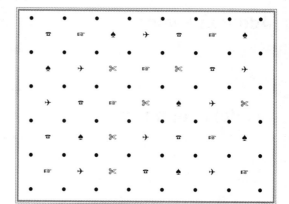

Directions

1. Decide who goes first. Take turns.

2. On your turn, draw a line by connecting one dot to another. You can only draw horizontal or vertical lines.

3. If you complete a square on your turn, mark your initials in the square and take another turn.

4. Continue playing until all the squares are completed.

5. The object of the game is to score the most points. The symbol inside the square tells you how many points the square is worth.

6. The player with the most points is the winner.

Discussion Questions

- What was your strategy for winning Corral?

- What are good moves? Why?

- What are bad moves? Why?

Variations

- Allow points for all squares created, regardless of size. In the original game, points are scored for "unit" squares. However, in this variation, students can score points for creating a 2 x 2, 3 x 3, or any other larger square. Points for each square are determined by summing all the symbols inside the square.

- Change the point values for the symbols to decimals or fractions for extra practice with these numbers.

- Have students make up their own game boards. See page 173 for a sample game board.

Corral (cont.)

Game Board

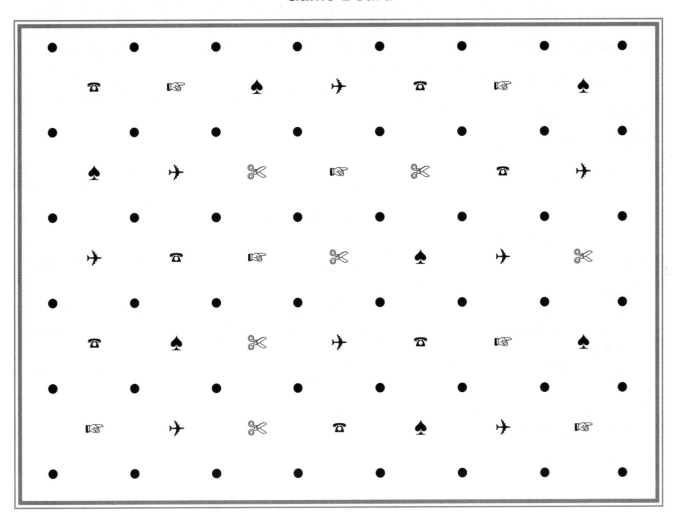

Points

$\ge 8 = 2$ $\widehat{\mathbf{T}} = 3$ $\spadesuit = 4$ $\mathbb{I}\mathbb{S} = 5$ $\nleftrightarrow = 6$

Player #1: _____   Points Earned: _____

Player #2: _____   Points Earned: _____

Resources

Allen, S. *How To Think*. Meadowlands Music, Inc. Sewell, NJ. Gifted and Talented Publications, Inc.

Armstrong, Thomas. *Multiple Intelligences in the Classroom*. Alexandria, VA. ASCD. 1994.

Bellanca, James. (1990) *The Cooperative Think Tank. Practical Techniques to Teaching Thinking in the Cooperative Classroom*. Palantine, IL. IRI/Skylight. 1990.

Black, Howard and Black, Sandra. *Organizing Thinking*. Pacific Grove, CA. Midwest Publications. 1990.

Black, Susan. *The American School Board Journal*. "The Musical Mind." 20-22. 1997.

Caine, Renate & Caine, Geoffrey. *Making Connections: Teaching and the Human Brain*. Alexandria, VA. ASCD. 1991.

Chapman, Carolyn. *If the Shoe Fits...How to Develop Multiple Intelligences in the Classroom*. Palatine, IL. IRI/Skylight. 1993.

Chapman, Carolyn. *Multiple Assessments for the Multiple Intelligences*. Palatine, IL. IRI/Skylight. 1996.

Costa, Art. Developing Minds. *A Resource Book for Teaching Thinking*. Alexandria, VA. ASCD. 1991

DeBono, Edward. *CoRT Thinking Skills*. New York, NY. Pergamon Press. 1985.

DeBono, Edward. *Six Thinking Hats*. New York, NY. Penguin. 1985.

DeBono, Edward. *Six Thinking Hats for Schools*. Logan, IA. Perfection Learning Corp. 1991.

Downie, Diane, Twila Slesnick, and Jean Stenmark. *Math for Girls and Other Problem Solvers*. University of CA. Equals. "Toothpick Puzzles". 66-8. "Balloon Ride." 16-7. 1981.

Epley, Thelma. *Models for Thinking: Activities to Enhance Modes of Thought*. Ventura, CA. Ventura Co. Supt. of Schools Office. 1982.

Evans, Brent R. *Instant Play and Learn Games. Lesson 18. Silly Perspective Puzzles. Life Cereal Learning Program*. Quaker Oats Company. 1975.

Flack, Jerry. TalentED. *Strategies for Developing the Talent in Every Learner*. Greeley, CO. ALPS. 1993.

Fogarty, Robin. *Keep Them Thinking*. Palantine, IL. IRI/Skylight. 1990.

Fogarty, Robin. *Problem-based Learning and Other Curriculum Models for the Multiple Intelligences Classroom*. Palantine, IL. IRI/Skylight. 1997.

Gardiner, Martin, Alan Fox, Faith Knowles, and Donna Jeffrey. *Nature. "Learning Improved by Arts Training."* 1996.

Gardner, Howard. *Frames of Mind: The Theory of Intelligences*. New York, NY. BasicBooks. 1983.

Gardner, Howard. *Multiple Intelligences: The Theory in Practice*. New York, NY. BasicBooks. 1993

Gardner, Howard. *To Open Minds*. New York, NY. BasicBooks. 1989.

Gardner, Howard. *The Unschooled Mind*. New York, NY. BasicBooks. 1991.

Resources *(cont.)*

Gold-Vukson, M. and M. *Invisible Unicorn.* Mobile, AL. GCT, Inc. 1989.

Goleman, Daniel. *Emotional Intelligence: Why It Can Matter More than IQ.* New York, NY. Bantam Books. 1995. Hanford, Martin. *Where's Waldo?* Boulder, CO. Character Imprints. 1991.

Hodges, Donald A. *Handbook of Music Psychology.* San Antonio, TX. University of Texas. IMR Press. 1996.

Hyerle, David. *Visual Tools for Constructing Knowledge.* Alexandria, VA. ASCD. 1996.

Jensen, Eric. *The Learning Brain.* San Diego, CA. Turning Point Publications. 1995.

Jensen, Eric. *Teaching with the Brain in Mind.* Alexandria, VA. ASCD. 1998.

Johnson, David W. and Johnson, Roger T. *Cooperation in the Classroom.* Edina, MN. Interaction Book Co. 1984.

Johnson, Dee & Kolbe, Kathy. *Options & Observations.* Phoenix, AZ. Think Ink Publications. 1980.

Johnson, Nancy. *Look Closer. Visual Thinking Skills & Activities.* Beavercreek, OH. Pieces of Learning. 1996.

Johnson, Nancy. *Questioning Makes the Difference.* Beavercreek, OH. Pieces of Learning. 1990.

Johnson, Nancy. *Thinking is the Key.* Beavercreek, OH. Pieces of Learning. 1992.

Johnson, Nancy. *The Best Teacher Stuff.* Beavercreek, OH. Pieces of Learning "Dot-to-Dot" Stories. 72-73. 1993

Kay, Keith. *The Little Giant Book of Optical Illusions.* New York, NY. Sterling Publishing Co. 1991.

Lazear, David. *Multiple Intelligence Approaches to Assessment.* Tucson, AZ. Aephyr. 1994.

Lazear, David. *Seven Ways of Teaching.* Palantine, IL. IRI/Skylight. 1991.

Margulies, Nancy. *Mapping Inner Space. Learning and Teaching Mind Mapping.* Tucson, AZ. Aephyr. "Brain Gloves". 66-67. Zephyr. 1991.

Nash, Cindy and Torrence, Janice. *Challenge. "Droodles" Good Apple.* Issue 41.34. 1990.

Oakes, B. *Illusions.* Kingston, NH. Acron Press, Inc.

Okun, M. *Peter, Paul and Mommy.* Los Angeles, CA. Warner Bros. Seven Arts Records.

O'Neil, Kate. Effective Schools. Vol. 12. No. 1. Research Abstracts. 1998-99 Series. Citation: Kelstrom

Joyce. J. NASSP Bulletin 82, 597. *"The Untapped Power of Music; Its Role in the Curriculum and Its Effect on Academic Achievement."* 34-43. 1998.

Rasmussen, Gretz. *Brain Stations. A Center Approach to Thinking Skills.* Stanwood, WA. Tin Man Press. 1989.

Resources

Rauscher, Frances. *"Pilot Study Indicates Music Training of Three-Year Olds Enhance Specific Spatial Reasoning Skills."* Irvine, CA. Center for the Neurobiology of Learning and Memory, University of California-Irvine. 1993.

Rauscher, Frances. *"Listening to Mozart Enhances Spatial-temporal Reasoning: Towards a Neurophysiological Basis."* Neuroscience Letters. 185, 44-7. 1995.

Rozakis, Laurie. *Critical Thinking for the Middle and Upper Grades.* New York, NY. Scholastic, Inc. 25. 1991.

Rauscher, Frances. *Nature. Music and Spatial Task Performance.* 365, 611. 1993.

Ruef, Kerry. *The Private Eye. Looking/thinking by Analogy.* Seattle, WA. The Private Eye Project. 1992.

Saxe, John. *Anthology of Children's Literary.* Modern Fables. "The Blind Men and the Elephant."

Slattery, Beth. *WOW: The Wonder of Wetlands.* St. Michaels, MD. Environmental Concern, Inc. 1991.

Sousa, David. *how the Brain Learns.* Reston, VA. NASSP. 1995.

Sternberg, Robert. *Successful Intelligence.* New York, NY. Simon & Schuster. 1996.

Synder, Neal. Teaching Music (40). *"Frances Rauscher: Music and Reasoning."* MENC. 1995.

Tomlinson, Carol Ann. *How to Differentiate Instruction in Mixed-Ability Classrooms.* Alexandria, VA. ASCD. 1995.

Tomlinson, Carol Ann. *The Differentiated Classroom.* Alexandria, VA. ASCD. 1999.

USA Weekend. *"Migrantes? Try Mozart."* 1997.

Vernon, Robert. *A Simulation of the Origins of Writing.* "Talking Rocks." Del Mar, CA. 1978.

Viadero, Debra. Teacher Magazine. "Bach to Basics." 1998.

Villalpando, Eleanor. *Simulations.* Phoenix, AZ. Kathy Kolbe Concept, Inc. "Design a Park." 50-53. "Talking It Up." 27-28. "Communicate." 31-32. 1984. Web site: www.kolbe.com.

Virginia Journal of Education. *"Piano Training May Boost Reasoning Skills, Math, Science Ability."* 1977.

Wineberger, Norman. MUSICA newsletter. Irvine, CA. University of California. 1994.

Winebrenner, Susan. *Super Sentences.* Mansfield Center, CT. Creative Learning Press, Inc. 1989.

Winebrenner, Susan. *Teaching Gifted Kids in the Regular Classroom.* Minneapolis, MN. Free Spirit. 1992.

Winebrenner, Susan. *Teaching Kids with Learning Difficulties in the Regular Classroom.* Minneapolis, MN. Free Spirit. 1996.

Wonderful Ideas. P.O. Box 64691. Burlington, VT 05406.